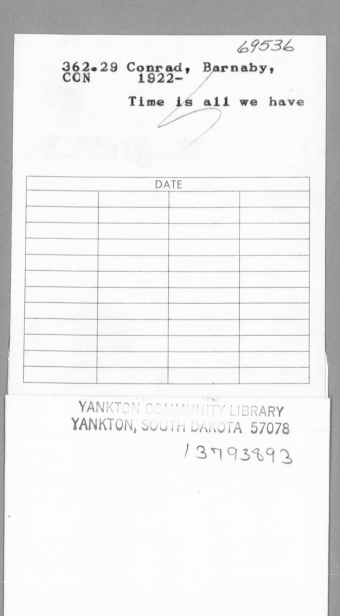

69536

362.29 Conrad, Barnaby,
CON   1922-

         Time is all we have

DATE		

by Barnaby Conrad

Fiction

THE INNOCENT VILLA
MATADOR
DANGERFIELD
ZORRO: A FOX IN THE CITY
ENDANGERED (with Niels Mortensen)
FIRE BELOW ZERO (with Nico Mastorakis)
KEEPERS OF THE SECRET (with Nico Mastorakis)

Translations

THE WOUNDS OF HUNGER (Spota)
THE SECOND LIFE OF CAPTAIN CONTRERAS (Luca de Tena)
MY LIFE AS A MATADOR (Autobiography of Carlos Arruza)

Nonfiction

A REVOLTING TRANSACTION
FUN WHILE IT LASTED
HOW TO FIGHT A BULL
ENCYCLOPEDIA OF BULLFIGHTING
TAHITI
FAMOUS LAST WORDS
SAN FRANCISCO—PROFILE IN WORDS AND PICTURES
DEATH OF MANOLETE
GATES OF FEAR
LA FIESTA BRAVA

BARNABY CONRAD

TIME IS ALL WE HAVE

Four Weeks at the Betty Ford Center

A Belvedere Book

ARBOR HOUSE   NEW YORK

Manufactured in the United States of America

10 9 8 7 6 5 4 3 2 1

Library of Congress Cataloging-in-Publication Data

Conrad, Barnaby, 1922–
Time is all we have.

"A Belvedere book."
1. Betty Ford Center.   I. Title.
RC564.74.C2C66   1986   362.2′9   86-14163
ISBN 0-87795-835-1

Grateful acknowledgment is made for permission to reprint:

From *The Times of My Life* by Betty Ford and Chris Chase. Copyright © 1978 by Betty Ford. Reprinted by permission of Harper & Row, Publishers Inc.

"The Twelve Steps," reprinted with permission of Alcoholics Anonymous World Services, Inc.

From *The Courage to Change* by Dennis Wholey. Copyright © 1984 by Dennis Wholey. Reprinted by permission of Houghton Mifflin Company.

From *Papa Hemingway* by A. E. Hotchner. Copyright © 1983 by A. E. Hotchner. Reprinted by permission of William Morrow & Co. Inc.

Quote from *Village Voice*. Reprinted with permission of Meryl C. and *Village Voice*, 1985.

Quote from *The New York Times*, "About Men: That Thirsty Animal," by Brian Manning, of October 13, 1985. Copyright © 1985 by The New York Times Company. Reprinted by permission.

"When I Have Fears," from *Collected Verse* by Noel Coward. Copyright © 1984 the Estate of the late Noel Coward. Reprinted by permission of Methuen London, Ltd.

For John Dodds,
inspired editor and friend
who said, Hey, write a book about it!

Author's Note

The experiences and impressions herein are as true and honest as I could make them. But in deference to AA's cherished and time-honored concept of anonymity among alcoholics, the cornerstone of the organization, events and names and characters have been changed and imagined to protect the privacy of the patients and the personnel at the Betty Ford Center.

F O R E W O R D

This is the best book on the treatment of alcoholism and drug addiction that I have read. In an exciting and highly readable fashion, it depicts treatment and recovery as a voyage that begins with tenuous acceptance and leads to honesty and gradual self-discovery. It lets you experience realistically the treatment techniques and exercises that tend to sound hokey or harsh when you see them described elsewhere.

Denial usually means fear. In the case of chemical dependency problems, denial hides our fear of what we think treatment is all about, and our fear that one couldn't possibly live without some alcohol or other drug use. By dispelling such apprehensions on the part of patients, their families, and their employers, this book will help enormously to make treatment acceptable.

In short, it's the best answer to the question, "What do they actually *do* in a rehabilitation program?" It should do a lot to dispel misapprehension on the part of patients and their families and thereby make treament acceptable.

JOSEPH PURSCH, M.D.
Member of the Presidential
Commission on Alcoholism,
and personal doctor to Betty
Ford and Billy Carter for
their recovery from alcoholism

TIME IS
ALL WE
HAVE

ONE

I was lost. "Where's the clinic for drugs and alcohol?" I asked.

"The Center?" the policeman said.

That particular morning I wasn't afraid to pull up alongside the Palm Springs policeman's car; I'd had a few, but I wasn't drunk, not according to their little Richter scale anyway. Just hung over and shaky from the day before—the days, weeks, months, the years before. "Hell, mister, you're a ways from Betty Ford's—that's over in Mirage. See that road right there—it'll take you directly to it."

"Good name," I said. "Mirage."

He didn't seem to hear me.

I turned my car around and got on the right road.

It had taken me a long time to find the right road. Fear, more than hope, had brought me here.

o   o   o

The Betty Ford Center ("Clinic sounds too threatening") for the rehabilitation of chemically dependent people was estab-

1

lished in 1982 by the wife of the thirty-eighth president of the United States, and in its few years it has established itself as the best known and perhaps the most successful institution of its kind in the world. It usually has a waiting list of some three hundred people from all over the world, and when I went there, it could only handle sixty patients at a time. Part of its renown is owing to the number of celebrities who have "graduated," such people as Robert Mitchum, Tony Curtis, Liza Minnelli, Elizabeth Taylor, Mary Tyler Moore, and a top astronaut, who requested anonymity. For anyone from any walk of life who had an alcohol or drug-related problem, the center's reputation for success, its geographical location, and its physical layout held an undeniable allure.

I was "established" in 1922, started drinking in college, and in the last two decades of my sixty-three years I had progressively proved to myself and my distressed family that I couldn't handle alcohol in any form and that my life had become unmanageable and endangered.

At sixty-three, I was an alcoholic. I had only semi-realized it, barely admitting it to myself, fighting the stigma of the opprobrious label, preferring the lighter sentence of "heavy drinker." I had even tried AA and two other highly publicized centers for alcohol rehabilitation. They proved to be unsuccessful in curing me of my addiction, and I continued to drink to excess on a regular basis.

For some years my work didn't suffer at all from my steady drinking. "Hell," I'd maintain defensively, "all creative people drink. Name me one famous American writer, one Nobel Prize winner, other than Pearl Buck, who wasn't a lush."

While having my first drink of the day, a double greyhound (gin and grapefruit juice), at eleven o'clock in the Mecca Cafe in Santa Barbara, I would console myself with the literary list and was ever trying to add new names to it: Capote, O'Hara, Hemingway, Millay, Parker, Williams, Faulkner, Steinbeck, Poe, Dreiser, Thurber, Benchley, O. Henry, Jack London . . . I was pleased to read that even Mark Twain was once jailed for drunkenness; it helped take the heat off me. And as for the painters . . .

I have always been a free-lance writer, painter, and teacher. I managed to keep writing for newspapers and magazines—everything from the *New York Times* to *Playboy* to the *Reader's Digest*—and to produce successful books, some twenty in all, though none were best-sellers in a class with my second novel, *Matador,* which received critical acclaim (Steinbeck in the *Saturday Review* picked it as his favorite novel of the year) and ultimately sold some 3 million copies in twenty-eight languages in its meteoric life. I also taught portrait painting at a California state university and continued as founder and director of the annual Santa Barbara Writers' Conference, for twelve years one of the most successful in the nation, though I was frequently in recent years too drunk to make the podium to address the 350 would-be writers. My portrait commissions were beginning to fall off because my shaking hands were unable to execute the exacting style of realism, which was my forte. My portraits of Sinclair Lewis, Steinbeck, and Truman Capote are in the University of Texas, the Steinbeck Library, and the National Gallery of Art of the Smithsonian, respectively; my portrait of William F. Buckley, Jr., graces the cover of his book *Atlantic High,* and my charcoal of the Baroness Pauline de Rothschild was featured in *Architectural Digest.*

For a couple of years I had lectured around the country at universities and women's clubs, usually on writing and my experience as Sinclair Lewis's secretary-companion or my early life in bullfighting in Spain, Mexico, and Peru. The fees were good, but I was finding I had to have more and more to drink before I could face the audiences, either the feckless youths of the campus, or the elderly "blue cotton field" of the average women's club. Once I found myself in Salt Lake City scheduled to address 750 people—and there was no liquor to be had. I was panicky but managed to agonize through my talk. With all the lectures it was the socializing with strangers before and after the talk that was so tough. Harry Golden used to answer, when asked how much he charged to speak, "A thousand dollars, unless I'm not met at the plane, in which case, nine hundred dollars, and if I don't have to go to the luncheon, eight hundred, and if I don't have to go to the tea afterward, seven hundred . . ."

Once at a reception after one of my lectures in Ohio, the hostess observed me belting down the scotch and sniffed haughtily, saying, "You know, Mr. Conrad, drinking does not make you more attractive." I bowed slightly and said, "Madame, I don't drink to make myself more attractive. I drink to make *you* more attractive."

I was not asked to speak to that club again, and my lecturing in general dwindled in proportion to the increase of my intake.

In spite of the blatant warning signs, I continued to drink. But now I was growing sick and tired of being sick and tired. I was ashamed of my three drunk-driving arrests and mortified by a jail sentence and loss of my driver's license. But I still kept on drinking. My health had deteriorated alarmingly. As captain of my college boxing team, I had weighed 160; as an amateur bullfighter, I had weighed 175 pounds. Now I carried 225 on my 6'2" frame, 50 extra pounds of fat and bloat. As a direct result of my alcoholic intake, I was suffering from insomnia, depression, anxiety, high blood pressure, swollen ankles, cramps in my legs, watery eyes, liver damage, rectal bleeding, sick hangovers with prolonged vomiting, shaky hands, and blackouts with the events of entire evenings sometimes erased.

I did not set out to be an alcoholic; no one does. It was just a condition that developed over the years. But now that it had, I had to do something—*I had to quit drinking*. But how? I would give it up for a few days, maybe a week or two, by a heroic effort, especially if I got a challenging portrait or writing assignment. But drinking never left my subconscious, and I would slip back to it voraciously. I would try limiting

4

myself to a certain amount of alcohol a day, but like Dr. Samuel Johnson, I found it easier to abstain than to moderate. But finally—I found I could not abstain. I tried the beer wagon, then the wine wagon, but I discovered I could do the same job of a pint of gin with two bottles of wine or a six-pack. So I abandoned wine and beer and went back to the hard stuff. I could cut way back for short periods if the motivation to do so was strong enough, greater than the thirst. For example, I love to sculpt in wood, but chisels and knives are tough to handle with alcoholic hands. Once I had a burning urge to do a rearing-horse like the one on the frieze of the Parthenon, so I cut out the Tanqueray while I cut out the two-foot figure in basswood. But in a couple of weeks it was finished; I sold it for $3,000, and went back to the booze.

Friends and family members urged me to quit. They begged, cajoled, prayed, and threatened, to no avail. What they didn't realize was that I'd come to a point where I couldn't stop drinking any more than I could stop breathing. The you'd-quit-if-you-loved-me tactic simply doesn't work on a true alcoholic, no matter how much he thinks he wants to. Even the threat of imminent death doesn't deter him.

"I fell off the wagon," I confessed to my doctor after one three-week try.

"You're going to fall off the world!" he exploded. "Just look at this report from the lab!"

In the face of everything, I persisted in getting drunk to various degrees nearly every day. I celebrated good tidings with drinks, bad news with more. There was no problem or situation, no matter how slight or how serious, that I couldn't make worse by drinking.

"Go to Betty Ford's," my concerned ex-father-in-law urged me.

"Four whole weeks?!" I exclaimed. "And all that money? No way. I'll quit myself."

"You have a disease," he said, "like diabetes. I had it, too. If

5

you have a disease, you go to a hospital. It's that simple."

I didn't buy that disease business, even though the American Medical Association, the World Health Organization, the U.S. Department of Health, the American Psychiatric Association, and the National Council on Alcoholism had so declared it. To me it was a character weakness that could be overcome simply by putting one's mind to it. My mother and father had "character," and so, by God, did I. I would quit next week, no problem, no sweat.

Of course, next week never came, and I had dozens of valid reasons why for myself, my family and friends. After all, I was still productive, wasn't I? I didn't just sit around in taverns and drink all day. I was still functioning reasonably well in all departments, like a frightening number of alcoholics out there in all walks of life, from surgeons to pilots to accountants. I didn't miss *many* appointments or deadlines, I answered all letters, and we had an active and far-flung social life. A few of those parties I couldn't quite make; my wife would come up with clever excuses and go alone. One time I went when I shouldn't have—a party attended by the old-time singer Helen O'Connell. A dream girl of mine from my teens, she still looked glamorous, and I was thrilled when I was asked to play the piano for her while she sang "Tangerine." I was unable to find the simplest chord, however, and she was forced to sing unaccompanied, to my intense chagrin, frustration, and embarrassment that only more drinks could assuage.

I fought drunkenly with my beautiful wife of twenty-five years a couple of times a week, but we could still make up and make love over a blenderful of margaritas of a Sunday morning, and we could still play tennis, quarreling across the net about nothing, about anything; what it was about, of course, unapparent to us, was always directly or indirectly related to alcoholic intake and behavior. We traveled extensively on cruise ships all around Europe and South America, where I would give art classes and lectures to earn our passage. Drinking was good on ships: early and frequent and continual and no damned cops, 502's, and flashing red lights to worry about and plenty of fellow imbibers and fresh salt air and a bullshot for the hangovers. I averaged about a book every three years, and I kept writing articles for top magazines (one, incidentally and ironically, for *Horizon* on America's alcoholic writers). I would average about six portraits a year, and in 1984 I did a 35 by 10 foot mural for a posh San Francisco restaurant named Harris', managing not to fall off the scaffolding in the process. I also managed to hang on to a close relationship to my four children and two step-children, twenty years old to thirty-two, though it was often strained to the limit by my drinking. For example, the two girls were very hurt but said they forgave me for being drunk at both their debut cotillions, their Big Night, held ten years apart in San Francisco.

I was not exclusively a solitary drinker and, in spite of my intake, we had a large circle of interesting, creative friends who entertained us and whom we entertained at our unique, rambling beach house south of Santa Barbara.

There was an apocryphal story going around among our hard-drinking friends that after one of our bibulous cocktail parties the blind pianist, George Shearing, was elected to drive everyone to the restaurant on the theory that "he was the best we had at the time." I went trout fishing like a normal father every summer in Montana with my brother and my oldest son, albeit with a pint of gin aslime in the creel among the fish, and often my fingers were too trembly to affix fly to tippet.

In other words, I wasn't on skid row, nor had I yet hit bottom. But all the signs were pointed that way. At my age was it possible to reverse the trend, to change my life?

"Yes," said my ex-father-in-law. "Try Betty Ford's."

One day in February, 1985, I decided to do it. No one

knows exactly what makes a drunk decide to stop drinking any more than they know what makes him decide to start. But, in addition to the increasingly disastrous effects on my marriage, there were five happenings over several weeks that helped me arrive at the decision.

The first was almost comical: One morning I was gargling with Listerine and instead of spitting it out I just swallowed it. Hey, why not? Twenty-six percent was 26 percent—why waste it? My wife had all the booze hidden or locked up. I took another swig. Then I looked in the mirror with loathing and asked myself, Jesus, why would anyone in his right mind do something like that?

And I knew the answer was in the question: *I wasn't in my right mind.* I thought of actor/sailor Sterling Hayden's telling me of a desperate deck hand breaking the compass to get the alcohol. I thought of my wife's uncle, the polo player, who shortly before his death from alcoholism used to drink his wife's perfume and whose actions used to be ridiculed by us in the old days.

A week later a note from the director-writer-musician Ian Bernard, a Santa Barbara friend, saying, "Dear Barny: This is tough to write, but I have to warn you that if I see you get in a car and drive off in the condition you did today after our lunch, I shall feel obliged, no matter how reluctantly, to call the cops and ask them to take you in as a menace to yourself and others."

Mind your own business, I thought. Hell, I'd made it home, hadn't I? But the note nagged at me; it was one thing for a friend to think that message, but to go to the trouble of sitting down and writing it took courage and genuine concern.

Then there was the evening at a party in San Francisco when I saw my great friend of thirty-three years, the writer Niels Mortensen, and asked how he was.

"Fine," he said, looking at me with infinite sadness. "That

is, as fine as I can feel while watching my best friend drink
himself to death."

Come on! I wasn't *that* bad, by a long shot. Was I? Hell, a lot
of people didn't even know I had a problem. But then, when
I thought about it, they were generally drinking pals who
liked to have good ol' buddies around who drank as much or
more than they. Besides which, Niels wasn't my best friend.
My best friend was the bottle. It never failed me. It always
brought relief quickly and whenever I asked for it. It never
rejected my manuscripts, never looked at one of my portraits
and said there was a little something wrong with the mouth,
never put me on hold, never said I was too fat, bald, or old,
never said I was a lousy lover, never took Wednesday off to
play golf like doctors, never threw things at me, and was
always available.

It was my indispensable friend, no matter how sick it might
make me. But Niels's words bothered me mightily in the next
days.

Shortly thereafter I had a call in midmorning from Artie
Shaw, the musician, a man I greatly admire, and upon hearing me talk, he said, not unkindly, "I'll call back when you're
sober. I suppose you know you're throwing a lot of talent
down the toilet. Hey, man, this is the real thing, this isn't the
dress rehearsal! I can't forgive you for all the time you're
wasting. Don't you realize that all you've got is time, that time
is all any of us has?"

There were tears in my eyes when he hung up. Why would
he do that to me? How could I be drunk? I'd only had two
drinks this morning.

But that phrase kept running through my head: Time is all
we have, time is all we have . . .

Maybe I did need some help—at least to cut down on the
drinking. Eliminating my best friend completely and forever
was unthinkable. I wasn't really an alcoholic—*they* lay in gut-
ters, clutching bottles in brown paper bags and went to

boring meetings—I was just an all-American two-fisted drinker. But I'd start tapering off tomorrow. For sure. Tomorrow.

Then the final and decisive event was a wrenching letter from my thirty-three-year-old son, who lives in Paris, where he is a free-lance writer:

Dear Dad: You simply have *got* to stop drinking. I could have cried when I saw the shape you were in when you met me at the airport. You are killing yourself. It is *terrible* for us, your children who love you so much. Do you realize how people at the Writers' Conference in June were making fun of you and laughing at you behind your back? People who used to admire you? You could have at least twenty great and productive years left if you quit—NOW. You say your main objection to getting help is that you can't spare the time or money to go to a rehabilitation place. But you could write in there, and maybe draw. I called the Betty Ford Center and the cost is $6,ooo for the four weeks. I enclose a check for that amount made out to the Center. I can spare it and don't worry about paying it back; it's a gift. Believe me, it's the easiest check I ever wrote—Cash it—soon.

I dissolved in tears. *Time is all we have.* When I was able, I reached for the phone. At the Betty Ford Center a deep friendly voice said his name was Malcolm and informed me that they could not take me for six weeks at least. I pleaded with him. I had made up my mind—I would drive down the four hours today. I didn't want all that time, six weeks in which I might change my mind. Malcolm was patient but firm—there was no room at that time. He would let me know if there was a cancellation.

I went out and got drunk.

The next day Malcolm called and said hooray, there was an

opening—a patient had quit after two days of treatment. I said I'd be there the next day. And went out and got drunk.

"Last drink of my life," I said to my friend the Mexican bartender on lower State Street.

"Oh, shit, yes," he said laconically.

The next morning, Valentine's Day, I said good-bye to my wife. She was sobbing.

"What are you crying about?" I asked. I hadn't anticipated this reaction.

"They say people come out of there all changed," she said. "We had some fun drinking, sometimes. It wasn't *all* bad. Maybe you won't want me when you come back."

I kissed her hard. "Maybe I'll want you more," I said distractedly. God, I felt so sick.

But there were doubts. What if the damned thing worked and I came out not drinking and she was still drinking? Could I handle that?

One thing at a time. And time is all we have, right?

o   o   o

I felt terrible and about to throw up. In front of my blood-shot eyes in Rancho Mirage was a mirage: Floating there in the desert in a sea of grass, newly cut, was what appeared to be a country club. Only there was no golf course. There are some sixty-five golf courses in the Palm Springs area, but this wasn't one of them. It looked like an elegant clubhouse in need of Robert Trent Jones. There were four other one-story buildings behind it, and off to the left was a large pond with three swans gliding gracefully on it.

How could any place with an address like 39000 Bob Hope Drive, Rancho Mirage, expect to be taken seriously?

A tall white-haired man opened the glass door for me. "Hi, I'm Edward," he said genially, shaking hands.

A week later he would joke, "My own hand shook for an

hour after that contact with yours!" One of several "graduate" volunteers, he took my suitcase to the registration desk. I
was in Firestone, the nucleus of the rehabilitation center. As I
looked around, my first thought was how very unlike a clinic
it appeared; there were no visible white-coated doctors in the
spacious lobby, no nurses in uniform, no patients in gowns,
no hospital smell. Just several normal-looking, informally
dressed people of various shapes and colors, wandering
around, going into the little gift and candy shop, the cafeteria, the office doors, sitting on the couches talking or
looking at the handsome framed prints on the wall.

Where were the drunkies, the alcoholics and addicts, the
dope fiends, the crazies, the inmates kept? Tucked out of the
way in wards?

After I signed in, a slim man in a sport coat and bow tie
introduced himself. He was Malcolm. He led me to an empty
office, put my suitcase on a table, and began to go through it
purposefully, saying, "Sorry about this—standard."

He confiscated a bottle of after-shave lotion, aspirin, and
some pills.

"I have to take those," I said. "Blood pressure."

"You can get them from the nurse every morning at eight
right here."

He took away the Listerine, saying with a laugh, "We get
some beauts in here who actually drink this stuff."

I took heart that I appeared so normal that he and I could
laugh about those others, those beauts.

I had six paperback books—two Elmore Leonards for fun,
and four for self-improvement I'd been "dying to read" for a
quarter of a century: *The Red and the Black, The Idiot, Lord Jim,*
and *Swann's Way*. Here, with four boring weeks staring me in
the face, I would finally get through them.

"Gotta take those," said Malcolm.

"No reading?" I exclaimed. "How about magazines and
newspapers?"

"You can read the paper after seven at night. No magazines. No books. No distractions."

Jesus. If I felt sick before, I felt sicker now.

Four weeks without reading! Not since I was a child had I gone a day without reading a book of some sort. I read at breakfast, even if only the cereal boxes. I read in the bathroom, in elevators, at stoplights.

Malcolm closed the suitcase. "Let's go see the doctor."

"I'd like to call my wife," I said. "Tell her I got here okay."

"We'll call her for you," he said. "No phone calls till after the fifth day. In or out. No visitors for a week either."

As we started out of the office, I asked gloomily, "Any good restaurants around here?"

"A few," he said, "but, of course, you can't leave the premises. Not for a month."

Lord, I was in a concentration camp!

But I reminded myself I could walk out of here anytime I wanted to. I hadn't signed anything that committed me to stay here. Give it a day, maybe two, then split. God, I needed a drink.

But what about the money? My son's $6,000—would they refund it? I'd signed several papers at the desk, but I hadn't read them; felt too sick, too busy worrying about whether my trembling fingers could work the pen. I didn't want them to see that—afraid they'd put me over at Eisenhower Hospital where I'd heard they put people for detox who arrived in bad condition. I'd been careful not to arrive too bent out of shape. Only had a half pint of Tanqueray that morning—didn't want to draw any extra days here in this looney bin. Thirty days was enough. Thirty days was appalling. And the newspapers had said that Liza Minnelli had done eight whole weeks. How had she stood it?

The doctor was a pleasant bearded man in his thirties. He did the usual physical checkup, blood pressure, and so forth. I felt awful.

"Now a few questions," he said, a pen poised over a form. "Last drink?"

I looked at him dumbly.

"You had your last drink when?"

"Yesterday," I said forthrightly. "Day before yesterday actually."

He wrote something down, then said cheerfully, "Know how you can tell when an alcoholic is lying?"

I shook my head.

"When you see his lips moving!" He laughed.

"That's a good one," I mumbled. "Lips moving."

I wondered how close the bathroom was.

"You're a writer," he said looking at my file. "I read *Death in the Afternoon.*"

"So did I," I said.

"Didn't you write it?"

"Hemingway," I said.

There was a *Ladies* down the hall. Could a *Gentlemen* be far behind?

"Excuse me," I said, getting up hastily.

I made the toilet, but just barely. I stayed there awhile, talking to God on the big white phone, as a drunk friend of mine always said, and when I went back to the doctor's office, I felt better, almost jaunty.

"Throw up often?" he asked matter-of-factly.

"Last few weeks," I said.

He looked at me.

Then I said to myself, Hell you're paying this money, you're stuck here for a while, you might as well try to tell the truth.

"Last year, last couple of years, actually."

I'd heard that all of the employees of the Betty Ford Clinic were ex-drunks.

"Sir," I said, "were you an alcoholic?"

"Still am," he said. "A recovering alcoholic. Once an alky,

14

always an alky. Once you become a pickle, you can never be a cucumber again, right? We can never again drink like"—he gestured toward the front door—"like the civilians out there." His voice put quotes around the word "civilian." "You see, you and I and everyone else in here, Mrs. Ford, all of us, have been singled out to have this incurable and ultimately fatal disease. But"—he smiled—"would you swap it for some other fatal disease, like AIDS or cancer, say? We know we can arrest *this* one in most cases."

He gave me some pills to take for withdrawal symptoms, and after a while two young men in sport shirts showed up at the doctor's office. Fellow patients, Walt and Tim, they were assigned to show me to my quarters and orient me.

"You're lucky," the older one said, picking up my suitcase. "You drew McCallum—it's the best of the three living quarters. The other two are separate, either all men or all women; ours is coed."

I'd show them I was one of the boys. "Are we allowed to . . . er . . . fraternize?"

"There are two easy ways to get kicked out of here," said Walt. "One is to bring booze or dope in, the other is to fraternize."

"There go my Liz Taylor fantasies," I said.

"She was a great gal," said Tim. "I'll tell you about her later."

As we went through the lobby, Walt explained that there were only sixty patients at a time, and these were broken up into three sections of twenty people each. There was a staff of seventy-five, including seven ministers, priests, and rabbis.

"We can mingle with the others occasionally, but you're supposed to eat and socialize with your own group, essentially."

Like at prep school, where we were arbitrarily divided into Alpha, Beta, and Gamma groups for intramural sports and activities.

I was surprised to walk past a door lettered "Mrs. Gerald Ford."

"Is she ever here?"

"Actually, just about every day," Tim said.

"What's she like?"

"You'll find out."

We walked out of the back of the building. "Men's"—Tim said, pointing to the structure to the right—"women straight ahead, and coed to the left."

The thick, recently watered grass felt and smelled good as we walked toward McCallum Hall. The desert lay beyond where the grass stopped and the beautiful jagged San Jacinto Mountains jutted up abruptly in the dazzling February sun.

"That's where Sinatra's plane ran into a peak and killed his mother," Walt volunteered.

"Bob Hope gave the eighty acres this place is built on," said Tim. "And a lot of bigwigs gave millions, like Annenberg and Firestone."

"How come all the stars come here?" I asked.

"It's the best," said Tim simply. "I've been to three other places, too. This one works."

"What do they do that's so special here?" I asked. "Hypnosis? Aversion techniques? Drugs?"

"Ah, it's too complicated to explain," said Walt. "You'll find out."

"Is the place loaded with celebrities now?"

"I'm not one. Are you? That's been blown all out of proportion. For every Liz Taylor or Bob Mitchum or Mary Tyler Moore or an astronaut, there's a hundred housewives or gardeners or insurance salesmen or doctors. But it does seem that more drunks jump out of penthouse windows than flophouses."

We went in a side door of the low building, down a corridor, and into room 20.

"Here we go!" said Walt, sliding the suitcase into the room.

"Welcome to the BFC. See you at lunch in half an hour. And punctuality in this place is rated right up there with godliness, cleanliness, and sobriety."

The two-bed room was like a nice motel. A short, shirtless hirsute man of about forty came in from the sunny porch. He held out his hand.

"Shalom," he said. "My name is Moishe—from Israel." With his prickly black beard he looked like an amiable hedgehog. "You are here why?"

"Excuse me?"

"For what reason you are here?"

"Alcohol."

He nodded. "Me—alcohol, drugs. Six weeks." He pointed at one of the beds. "Dis guy—three days, he don't like"—he slapped his hands together—"he go to Las Vegas. Hah!"

"You like?" I asked. "You like it here?"

He nodded. "What you do?"

"Writer. And you?"

"Diamonds." He grinned. "This place worth two Kohinoors!"

He put on a shirt and led the way down the hall to the main room. There was an office and meeting rooms and a big open kitchen area adjacent to a sunken lounge. A dozen or so men and women were at tables writing or conversing over coffee on the sofas or reading textbooks or pamphlets on alcoholism. They looked up and smiled at me. It seemed all were smoking. Only one, a florid-faced Irishman, looked anything like the standard idea of a drunk.

A short woman with bobbed gray hair came out of her office and walked up to me with a smile. "Hi, I'm Jerry, your counselor. Come on in. We'll talk a bit before lunch."

I liked her immediately but was intimidated by her. Afraid of her. And why not? She held the key, I knew, that would ultimately get me out of here.

She was dressed in a suede skirt, cashmere sweater, and flat no-nonsense shoes. Her direct manner was also no-nonsense. I followed her into her office and sat down by her desk. There was an Audubon print on the wall of a swan.

"Like the ones on the pond," I said to be saying something.

"Oh, those?" she said briskly. "Those are plastic."

"Plastic?" I asked numbly.

"They're there to scare away the migrating ducks and geese, who mess up the place."

I felt stupid. "Thought they were real," I mumbled.

"Don't worry. Everything's going to be a bit confusing for a few days while you dry out." She turned her wise penetrating eyes on me after opening my file folder. "Here's the routine except for Sundays. Up at six-fifteen, make your bed, breakfast, walk, therapeutic chore, that is, whatever you're assigned to do on the bulletin board, like vacuuming or setting the tables—some columnist said we put Liz Taylor on the 'toilet detail'—there's no such thing. We've found that a little menial chore is therapeutic. Morning lecture's at nine. At ten you and five others meet here in my office for group. Then lunch, afternoon lecture, and your group meets in here again. Then exercise in the pool or aerobics, dinner at five-fifteen, evening lecture, reading and writing assignments, bed." She gave me her good smile. "Think you can stand it?"

I wasn't exactly sure, but I said, "Better than the options, I guess."

"You *guess?*" She picked up some of my documents. "You were on a toboggan ride to nowhere it appears. Why are you here, Barny?"

"Well, you see, my son who lives in Paris—"

"Why are you here?"

"Well, my wife and my son, they—"

"Why're you here?"

I sighed. "I was sick and tired of being sick and tired."

She nodded. "So why're you here?"

"Alcohol," I said.

She applauded silently. "And we're not going to let you

forget it. For the next thirty days, maybe longer—you've got quite a history here. How long have you been having a problem with alcohol?"

"Well, the last couple of years I've—"

She looked down at the file. "You were arrested almost twenty years ago for drunk driving."

"Yes, but then I gave it up for at least—"

"Are you an alcoholic, Barny?"

"Well, I can go—I have gone—long periods where—"

"Are you an alcoholic?"

"Once, about three, four years ago, I went four months without—"

"Are you an alcoholic?"

"I suppose so or I wouldn't be here, right?"

She sighed. "Still some denial there. Well, go get some lunch and after the lecture I'll see you here for group. Now here's your *Alcoholics Anonymous* book." She handed me a large blue book. "We'll be using it a lot. Plus a notebook; you are to write your feelings in it every night and turn it in to me before eight every morning. Plus your *Twenty-Four Hour Book*. Plus the *Twelve Steps and Traditions* book."

Homework. I was a third grader again. It was demeaning.

A voice called out over a loudspeaker, "Circle time." In the lounge people got up from the tables and couches and went outside the glass doors onto the lawn.

"Where's Larry?" asked a girl.

"Saw him in his room."

"I'll go get him."

"Never mind. Here he comes."

Twenty of us—about half men and half women, ranging in age from sixty-four to twenty-two—stood in a circle holding hands. One man led off with Reinhold Niebuhr's prayer and the others joined in: "God grant me the serenity to accept the things I cannot change, the courage to change the things I can, and the wisdom to know the difference."

We broke the circle and set off across the lawn. Everyone

seemed cheery and friendly, doggedly so, and I exchanged polite where-are-you-froms with several people on the way over to the cafeteria in the main building. There was a kind of collegiate rah-rah gaiety in the air that I seriously doubted that I would ever become a part of.

I felt sick again. I let them go on and headed for the bathroom.

Twenty-nine days to go and this one wasn't even over yet. I still didn't know what the hell they did in this place, and I wasn't at all sure I was going to stick around and find out. My suitcase wasn't unpacked yet. I wanted to go home. Why not just give me some sort of pill to keep me sober, something I could take every day to make alcohol an anathema to me, something like Antabuse?

I didn't want lunch in their bloody cafeteria; I wanted a drink, a double greyhound.

T W O

As I started into the sunny cafeteria, Mrs. Ford came out of her office. Elegantly dressed in a robin's-egg-blue suit, she carried a manila file folder and was flanked by two people, who I assumed were part of her staff. She was busy talking to them but flashed me a warm "welcome, Mr. Newface" smile in passing. A young patient stood aside to usher her in the door.

"Mrs. President, the cafeteria itself is nice," he said boldly in his Brooklyn accent. "But stay away from the food."

His face flushed after he'd made his daring little joke, but Mrs. Ford laughed easily. "But what's the alternative?" she quipped and kept going, turning left into a room where the staff, counselors, and important visitors ate. I was impressed by her general looks and demeanor, which I hadn't been particularly before in public appearances when she was in the White House. There were a few more wrinkles than the photos showed, but she was still very handsome, with serious vulnerable blue eyes above a Hollywood smile.

I got a trayful of food, though my stomach churned at the sight of anything to eat, and looked around the crowded room. People from McCallum, my dorm, sat over on the right third of the cafeteria, and some groups at the different tables for four motioned to me to sit down. Friendliness and smiles were the order of the day, talking back and forth between tables, in-jokes. We introduced ourselves.

Tolstoy's famous opening line of Anna Karenina, "All happy families are happy in the same way—all unhappy families are unhappy in different ways," could be paraphrased "All sober people are sober in the same way—all drunks are drunken in different ways."

I was discovering that alcoholics and druggies came in startlingly different shapes, ages, colors, and origins. The group I sat with included—and I'm changing the names to protect anonymity—Dave, a sixty-four-year-old Stanford science professor. Tall, slim, with a shock of white hair, he grinned and joked through lunch, acted as though he'd been here for months though it was less than a week. He looked like everyone's favorite New England rector. Could he really be a drunk?

"Pills and booze," he explained jovially.

"You look so healthy."

"I quit for a month before coming in here."

"If you could quit on your own, why'd you come here?"

"Afraid I might go back."

I found that no one seemed reticent to state his addiction. The handsome Sacramento Mexican, Chico, mumbled simply, "Heroin." He was only twenty-six, strong and athletic, and here but a few days; his face was still gray and tight, and his eyes were nervous and fearful from the withdrawal.

The other person at the table was Beth, twenty-seven years old, short and stout, with fat that looked applied and unnatural. She had a very pretty face. "I used to be a star swimmer, believe it or not. Then the beer got to me—a case a weekend seemed about right. But no hard stuff or dope," she added defensively. Alcohol hadn't yet done any damage to her pretty face. She said she had a loving husband back in Connecticut who had persuaded her to come to Betty Ford's. I liked her immediately.

They chatted and filled me in on the routine and procedures of the clinic at dessert time. Some others brought their coffee to the table to say hello to the newcomer. Everyone seemed so damned helpful and warm it was sickening to an already sick person. These poor bastards—not only could they not drink, they had to pretend to be happy about it.

And all they talked about was one subject. It was like a writers' conference, where every conversation is about writing. Or a dog show, where nothing but canine matters is admissible. Here it was alcohol in all its forms that was discussed, objectively or subjectively, past or present or future. I made notes later of some fragments, many of which were in a jargon I didn't understand then, the recovering alcoholic's special slogan language:

"I'm having a hard time with my Higher Power concept, being I'm an agnostic."

"No problem. Your Higher Power doesn't have to be God. My counselor says it doesn't have to be God—it can be your group or this clinic or a doorknob."

"I can't see asking a doorknob for guidance in helping me give up booze."

"Your God can be anything or anyone just as long as you're not Him."

"Did you see Laurie's sign in her room: 'God grant me patience—right *now*'?"

"How about the new one on the bulletin board: 'Let's get together and call it alcohol-wasm'? Get it? Ism? Wasm?"

"Nah, too cute. I like that new Irish guy's bumper sticker: 'Reality is an illusion created by a shortage of alcohol.' "

And there was lots of gossip.

23

"Didja hear about what Larry told Mrs. Ford just now about the crummy food?"

"Yeah? How'd she take it?"

"Bill just told me in the chow line that she was real upset."

"She should be."

"I heard on the grapevine that Liza Minnelli went back out there." (A euphemism for drinking or using, I gathered.)

"Not true. Read where Liz Taylor said this place saved her life. Said, 'Where oh where was Betty Ford five years ago when I really needed her!'"

"Dead drunk, that's where!" someone volunteered gratuitously.

"How about Bob Mitchum being interviewed the other day and they asked him if he got much out of his four weeks here and he said 'Sure, I learned to put more ice in my drinks.'"

"My counselor was his when he was here and he says he's a really good guy."

"How come I've got Colette for a roommate instead of him?" said Beth.

"Read that article by that young superstar? About her father? She tells how she'd look forward to the mornings because her father'd be hung over but sober. Breaks your heart when she tells her father, 'I wish I knew you only in the morning.'"

"Sounds just like my daughter when she put me in here. God, what we did to our families!"

"I was just in group and it was so funny! Fred, the doctor, y'know? Well, the counselor was running on about alcoholics' denial—denial this and denial that—and Fred pipes up solemnly in a Southern accent, 'Suh, I done always thought denial was a ribber in Egypt!' Even Patty cracked up."

Lord, was I going to be able to take a month of this sophomoric banter?

I hadn't touched my food, but managed to get down and keep down some iced coffee before we broke up. "Now what?" I asked.

"One o'clock lecture," I was told.

But first we had to go back to McCallum, make the circle, and say the Serenity Prayer.

"Is it always the same boring prayer? Don't they vary it?"

"Sometimes you get the Lord's Prayer—it's done before every group activity without fail."

"Why?"

"Don't ask, just do," said Dave, the nice college professor. "It works. Might seem dumb at first, but it all works. And no one seems quite sure why. Just got to trust it—and them. They know what they're about. Ours but to do or die."

The talk took place in the lecture room across from the cafeteria. All sixty patients assembled there, the three dorms' inhabitants sticking with each other. The lecturer, an energetic research scientist of forty dressed in sports clothes, explained that he'd been working for several years with a large colony of white rats in an attempt to learn more about man's relationship to alcohol. Some of the rats would not touch alcohol, even when deprived of all water. They would die of thirst before drinking alcohol. Some would tolerate alcohol when mixed with water, and some others grew to prefer it to plain water. He showed films of the colony before the "dinner hour." When the "dining room" and "bar" were opened, most would head for the food, while some would stop off for a few sips from the alcohol siphon before going in. A small number would stay in "the bar," skip their food, and become intoxicated, reeling around and disoriented. The next day the same rats would repeat the process, eager for some "hair of the dog" to alleviate their hangovers. The audience laughed repeatedly with recognition.

"I guess we know what category we fit into, don't we?" said the doctor, a recovering alcoholic, as he joined in the laughter. "Now, that long ongoing experiment has a point and a goal. Like so many people, certain of those rats have an X factor in their makeup that makes them not be able to assimilate alcohol and also makes them susceptible to alcohol and to

25

crave alcohol. They do not have weak characters, they are not less moral than their fellows. They have a disease, and we are trying to determine what it is in their physical makeup that makes them react differently to the intake of ethyl alcohol. We are hoping to pinpoint that X chromosome so that we can spot it in humans and determine early on who among us is prone to contract the disease and then do something about it."

He told about experiments and studies in Denmark where identical twins were separated at birth and brought up in totally different environments in loving, nondrinking, foster homes hundreds of miles from each other and their alcoholic natural parents, and how they still would turn into alcoholics themselves.

"They had the X factor in their genes," the lecturer said simply.

At question time, Dave, the science professor, asked, "If it is so related to the genes we inherit and if it is indeed a disease, why all the emphasis here on uncovering the reasons why we drink?"

"That is a good and ongoing question, never quite clear-cut in this baffling affliction that we are only just beginning to understand. In most cases alcoholism is both psychological and physical. It is both psychological dependence and physiological addiction. And it *is* a disease because we can recognize it, diagnose it, and, unless it is treated, the prognosis is always the same: death. Either the heart, liver, or kidneys fail, or the alcoholic kills himself in a fall or with a pistol or an automobile."

Then he looked over the audience of sixty and said chillingly but in a matter-of-fact voice, "Look around you, ladies and gentlemen. One year from now one-third of you will probably be drinking and using again. And five years from now one-half of those will be dead."

Lord, which percentage would I be in? Would I see my

kids get married and have children? Or would I end up a statistic in this guy's computer software?

The hour was up, and I left the room a trifle shaken. I saw that the little candy and notion shop was open and I wandered in, attracted by all the books and magazines. At last some reading matter! Some escape from this incessant talk about alcohol!

Alas, all the publications were about that liquid. Hundreds of books and pamphlets, from the magazine *The A. A. Grapevine* to the famous Dr. Joseph Pursch's *Dear Doc.* (It was he who first got Betty Ford herself into treatment.) Her best-selling *The Times of My Life* was, of course, prominently displayed. As were T-shirts with slogans so dear to alcoholics on them: "One Day at a Time," "Easy Does It," "Let Go and Let God," the Serenity Prayer, and so forth.

I bought a large Hershey bar—like most alcoholics deprived of alcohol, I was beginning to crave sugar already—and ate it on the way back to McCallum Hall.

It was a stunningly beautiful day—the sky looked like the sky in a child's painting, the same bright blue all the way down from the top to the horizon and only one small Magritte cloud in the center. I longed to go sit alone by the pond, with its plastic swans, but it was time for group. Just as I turned into the building I saw a young bearded man run to the edge of the pond, cup his hands, and shout to the heavens, "Fuck you!"

Then he turned and repeated the alarming yell in a different direction and then once more, before turning and loping up to the dorm.

"Good afternoon," he panted pleasantly as he went past me.

Patients were gathering in Jerry's office. There were seven of us: Dave, the college professor, and Chico, the twenty-two-year-old heroin addict among them. The other three were Tim, the fortyish airline pilot; Terry, a black nurse with dyed blond hair from Arizona; and Willy, a fat architect from Iowa. And finally, Bill, the young bearded man from the pond came in. I would find out he was a surgeon from Chicago.

"Hi, I'm Jerry," our counselor started. "And I'm an alcoholic."

"Hi, Jerry!" was the automatic and expected response.

"Well, Bill, you certainly were in fine voice today."

The bearded man grinned and I could see he was not as young as I'd first thought—perhaps thirty-eight or forty years old. "Only two more days. I'll sort of miss it. Damned therapeutic."

"Well, you can always do it on your own, you know."

"Somehow it's more fun this way. It'd be kind of embarrassing if it weren't an assignment. They'd lock me up back in my home state."

"Speaking of assignments"—Jerry took a sleep shade off her desk—"Dave, I want you to wear this for thirty-six hours. Group, any idea why?"

Someone suggested tentatively, "So he'll have to depend on other people?"

Jerry nodded. "He's got to learn the humility of being blind and having to ask other people for help. All your life, Dave, you've thought you were too damned big and important to have to stoop to ask for help."

Dave flushed and took the mask.

"And Chico? You will be in charge of David, of seeing he gets to meals and lectures and exercise. Why Chico, group?"

"To learn some responsibility," said Bill.

"Right."

Dave donned his mask with good humor. Chico looked detached and pained.

"Well, Tim," Jerry said with her good smile as she turned to the airline pilot. "You graduate tomorrow. How does it feel?"

"I think that—" Tim began but was interrupted by Dave with mock reprimand.

"No, Tim, how do you *feel*. 'Think that' always precedes an intellectualizing, not an emotional, reaction!"

Everyone laughed, including Jerry, at the in-joke.

"You're right," said Tim. It was hard to imagine that this intelligent-looking, healthy young man was ever a drunk or a junkie or both. "Okay, how do I *feel*? I feel—great—but . . ."

"Apprehensive?"

He nodded. "Slightly. And a little sad. Hell, a lot. I've come to love this place in my time here. All you guys. I can't believe what a mess I was when I came in. I can't believe how different I feel now."

"But?" said Jerry.

"I'm going back to that big wide drinkin', usin' world out there. And how will my wife and kids adjust to a sober husband and daddy?"

"You'll do fine," said Terry, the nurse, patting his leg. The others murmured in agreement.

"Do you think you'll drink and use again?" Jerry asked.

"No way." Tim shook his head. "I hope and pray my Higher Power sees to it that I never take another drink as long as I live. I'm a different person."

"Amen."

"Look, Tim, you can make not drinking a great big mountain you'll never be able to climb, or you can make it a little pebble you step over every day. So just don't drink one day at a time."

Jerry turned to the group. "And speaking of that, what was the entry for today in this?" She held up the small *Twenty-Four Hour Book*. "Chico?"

The young man shook his head unhappily. "I didn't read it this morning."

"Why not?"

"Didn't have time," he mumbled.

"Listen, Chico, and this applies to all of you." Her voice was suddenly schoolmistress stern. "The money you paid to get here doesn't in any way automatically guarantee you your medallion at the end of your time. It also doesn't mean we can't ask you to leave at any damn time—expel you—if we feel you aren't doing the assignments or are in any way interfering with the other patients' recovery. Part of your assignment, a very small part, is to read the daily entry in this book. For your information, here is today's, February 14, which all of you when you get out should have emblazoned on your forehead. I'm not going to be around to harp on it." She read from the book: "'After that first drink, we had a single-track mind. It was like a railroad train. The first drink started it off and it kept going on the single track until it got to the end of the line, drunkenness. We alcoholics knew this was the inevitable result when we took the first drink, but still we couldn't keep away from liquor. Our willpower was gone. We had become helpless and hopeless.'"

Jerry turned to Willy, a pudgy thirty-five-year-old man with an unlined cherubic face. "Willy, anything on your mind today? You look down."

"I'm Willy, an alcoholic and addict." He shifted uncomfortably in his chair. "Had a bad night last night. Thinkin' of Janine again. If I'da had the access last night, I mighta used or drank. Janine was the girl I loved—only girl I ever loved. And she's dead and I feel like shit."

"Tell us about her, Willy."

"I told you once."

"Some of us didn't hear it. That was over a month ago."

Over a month ago! How long had this guy been here? So they could keep you here indefinitely! Fear gripped my already sick intestines.

"Well, I was studying architecture in San Francisco and I was in love with Janine and I wanted to marry her, and she said okay, she loved me, and we were going to get married.

30

Then one day I phoned her—she lived across the bay in Berkeley—and, shit, her line was busy and busy, so I skipped my last class that afternoon and drove over there and walked into her house and there Janine was in bed and the phone was off the hook and there with her was one of my teachers at the college. He was dressed and sitting on the end of the bed and nothing was going on at the moment, but his coat and tie was off, and I called him every kind of name, accused him of knowing my schedule so he'da knowed I wouldn't be there and could come over and bang Janine into orbit, and I called her every kind of a deceivin' slut and whore, and, hell, I ran outta there cryin' like a fool. Then later I got holda myself and phoned her and said I was sorry, and she said listen that guy is just a friend who dropped by when she was takin' a nap and nothin' happened at all and I said some drop-by, all the way to Berkeley from San Francisco, but she said she loved me and still wanted to marry me, and I said why don't you come over to the city tonight and we'll have dinner at Gino's, and she said fine, okay. And then on the way over she stopped her car on the Bay Bridge and—and—"

Tears were coursing down his cheeks.

"And she jumped, and I can't get her out of my mind, what I shoulda done, what I shoulda said to stop her. It was the end of my world, my life."

"And that's what started you drinking and using?" asked Jerry, looking deep into his eyes.

Willy nodded and caught a sob. "Yes, I wanted to forget it all and got stoned and stayed stoned or drunk, and just when I think it's gone from my mind, it comes back and I feel like hell and I drink and use."

Jerry ran her fingers through her bobbed gray hair and turned to us. "What are you hearing, group?"

"Bullshit," said Terry, the nurse.

"Bullshit," echoed Bill, the doctor.

Willy looked as though he'd been struck in his fat face. His mouth began to work and he started to sputter. "But—but—"

Jerry put her hand on his shoulder. "Be quiet and listen, Willy."

"A lot of PP," said Dave. "Sounds as though he's on the pity pot."

"God, Willy," said Tim. "You're talking about an event that happened—what?—fifteen years ago! And you mean you've been loaded over that for all these years? Blaming yourself?"

"Are you sure it really happened at all?" asked Bill.

Chico, Willy's roommate, said, "What about Anne, the girl you've had for two years now? You seem to love her. How come you're flashing back to Janine all of a sudden?"

"I don't think Janine has anything to do with the way you are feeling, Willy," said Jerry. "I think it makes a good cop-out. What do you think?"

She handed him a Kleenex, and he sniffed and said, "I think you're all a bunch of heartless bastards who don't understand, that's what I think."

"Willy, how old were you when you first got drunk?" asked Jerry. "Wasn't it in your early teens?"

Willy nodded sullenly.

"Well, that was long before Janine, wasn't it? And you used marijuana and beer constantly all through high school to make the pain go away, didn't you? What was the pain, Willy? Was it because you were fat and unathletic and didn't hunt and fish the way other boys did—was that it, Willy? The way your brothers did? I've got a questionnaire here from your brother Ted that he filled out at our request and that's the picture he gives."

Willy looked stricken.

"The way your father wanted you to be?"

He closed his eyes and his lips compressed.

"Your father didn't understand you at all, did he?"

Willy's thick red lips trembled and he whispered, "He called me a poet as though that was a bad word. He implied that I was a faggot, though I liked girls plenty. He looked down on me 'cause I used pot even though he'd go out and get drunk with the fellas all the time."

"What would you say to him if he were here, right in this room now?"

Willy was trembling, but he thought and then swallowed twice. "I'd ask him why he didn't love me the way he loved my brothers."

"Pretend this chair here is your father. Get down on your knees and pretend it's your father, Willy, and say to it what you'd say to your father."

Willy got off his chair and clumsily knelt in front of the empty chair and looked at Jerry.

"Now, Willy, tell him. Look at the chair and tell him."

Willy cleared his throat. "Why didn't you love me like the others?" he began quietly.

"Use the words you'd use!" Jerry commanded. She took out two stuffed cloth baseball bats from the shelf.

"Daddy, I loved you!" blurted out Willy. "Goddamn it, why didn't you love me?"

"Tell him!" said Jerry, putting the cloth bats in his hands. "Tell him and hit him!"

Willy struck the chair seat with one of the bats. "You hated me, damn you!" He struck it with the other. "You made me feel like a fuckin' worm, you sonofabitch."

"Tell him!" Jerry encouraged him.

"Goddamn you to hell!" Willy cried, tears spurting from his eyes, as he beat the chair. "Why couldn't you have loved me just a little? I loved you, I loved you, Daddy. I really loved you! If you'd given me a chance I coulda learned to hunt and fish, if you'd only just taken me along!"

"That's it, Willy!" Jerry shouted.

"Oh Daddy, please take me along!"

The emotional scene went on for several minutes, and then Willy dropped the bats, flung his arms around the chair, and collapsed, his head on the seat, sobbing piteously.

Jerry knelt and put her arms around him and whispered, "We love you, Willy. Everything's all right."

We helped him back to his seat and several people said, "We love you."

"Thank you," he murmured weakly, gasping for breath. "I love you and this was good—and—and—and I feel okay now. I think maybe—maybe I've been using Janine for a crutch for a long time. I don't know. Maybe. She was plenty neurotic. She'd talked suicide and probably would have done it anyway. I'm glad I got this out about my father."

"That's the important part," said Jerry. "We'll quit for now."

We made a circle holding hands, said the Serenity Prayer, and the meeting broke up and people began to file out.

"Is it always like this?" I asked Tim.

"Sometimes," he said.

Blindfolded, Dave was being led out by Chico. "All things being equal," Dave said, "I'd prefer a good German shepherd with a harness."

"Stay," Jerry said to me, sitting at her desk and motioning me to a chair. She had my folder in front of her. "You went through an alcoholic program before. What was it like? And why didn't it work for you?"

I told her about the experience at the Schick-Shadel hospital in Santa Barbara four years before. This is a small, cozy clinic that advertises on television, assuring people with alcoholic problems that in "ten days plus a couple of two-day followups" it can rid people of their chemical dependence. It claims a very high rate of success and, though much smaller than Betty Ford's, people come from all over to the treatment centers in Seattle, Dallas, and Santa Barbara.

The "cure" consists mainly of what they call "duffys," after the old radio show *Duffy's Tavern*. A duffy takes place every other day during the person's stay. In a hospital-like setting and atmosphere, the patient is taken down the corridor in his bathrobe and slippers to a small room where a nurse in

34

uniform awaits him. The room is outfitted to look like a small, private bar—the best-stocked bar imaginable. Every kind of liquor, from Glenlivet to Jack Daniel's to Beefeater to Herradura tequila, is available. An injection is given to you in the shoulder that makes you allergic to alcohol. Then the nurse says something like, "Isn't this a lovely little bar? Let's have a little of your favorite gin and tonic, shall we?"

She pours it for you, a really stiff shot, makes you smell deeply of it, and says, "Doesn't it smell *good?* Down the hatch!"

You are seated with a large crescent-shaped basin around you, and that is lucky because the drink barely gets half swallowed before it comes up.

"Come on, now, drink up the rest!"

And in a moment she has another glass in your hand, this time perhaps beer. Then wine. Then Kahlua. Then Grand Marnier. Then bourbon. It makes no difference—it all comes up almost immediately. In thirty or forty minutes you ingest, or try to, about twenty drinks. You are gasping and pleading "No more, no more" by the end of the session. The taste is awful and just the smell of the alcohol as it comes near your nose and mouth triggers the vomitous response.

"Vile, nasty, stuff!" the nurse is saying toward the end. "Rotten, stinking poison! Have some more!"

Finally you are helped down the hall to your room, and for good measure a "butterfly" is given you—a doctored beer that causes violent retching and diarrhea for the rest of the day.

The next day you are given sodium pentathol and allowed to sleep, rest up from the grueling duffy, and prepare for the next one. In between one receives tender loving care, counseling, and programs based on Alcoholics Anonymous principles. Dr. Joseph Frawley, the son of the founder, is a concerned and conscientious mentor to all the patients during their stay. Ten days later you are discharged.

"Did it work?" asked Jerry.

"They claim a terrific success rate," I said, "and it worked for me—for a while."

I couldn't stand the sight or smell or alcohol for many weeks. Even detecting wine on a person's breath made me queasy. But the desire to drink was still there. After a month I tried a sip of wine at a party and had to run for the bathroom. But one day, six weeks later, I was passing my favorite low-down Mexican bar at about eleven in the morning. I decided to see if I could actually get down a drink. It wasn't a craving for alcohol, you understand. Purely an experiment. A challenge.

I walked into the stale air of the bar, past the faded bullfight posters, past the bowling game, down the line of habitual drinkers at the ancient bar, and got on my favorite stool.

"Where ya been?" the old barman greeted me.

"Away," I said.

I ordered the greyhound, a single shot of gin, well disguised with grapefruit juice. I took a sip. It stayed south. I took another. Just then a remarkable coincidence took place: I saw what looked like Dr. Joseph Frawley walk in. But it simply couldn't be—the head of Schick-Shadel Clinic for alcoholism in this part of town, and in a low-down bar?! Life's darkest and most humiliating moment—it *was* Dr. Frawley.

He walked by me, and I had one shoulder up and was trying to hide behind it.

"Car broke down," he said to the barman. "Use your phone?"

On his way out, he smiled at me and said, "Hi, Barny," with no malice or surprise in his voice. I ordered another drink, a double, and Operation Schick was over.

Jerry gave a little shudder. "I can't see paying someone to make one vomit, especially with all the free throwing up I did in my alcoholic career."

"Then you don't approve of the aversion method?"

"We approve of anything that works for you—anything

that gets you through the night, as Sinatra says. We just don't feel the aversion technique gets to the heart of the matter, so we don't use it here." She looked at her watch. "You'd better get to the exercise session—circle's about to begin."

As I got up, she added sincerely, "Oh, and in case I didn't tell you, we're very glad you're here, Barny."

"So am I," I said.

And I almost meant it.

T H R E E

Even in the swimming pool, between aerobic gyrations, the talk among the patients was of their disease—talk in their own Esperanto:

"Angie's got her Fifth Step tomorrow and she's all nervous."

"Coming to Tim's burning tonight?"

"Peter went to a gay AA meeting last night in Palm Springs."

"I hear Mrs. Ford's speaking tonight."

"Bullshit, I've been hearing that every day during my three weeks in this place."

It wasn't a regular pool, just a four-foot-deep exercise pool at the edge of the buildings. The instructor was a trim little blonde in a bikini who stood on the side of the pool executing the stretching, reaching, jumping maneuvers while twenty of us in the water imitated her to the rhythm of a rock and roll tape and her "anna-four-five-six-seven-eight . . . anna stretch those arms uppa to the sky . . ."

It was pleasant in the warm water and the late-afternoon sun, but the exercises were deceptively strenuous, and I soon found myself clinging to the side and gasping. Lord, I was in terrible shape, but so were many others. Only Dave, his lean jogger's body belying his sixty-four years, and Chico, once a high school basketball star until heroin and tequila got him, were doing the exercises vigorously to the end of the forty-five minutes.

There followed a brief volleyball game, and I watched in admiration as Chico would leap out of the water across the entire court to smash back an impossible volley.

Afterward, pretty Beth swam two fast laps, and as she propelled her body, chunky with the years of beer consumption, through the water, one could see that she had been a fine athlete at one time. When she came out of the pool panting and knocking the side of her head with the heel of her hand, I said, "Well, Esther Willims is in deep trouble."

"Who?" she asked brightly.

Oh, dear. I'd forgotten she was only twenty-seven.

We walked back across the grass to McCallum with Chico leading Dave, blindfolded again after a brief respite. Dave confirmed the fact that Betty Ford was the evening speaker.

"She speaks at least once every month so everyone gets to hear her before they leave."

Moishe was praying and reading the Torah when I got to my room. He had a yarmulke on his head and nodded without stopping his chant. I just had time to shave with my trembling hands and dress in slacks and a sweater when at five-fifteen the loud-speakers announced, "Circle for dinner."

I was exhausted and could have gladly fallen in bed.

After making the circle and once again reciting the Serenity Prayer, we walked over to the dining room in Firestone, where Beth, Dave, and Chico held a place for me at their table. As we ate, we compared our histories. No one seemed the least shy about disclosing his or her "drunk-alogue."

"My employer paid for me to come here," said Chico. "I've been in an aircraft factory, had a good job considering I'm only twenty-two."

He seemed brighter and less morose since the exercise.

"Didn't you say you stole money from him for your habit?" asked Beth.

"No—I stole from my parents' feed store, where I worked on the weekends." His handsome face went grim. "Heroin costs a lot of money. I want to pay them back."

"Are they giving you methadone here to get you away from the dope?" Dave inquired.

"I asked for it but the doctor said that prescribing meth-adone to a junkie is like treating an alcoholic with bourbon."

"So you went cold turkey?"

"No, I was in detox over at Eisenhower for a week, and they're giving me some pills now and phasing me out. But man, I could use a fix."

I knew how he felt; my body and mind were yelling for gin.

I tried talking to Chico about Mexico, a country I love, but he was totally American, knew little of Mexico, and barely spoke Spanish.

"My employers, Stanford, don't even know I'm here," said Dave. Chico brought him some coffee. "Nor do my students. They think I'm on a scientific dig in Egypt. They never saw me drunk. Most people didn't know. But my wife sure knew. And I sure knew."

After dinner there was just time to go back to McCallum, find out that my work assignment for that week was setting and cleaning tables, and then it was time for the evening lecture.

The speaker *was* indeed Betty Ford, and when she came into the room and went to the podium, everyone clapped and stood up.

"Hello," she said. "My name is Betty Ford and I'm an alcoholic and an addict."

The AA-indoctrinated group chorused in unison, "Hi, Betty!"

"Welcome to newcomers and good luck and bon voyage to those of you preparing to go back to reality. I fervently hope that a new life is awaiting you all."

Flushed and smiling shyly as though it were her first time to speak here, she went on, "Not one of us set out to be an alcoholic or addict, did we? We have a lot in common, you and I. You wouldn't be here if you didn't have the same disease as I, if you didn't suffer from chemical dependency. It's no stigma; but believe me, you couldn't have convinced me of that back then. Let me tell you about it. Perhaps you'll recognize yourself here and there."

She entwined her fingers and leaned her forearms on the podium. In an informal, almost casual way, she gave her "drunkalogue." There was little variety in the inflection, the tone was colorless, yet the sincerity and caring were undeniable. No one coughed or rustled for the next hour as she told her story, much as she had in her autobiography, *The Time of My Life*. (I bought the book at the Center's little store later and quote from it here.)

She turned to the last chapter. "I had thought my book was finished. I had not expected to write this chapter. But neither had I expected to wind up in the Long Beach Naval Hospital's Alcohol and Drug Rehabilitation Service. So much for my crystal ball.

"Lately, some stories have surfaced about my drinking in the White House, and having behaved on certain public occasions like a 'zombie.' Bull. (That's part of my new Navy vocabulary.) I was fine when I was in the White House. I had no problem handling myself, despite my present conviction—painfully gained, and offered with hindsight—that I'd have been better off to have thrown away my pills, turned down my glass, and gone for a long walk whenever I was hurting."

She didn't realize that she was in trouble until after she'd retired to Palm Springs and private life with her husband, and only then because her family was worried.

"For fourteen years I'd been on medications for the pinched nerve, the arthritis, the muscle spasms in my neck, and I'd lost my tolerance for pills. If I had a single drink, the alcohol, on top of the pills, would make me groggy. In the fall of 1977, I went to Moscow to narrate *The Nutcracker* ballet for television, and later there were comments about my 'sloe-eyed, sleepy-tongued' performance. Still, I can't say I knew what was happening to me. Jerry and the children were worried, but I had no idea how much I had changed."

It was her daughter, Susan, who first went into action and arranged for an "intervention"—a confrontation between family, friends, and a medical adviser.

"The thinking used to be that a chemically addicted person—either on pills or alcohol—had to hit bottom, decide *he* wanted to get well, before he could begin to recover; but it's now been demonstrated that a sick person's family, along with others significant and important to the patient, can intervene to help him despite himself. With this new intervention method the recovery rate has increased significantly."

But the scheme didn't work.

"It was brave of them, but I wasn't in the mood to admire them for their courage: I was completely turned off. I got very mad, and was so upset that, after everyone had left, I called a friend and complained about the terrible invasion of my privacy. I don't remember making the telephone call; the friend has told me about it."

The family persisted and a second intervention was sprung on her in her living room.

"Besides Jerry and the boys and Susan and Gayle [Betty Ford's daughter-in-law], Captain Joe Pursch, the Navy doctor who's head of the Alcohol and Drug Rehabilitation Service at Long Beach, was there, and so was a Navy nurse. And they all proceeded to confront me with a second intervention. Only this time, they meant business. They'd met together, and with Captain Pursch's guidance, the family had prepared what they were going to say.

"I can't remember the words. I was in shock. I've been told that Susan harked back to the days before I'd stopped drinking the first time, and said she'd had to turn to Clara [the housekeeper] when I wasn't available, and Mike and Gayle spoke of wanting children, and wanting those children's grandmother to be healthy and in charge of her own life, and Jerry mentioned times when I'd fallen asleep in the chair at night, and times when my speech had slurred, and Steve brought up a recent weekend when he and a girlfriend had cooked dinner for me and I wouldn't come to the table on time. 'You just sat in front of the TV,' Steve said, 'and you had one drink, two drinks, three drinks. You hurt me.' Well, he hurt me back. All of them hurt me. I collapsed into tears. But I still had enough sense to realize they hadn't come around just to make me cry; they were there because they loved me and wanted to help me."

Yet she continued to deny that she was an alcoholic and would only admit to "some overmedication." Captain Pursch told her there was little difference between pill and booze addiction and gave her books to read.

"My sixtieth birthday came at the end of that week that had begun with the intervention in Palm Springs. We celebrated at a luncheon with presents and friends and family. We drank fruit juice. Two days later, I went to Long Beach—partly because I was so impressed with Captain Pursch, partly because Long Beach was only two and a half hours from home, and I wanted to be near my family."

She smiled at her audience.

"No need to tell you people about the treatment I received. You're going through roughly the same thing. The Betty Ford Clinic is an outgrowth of the Navy Hospital's program and Hazelden in Minnesota. But no two patients ever take the same treatment or react the same. It can be rough. Here's an entry in the diary I kept at Long Beach.

"'At first, I loathed the sessions. I was uncomfortable, unwilling to speak up. Then one day another woman said she didn't think that drinking was a problem, and I became very emotional. I got to my feet. 'I'm Betty, and I'm an alcoholic, and I know my drinking has hurt my family,' I said. I heard myself, and I couldn't believe it. I was trembling; another defense had cracked.'"

She looked around the audience and smiled. "Sound familiar? At first, growth is slow; it takes patience. If you expect a party with balloons and confetti and music the minute you get off the pills, the booze, whatever your poison is, you'll be disappointed. No lights flash, no siren screams. But the process of healing is interesting in itself, and peace is its reward. With peace comes new energy; I am filled with vitality I haven't known since I was a young girl."

She went into the many activities she was involved in now, the traveling, and the plans for her own future and that of the BFC.

She straightened and gazed over the attentive group.

"And so there you have my saga. I very much want to live this beautiful new life of mine to the fullest, and I will do anything to help you and others with this destructive disease do the same. Good-night."

As she stepped down, the room burst alive with applause. Several people crowded around her with copies of her book, and she autographed them graciously and with a personal touch to each.

When she went by me, she said, "You're new, aren't you?"

I smiled wanly. "First day, Mrs. Ford."

She patted my arm. "It should be all downhill from here."

David said, "That woman is going to be long remembered—and not as the wife of a president of the United States."

I walked back to McCallum eager to go to bed after an emotional day that had begun at five in the morning. But there was still a little more to come.

In the lounge, people started writing in notebooks, doing their assignments. Dave explained that every night we had to make an entry.

"What about?" I asked.

"Anything—how you felt about the day or something that happened to you. Couple of pages at the most."

I went to my room. Moishe had his cap on and was chanting at his desk.

"I trust pray no offend," he said.

"Not at all," I said. But I couldn't concentrate.

I took my notebook and went back to the lounge and tried to write at one of the end tables. People around me were doing the same or were engaged in reading assignments. On the upper level, where the sink and refrigerator were, groups drank endless cups of coffee, chain-smoked, read newspapers, and talked about their assignments.

In a little while someone announced, "Time for Tim's burning."

Everyone got up and went out onto the patio. An empty flower urn had some burning papers in it, and Tim was tearing out pages from his notebook and feeding them to the flames. A girl handed us Xeroxed pages with a verse on it.

"What is this?" I asked Dave loftily. "This little campfire groupie?"

"Tim's completed his Fourth and Fifth steps today."

"Which is?"

"Made a complete inventory of the wrongs he did to other people through his drinking and recited them to his God and another human being—in this case, Craig, one of the Protestant ministers. It's part of the Alcoholics Anonymous creed and program."

"So now he burns the list and is made whole again? Sounds pretty simplistic."

"Don't knock it; it works. AA has worked where all the psychiatrists in the world have failed."

"So why didn't we just stay home and go to AA and save the money?"

"Betty Ford gives you the equivalent of about two years of AA in one month."

Someone started singing the lyrics on the paper to the tune of "Bye Bye Blackbird":

"Burn up all my cares and woes . . ."

The voices grew in enthusiasm:

"All my peers can love and understand me,
I've heard all the bullshit they can hand me.
Make resentments, take a hike,
Se-re-nity is mine tonight,
Anger, bye-bye."

The phrase "all the bullshit" was shouted gleefully. They sang it twice more until all of Tim's papers were burned. He seemed jubilantly happy, and when the last page was gone, he was hugged by several people. He had ordered celebratory pizza sent in from Palm Springs, and we went back inside to eat it.

"Why do I keep thinking I'm twelve years old and at summer camp?" I asked Dave.

I was exhausted, but I had my assignment to do, so I went to my room. Moishe was out in the lobby now, so I sat at the desk and wrote a page describing my first day at BFC, as everyone called it. It was pretty cut and dried, in the how-I-spent-my-summer style. I wasn't quite sure yet how I felt about my being here. It was humiliating to be committed to an alcoholic institution. On the other hand, everyone had been so damn nice. And I reminded myself I could walk out any time I wanted to.

I missed my wife, and my beloved dog Addie wasn't lying on the bed waiting for me, and there was no pounding of waves beyond the veranda. I felt very alone.

I still hadn't unpacked. I took off my shoes, coat, and tie, and fell across the bed.

Why in God's name did I have to be here? Couldn't I just go home and—and *quit drinking?* Was I so lacking in resolve, so weak, so spineless, so morally bankrupt, that I had to have other people supply my willpower and monitor and control my intake of alcohol? I didn't need a battery of doctors and nurses and psychologists and clergymen to pound into me that alcohol was bad and was ruining my life. Okay, okay, I admit it! And I didn't need them to tell me what to do about it. Jesus, it was no big deal—all you had to do was just tell yourself each morning, Hey, I'm not going to drink today! I'm going to skip the preprandial shooter altogether, ditto the five o'clocker; I'm not going to have the dressing drink, and at the party tonight I'll have a Perrier before and one glass of wine with dinner.

But I'd tried that before, hadn't I? A dozen, two dozen times, at least. And maybe it worked for a few days or even a few weeks, and then the glass of wine became two or three, and there was always some kind of special occasion and, hell, you can't drink ginger ale at a wedding reception—it's almost insulting—and when your old friend, the bartender, forgets and makes you a scotch and soda out of habit, hell, he'd made it already, so you couldn't throw it out, and Mary's okay to drive home, so I'll have a couple more, and so there you were the next day with a hangover and wondering exactly how the evening had turned out, whom you'd insulted or made a pass at, and craving a little hair of the dog, and there you were back on the old merry-go-round, the only carousel with no brass ring.

So maybe I *was* in the right place, I told myself. Give it a chance. Everyone said it works for most people. But—the $64,000 question—maybe I didn't want it to work; maybe I didn't really want to quit drinking quite yet.

"Burn up all my cares and woes . . ."

Oh, Lord. Spare me.
I fell into a deep and dreamless and sober sleep.

F O U R

The next morning, my first morning at BFC, there occurred what for some time afterward was known as the Event. It was the talk of the campus.

The day started for us at six-fifteen, when a patient rapped on our door. (The waker-upper had what was considered to be one of the cushier work assignments.)

I glanced at my watch in disbelief. It seemed I had just gone to sleep. Moishe was dressed and just finishing his prayers.

I dressed and went into the lounge.

I handed in my notebook at the same time as Terry, the black woman, did. She had a blond Dutch haircut and a stocky body and a worried but unlined café au lait face. She had a tough, aggressive manner, and I didn't like her.

"Let's go," she ordered. "We've got the duty."

We walked over toward the cafeteria across the grass, and without prompting she volunteered her story. She was thirty-four, head nurse in a small Arizona hospital, and had gotten hooked on pills and drugs.

"Who wouldn't?" she said. "I found out my husband, Ted, was sleeping with my daughter."

"Wait a minute—"

"No, it wasn't incest," she said. "Carla's by my first husband. She's fifteen."

"I take it you're divorced now."

She shrugged. "Still together. Ted says they don't do it anymore. But I don't know. I've been here six weeks and they're home alone. They're coming up here day after tomorrow. For family week. Nervous as hell. Also, I got a six-year-old the authorities've taken away from me. That's why I've got to shape up, get my medallion, graduate from here with flying colors, get my shit together, get my kid back." Her voice was trembling. "I've just got to. Got another problem also facing me when I get out. Criminal charges. Accused of stealing, taking drugs from the hospital dispensary for my own use."

"And did you?"

"Shit, yes! Every day, when I went to work, there it all was, laid out as pretty as you please, like a smorgasbord. But if I can just complete this program to Jerry's satisfaction, then I can maybe talk the hospital into dropping the charges. Maybe keeping my nursing license, too. I'm a dead duck without it. I've been supporting the family by myself. Ted's an artist, a really good one, honestly, but he says he doesn't want to sell his babies, as he calls them, for anything less than fifteen hundred dollars. They're really good, too good for the public. Actually, I don't always understand them; they're kinda weird."

We went into the cafeteria, and as we were setting the five tables allotted to McCallum, Terry said sheepishly, "You know something, I lied to you back there. That's one of my lifelong problems—I lie a lot. Not only to other people, but

50

to myself. They say that's a very common trait among alkies and junkies—we lie a lot. Jerry says I'm never going to get well and get out of here until I start telling myself and others nothing but the truth."

As she talked, she swiftly took the knives, forks, spoons, and napkins off her tray and precisely set three places at each table in the time it took me to set one. I could see how she would be a valuable nurse in an operating room.

"What part did you lie about?" I asked.

"When I said—when I implied—that I began drinking and using when I found out about Ted and Carla. Actually, I just stepped up my intake then. I was a drunk by the time I was thirteen. On my way, anyway. Drank all the way through high school, then started using at nursing school. Never looked back."

"You didn't drink on duty, though."

"You kidding? I've been stoned through so many operations you wouldn't believe it. The public would die if they knew how many nurses and doctors have to have their booze or junk before they go into the operating room. Did you read about that doctor last month who took the wrong leg off a patient? Sure! The X-rays had been taken with the guy on his stomach. He comes into the operating room on a gurney on his back; doc's so stoned he can't adjust and takes off the wrong leg. Patient's lucky he's still got his dick, but he's suing."

We finished and started back to McCallum.

"Anyway, I'm sorry I lied."

"But the rest of it is true," I said, "about Ted . . ."

"You mean about Ted being an artist and all?"

"No—I meant—"

"Oh, about Ted and Carla?" she said. "I caught 'em. Right in the old acteroo right in the old guest room. I thought it was rape, but apparently it was seduction and she had taken to it like a duck to water." She gave a mirthless laugh. "I'm not

51

so sure she even wants me to get out of here! Maybe she's paying me back in spades for having been such a rotten mother all these years."

"How were you rotten? You've been supporting her."

"Yeah, and I loved her in my fashion. But you can't really love or be a good mother or a good nurse or a good wife or a good anything when you're plastered round the clock. Do you know how rotten I was? If I needed a fix and I couldn't get the stuff I wanted, I'd take it from the patients. Instead of giving the shot a doctor had ordered for a patient, I'd give it to myself. You know, I could have caused someone's death?"

She was trembling and close to tears. I put my hand on her shoulder and said lamely, "Well, you're here now and that's the past."

We arrived in time to make the circle, say the prayer, and head back to the cafeteria.

"Don't they overdo the Serenity Prayer a bit?" I asked Beth.

"It's part of the togetherness concept. You know the trip: The peers that pray together, stay together in sobriety."

At breakfast I was pleased to see that I could get a coffee cup to my lips—using both hands and shaking, but at least I could do it.

When everyone was through eating, Terry and I picked up the dishes and brought them to the kitchen and walked back to McCallum.

After straightening up our rooms it was time for the meditation walk. As usual before any event, we gathered outside the hall, made a circle, and said the Serenity Prayer. Then we were off for a mile walk around the periphery of the clinic's grounds. Some of the younger patients were jogging in sweat suits, some fast-walking, most just strolling silently and enjoying the clean, antrum-clearing desert air, meditating on the day to come. We had a chuckle when we saw Dr. Bill down by the pond yelling out "Fuck you!" to the heavens. I wondered what odious assignment would befall me. Dave still had on his sleep shade and was being led by Chico around our exercise track. Another man was wearing an ornate crown everywhere. "To remind him of his King Baby complex," someone unexplained to me.

As I walked, I thought about Terry and her story. She was not very likable, but I felt sorry for her and her mutilated life so rife with problems. Mine were nothing by comparison. When and if Terry licked the pressing problem of addiction, she would still be facing horrendous obstacles—criminal charges, career problems, monetary worries, and domestic chaos.

An important revelation came to me: I had only one real problem in the world—ethyl alcohol. Any health, financial, or domestic problems were intertwined with booze; remove it and presumably I would be one of the most fortunate of men.

So get on with it, I urged myself, do whatever you have to do here to get rid of your addiction and, thank God, you're not poor Terry with seemingly unsolvable problems.

When I came back into the lounge at McCallum, Jerry beckoned me into her office and motioned for me to sit. She was chic in a suede outfit and a blue silk scarf around her neck.

"This is unacceptable," she said, handing me back the notebook I'd written in the night before.

"What's wrong with it?" I said defensively. I hadn't had a literary rejection for a long time.

"No feelings," she said. "You've been way out of touch with your feelings for years. Maybe decades. Your feelings, like those of most drunks, have been anesthetized."

"I did what you told me," I said sulkily. I hadn't quite gotten used to being called a drunk.

"You described everything well enough. But I want to know how you *felt* emotionally, not what you thought intellectually."

"Feelings?"

"Yes, you know, like anger, anxiety, happiness, loneliness, hate, love, resentment, apprehension, and so forth. Do it over. Now, Barny, did you ever do anything while under the influence that you were ashamed of?"

"Plenty," I said.

"Didn't we all?" she said with a smile. "I want you to write in detail about one of those episodes. And—important—how you felt about it. For Monday."

She handed me a book called *Twelve Steps and Twelve Traditions*, published by Alcoholics Anonymous.

"As you probably know, we are totally AA-minded here at BFC. We believe the Twelve Steps program is often the only thing that works for the alcoholic and the addict. AA has the very best record of any program in history; on that everyone agrees."

"Why didn't I just stay home and go to AA?"

"You tried that once, didn't you? I saw that on your record sheet. Few years ago, wasn't it?"

"I tried going to meetings for a while."

"And?"

"It didn't take. I went because other people thought I should."

"I'll bet you'd go to a meeting, and then go to a bar afterward."

"Sometimes before, too. How'd you know?"

"Don't forget that everyone in this place has been where you've been, where you are now. We've all done things as bad and bizarre as you, and in my case, I know, a helluva lot worse. Why do you think AA didn't work for you?"

I shrugged. "I didn't take it seriously, I guess."

"When you get out of here, you will. Now, we only have time in four weeks to cover the first five steps. You'll start this weekend with the first. Know what it is?"

"Giving up booze."

"Right. The First Step says, 'We admitted we were powerless over alcohol—that our lives had become unmanageable.' Is that hard for you to admit?"

54

I hesitated. " 'Powerless' seems a bit strong. Sounds as though I was lying drunk in a gutter someplace."

"But, you must be powerless over it! Otherwise why haven't you been able to quit? Isn't the urge and habit of drinking stronger than your resolutions to quit? You've proved it over and over."

"All right. I'll admit that much."

"Secretly, you think that one day you'll lick alcohol, that one day you'll be able to go back to drinking, that one day you'll be able to handle it the way you once did. But you're wrong. You're fighting it inside still, even though you're here in this clinic. Way down deep you think you'll be able to drink again someday like normal people, maybe that you'll learn the secret of moderation here. But we don't teach moderation because there is no such thing as moderation for us drunks. Look, I went back out there and tried it again after years of sobriety, and you know what? In a couple of weeks I was right back where I started from. It's an amazing thing— all that time while I wasn't drinking, my disease kept progressing! I was worse than when I quit, my body was even less tolerant. So, your very first step and my very first step is the most important one—to accept the fact that we can never drink again, that alcohol has disturbed our lives enormously, that alcohol in any form is poison to us, and that we are helpless before it."

She looked at her watch. "Time for the lecture. I want you to read about the first step in this book and also in the big blue book, and write your feelings about it for Monday. Plus, of course, your daily impressions, and a complete revision of your first entry."

"That's quite a bit!" I said.

"What'd you think you were signing up for—a country club? Oh, and instead of coming to group this morning, you'll be taking a test."

"What kind of test?"

"Mental test, personality test. See you this afternoon at group."

I went out to join the inescapable Serenity circle and then we went over to Firestone for the lecture.

The lecturer was Dr. James West, medical director of the clinic. He was tan, trim, sixty, with bushy dark eyebrows and iron-gray hair, and dressed in a natty gabardine suit. He started out with a fine description of alcoholism and the alcoholic in general in understandable terms. He spoke without notes in an impressive and decisive way, and we had to scribble our notes in our binders fast to keep up with him. He didn't talk down to his audience, but his section on alcohol and the brain was a model of science made understandable to the layman. "The brain is the target organ for the pharmacological effect of the sedative-hypnotic chemical alcohol. Alcohol is closely related to the anesthetic ether.

"The biochemical reaction that takes place in the brain when alcohol is presented to the tissues of the brain is euphoria, and if not euphoria, at least a mood change. It is for this purpose the beverage alcohol is drunk.

"Alcohol affects the brain in a descending order starting with its effect on the cortex, where the higher centers of the brain are located. There is also simultaneously an effect on a very important part of the brain stem called the reticular activating system. Small amounts of alcohol will affect mood and slightly affect behavior, but as the dose of alcohol is increased, further behavioral changes occur in the area of the reticular activating system in the brain stem.

"This part of the brain is associated with keeping the person alert and aware of his environment. It is the harmful effect on this particular part of the brain that even a small dose of alcohol can produce to impair a person's driving. Those immediate reflexes, which have been learned, are dulled and dampened down so that a person doesn't respond as quickly as he or she should while driving.

"As more alcohol is drunk during a drinking episode, the cerebellum, or the balancing center of the brain, is affected, certainly by the time a person has imbibed five drinks. The concentration of alcohol in the blood is one hundred milligrams percent after the average person has drunk five drinks. The person with this blood alcohol level is considered legally drunk in most states.

"With more alcohol, a central portion, or the limbic center of the brain, becomes affected. This center is directly related to emotional behavior, such as rage, fear, and an inappropriate maudlin kind of behavior. After a person has drunk sufficiently to obtain a blood alcohol level of three hundred milligrams percent, unconsciousness develops. If a person drinks a large amount of alcohol in a very short time, one passes rapidly through all these stages of intoxification, or anesthesia, and becomes unconscious. This adversely affects the function of the respiratory center of the brain. Death may occur from respiratory failure.

"One of the brain functions most obviously affected by alcohol use is memory. It is thought by many authorities that short-term memory is primarily a transitory phenomenon that can be compared to an electrical charge, but that over a period of time, usually after about fifteen minutes, certain changes begin to occur in the brain that make these short-term memories, or electrical charges, permanent and convert them to chemical or permanent memory engrams. The process by which this takes place is called encoding.

"After the circuitry of memory has been exposed to alcohol repeatedly and over a long period of time, and in relatively large amounts, the encoding process, as a physiological function of the brain, begins to fail. This failure results in the drinking person not being able to recall what occurred during his or her drinking episode. As time goes on, it requires less and less alcohol to bring about this so-called blackout. Eventually the circuitry of the brain becomes so damaged that the patient is incapable of remembering anything beyond a very short time. This condition is referred to as Korsakoff's syndrome. It is usually an irreversible state.

"If a person continues to drink, the capability to encode information and make it permanent, so that it can be retrieved, or recalled, becomes less a capability of the brain.

"Certainly, then, this is one of the most important inducements to the person suffering from alcoholism to reach for and work to maintain abstinence and recovery."

He then started in on the specific damage that alcohol can do to the rest of the human body. "When alcohol enters the body, not a single cell remains unaffected."

He showed horrific enlarged photos of the liver from its normal pliable condition to a grotesquely enlarged mass hardened by alcohol intake to such a degree that "if it were dropped on this platform, it would sound like a stone when it landed."

He had just started on the effect of alcohol on the stomach and digestive system when someone in the lecture room broke wind audibly. The social offense was not only audible, it was stentorian, Homeric, and prolonged. It simply could not be politely ignored—it would have been like ignoring Krakatoa's explosion.

Starting with a low, oboe moan, the note ascended into the room in a glissando worthy of Tommy Dorsey, attained and held a Rampal-like peak, then gracefully slid down to a mellow shofar tone, which ended abruptly with a shattering, Wagnerian clap.

A collective gasp, and a stunned second-long silence followed; a superb lecture was in immediate danger of being ruined by a primitive reaction to a basic vulgar occurrence. I held my breath, but before anyone could snicker, titter, or guffaw, the suave Dr. West, in a show of alchemy, incorporated the happening into his talk in a skillful and effortless manner. We heard him saying, without missing a beat, "And thus, as I was saying, the alcohol-exacerbated gastrointestinal system is frequently subjected to insults and releases as put in evidence so recently here by the Event."

And so instead of roaring with childish and interruptive laughter as they might have done, the audience was defused and smiled and chuckled appreciatively at Dr. West's adroit legerdemain in the handling of the unscheduled intrusion. Several more times in the rest of his task, Dr. West slyly worked in pertinent references to the "Recent Event" as it pertained to pernicious inroads of alcohol on bodily functions, and when he finished, he was rewarded by an enthusiastic standing ovation.

At lunch the main topic of conversation would be the lecture, and for several days any mention of the Event would bring a smile to the listener's face.

Of such small happenings is institutional humor made.

o   o   o

There were seven of us taking the test, billed as "Personality and Intelligence and Vocabulary Evaluation." We were in a room off the cafeteria.

"Just use your common sense," advised the counselor as he handed out pages.

"If I had any of that, I wouldn't have landed here in the first place!" Beth cracked.

"I don't think it will be too tough," said Chico glancing at the first page. "I've always tested pretty good."

"So have I," I said. And then I wondered why I said that; except for a driver's license test, which I usually had to take three times to pass, and roadside sobriety tests by the highway patrol, which I usually flunked, the last test I remembered taking was back in 1943 for the State Department! I must have done all right then, for I was subsequently sent to Spain, at twenty-one, as a vice-consul in the Foreign Service, but that was a long time and a lot of drinks ago.

"Start anytime," said the counselor, who looked like Captain Kangaroo. "You have two hours."

I started in, and at first the problems and word games and puzzles seemed fairly easy. But then they got tougher, especially when they involved any kind of mathematics, my bête noire all through school.

Half an hour into the test Beth smiled over at me and whispered, "How ya doin', Geezer?" She had decided that was to be my nickname.

"Fine," I said. "Doing great."

But it was said without conviction.

In ten minutes I came to this beaut:

"Rearrange the letters to make a simple everyday word out of each of the following:

TICFEN	CYMALL	BIFCAR
WETIC	TAUMAR	EAPSU
INMAYL	ARREM	EXTUDO
RAYLEY	LIDBOY	PEBID

And on and on.

I read them over and then again. And then once more. It was the Rosetta Stone. Surely they jested. There were no words within these letters, at least not in English.

I remembered that I was never good at the games on the backs of cereal boxes. I tried saying them aloud: "Extudo . . . extudo." It sounded like a pretty good word just the way it was. Why fool around with it? Remember, I was still in the confused condition of the alcoholic deprived of his fuel.

"Pebid, pebid, pebid," I murmured over and over like some mournful shorebird.

I began rearranging the letters on a piece of scratch paper. They resisted all the combinations I tried. I glanced over at Beth. She had apparently deciphered them all and gone ahead, for she was on the next page. So was Chico.

I wondered if I could have suffered brain damage. Dr. West in his lecture had said that the "liver is a forgiving organ" and if caught in time can reconstitute itself and become almost as good as new, while once the brain cells are damaged, they are gone for good. "Every bender a drunk goes on destroys thousands of cells in the brain. Luckily, that organ has a great many cells, but they are not inexhaustible."

Was my brain so gone that it couldn't function well enough to decode these simple words that the others were breezing through? I, who once did a stint in the State Department's code room? I, who had appeared on William F. Buckley's *Firing Line* program? I, who had graduated from Yale on the dean's list? I would show them that I was no brain-damaged drunk!

I tried starting with the different consonants of a word and then following it with the vowels. Finally, I got one.

"Tuxedo!" I exclaimed, and the others, writing away furiously, looked up and glared. It was so easy when once you saw the word within a word.

But that was it. I had to go on to the next section. But I was bugged and frustrated, and after I had finished the vocabulary test, I went back to the scrambled words and worried and fretted over them. I got two more, "biped" and "calmly," but it was a Pyrrhic victory—I had to race through the other sections to catch up, skimping on important parts. One by one, the others finished and left for lunch.

"Stay with it, Geezer," Beth said with an encouraging pat on the shoulder as she left.

I was the last to leave—the time was up—and I still hadn't finished the whole test. The terrible thought came to me that I'd come to the BFC too late—I did have some brain damage. Was I suffering from *unalterable* brain damage, what Dr. West had called Korsakoff's syndrome?

I went gloomily to lunch still worrying about what the hell possible word could be lurking inside RAYLEY.

F I V E

It seems that I was well advised to be worried about brain damage. I got a preview of the results of the IQ test after the one o'clock lecture.

Before that, at lunch, the dining-room chatter had been all about the test and the varied difficulties of certain sections.

"What, may I ask, does RAYLEY spell?" I asked. "It *was* a misprint, wasn't it? They *did* leave some letters out, didn't they?"

Beth and Chico chorused, "Yearly!"

Oh, my Lord, of course.

"How about NECCIS?"

"Easy—scenic."

"And TOCVAR?"

"That was tougher," said Beth. "Cavort."

How come I didn't see that?

"How about the guy rowing up the inlet at five miles an hour," said Chico, "and the current is going two miles an hour against him and the lighthouse is—"

"The answer was *x* equaled twenty-two minutes," said Beth. "Smartass," said Dave. He finally had been given permission to take the sleep shade off.

I hadn't even tried that one. I remembered my days when I was fifteen at the Taft prep school in Connecticut. I had good marks in everything but algebra, and try as I might, I hovered between barely passing and flunking. "Do a picture of me and I'll pass you for the year," the teacher said semi-jokingly. The next day a life-size charcoal portrait was on his desk; it pleased him and he gave me a passing mark. Then in my junior year, I came head-on, *mano a mano,* with geometry, and Pythagoras won. I simply couldn't fathom what the teacher wanted me to do with these silly little corners of triangles, though I was perfectly willing to admit that two things equal to something else were equal to each other. That was the only thing I ever understood about the subject, and it was a requirement for graduation. But the headmaster, archetypical of the strict New England breed, somehow wanted very much for me to be graduated; his surprisingly ardent admiration for Rockwell Kent's pictures was the only factor that marred Mr. Cruikshank's total artistic insensibility, and he was dazzled by what he considered my major talent in draftsmanship. One had to have passed geometry in order to graduate, but Mr. Cruikshank created a special art course for me alone (the first assignment being a portrait of the founder, old Mr. Taft), which, to the horror of the math department and envy of the other students, he declared the equivalent of plane geometry. Thus it was that I became the only student before or since to be graduated theoremless, as it were, from the Taft school. (Some forty-two years later, I would be commissioned to do a life-size portrait of Mr. Cruikshank himself.)

And thus it was also that I arrived, almost five decades later, clueless to any section of the Betty Ford test that smacked of math or algebraic reasoning. My sins and omissions had come home to roost.

Over the years I used my ability to capture a likeness on paper to extricate myself from difficulties more than once, most spectacularly in Lima, Peru, when I found myself broke in that city at the age of twenty-four. I had gone there in 1946 following in the glamorous shadow of the legendary matador, Manolete. I tried to continue bullfighting as I had done in Spain, but, with an injured knee, I managed to fight only three times before giving it up. In order to live, I had wangled a job as a piano player in the Hotel Bolívar, the most elegant in South America, mainly because I could play "Gloomy Sunday," a favorite of the Hungarian manager. But I was fired after a couple of months, not because of drinking—I didn't imbibe much in those days—but I suppose the clientele got tired of my repertoire, especially "Gloomy Sunday." I needed to make money, but how in this foreign country? I had done a portrait of the beautiful girl I was living with; she took it to Señor Marini's shop to be framed, and a rich Peruvian woman saw it. "I want him to do my portrait. How much does he charge?"

Marini, who didn't even know my name, thought quickly. "He is very famous, señora," he said. "He charges one hundred soles."

"That's not bad," she made the mistake of saying.

"Ah, but with hands," said Marini, "it is two hundred soles! And life-size it is three hundred soles."

So all of a sudden I had a profession and an agent and a client. In the next year I executed some twenty portrait commissions in Lima. My portrait studies would save my neck in future situations. I was not above doing portraits at sidewalk cafés or in nightclubs. Or, most recently, in jail.

As our luncheon progressed, I was glad when Beth and Chico got off the subject of the math and logic sections and on to the vocabulary. At least I knew I'd done well there.

"How about 'pristine'?" said Beth. "I always thought it meant prim and proper. But nothing fit."

"I went for 'original.'"

"And 'meretricious'?" asked Beth. "Doesn't that mean when you do something good, some good service?"

"It means more like the opposite," said Dave. "By the way, you sure look pretty today. With my mask off, I'm observing more."

And she did, in a dark blue sport shirt and slacks.

"Did anyone ever tell you you looked like Elizabeth Taylor?" said Chico. I'd noticed he hung on her every word.

"Yes, as a matter of fact, the doctor, did last week," said Beth. "He exclaimed, 'Wow, exactly like Elizabeth Taylor!' Unfortunately, he was examining my liver at the time."

"There's a good article by Elizabeth Taylor in the *New York Times* about her experience here," said Dave. "I'll give it to you." He was an inveterate cutter-outer and Xeroxer.

Then we broke up, and after Terry and I cleared the tables and we made the circle and said the Serenity Prayer, we all went to the one o'clock lecture.

A drab woman was talking about nutrition and alcohol and absorption of same through the stomach and I didn't pay much attention. I thought of the beginning of a Hemingway story called "The Ash Heel's Tendon" that mentions absorbent stomachs:

In a former unenlightened time there was a saying "In vino veritas," which meant roughly that under the influence of the cup that queers, a man sloughed off his dross of reserve and conventionality and showed the true metal of his self. The true self might be happy, might be poetic, might be morbid, or might be extremely pugnacious. In the rude nomenclature of our forefathers these revealed conditions were denominated in order— laughing, sloppy crying and fighting jags.

A man with his shell removed by the corrosive action of alcohol might present as unattractive an appearance as the shrunken, misshapen nudity of an unprotected hermit crab. Another with a rock-like exterior might prove to be genial, generous and companionable under the influence. But there were men in those days on whose inner personality alcohol had no more effect than a sluicing of the pyramids with vinegar would have on the caskets within.

Such men were spoken of as having wonderful heads; the head being popularly misconceived as the spot of greatest resistance in the body's fight against alcohol. As a matter of physiological fact, they were the possessors of non-absorbent stomachs. But you couldn't build a bar-room saga around a non-absorbent stomach.

I'd read somewhere that Patrick Hemingway had said his father drank a quart of whiskey a day for twenty years and without it was "morose, silent, depressed." Irrelevant and unverified fact number 62.

I went back to rehashing the test in my mind. The nagging phrase "Korsakoff's syndrome" kept running through my brain. Just the name was chilling. Was my brain damaged? It seemed fine to me. It didn't seem any different than it had ever been. But maybe all heavy drinkers think that way.

I didn't take notes (and Rita the Stew wasn't there that day; she always took complete transcriptions in shorthand of every talk and gave them to the rest of us). But I do remember a couple of facts the nutritionist brought out. One about the myth that if a drunk eats well, he'll be okay.

"Alcohol inhibits the assimilation by the body of the food's nutrients," she said, "so eating properly does the alcoholic little good when he's drinking. Few of the vitamins reach their destination."

On the subject of absorption, she addressed herself to the strength of drinks. "The famous Dr. Pursch says this about the idea and the physiology of the double drink, which so many advanced alcoholics favor: 'The normal liver can neutralize (detoxify) eighty proof booze at the rate of one drink per hour. Thus, when you start *sipping* a drink, the liver immediately gets busy, clearing the blood and leaving the brain relatively unaffected. The alcoholic—sly devil that he is, and wanting a more noticeable, immediate effect—soon discovers that he can beat his own system by gulping a double: "One for my liver, and one for me," he is in effect saying, as his liver gets overwhelmed, and the sizable overload heads for the brain.'"

I thought about doubles. When had I given up singles in favor of doubles? That might have been the turning point, an indication of when I crossed the line from social drinking to pathological drinking.

The nutritionist concluded her talk with a vapid smile and, "Remember, we're not bad people trying to be good, we're sick people trying to get well."

After the lecture, Jerry intercepted me at the entrance to McCallum and led me into her office.

"How are you doing, Barny?" she asked as she sat down and opened my folder.

"Fine," I said.

"Why are you smiling?"

I was taken aback. "Is that against the rules?"

"No," she said, "but there was no reason to smile just then. I figure you've gotten through life pretty much on the basis of that smile."

"Would you rather I frowned?" I said still smiling, but aggressively.

"I'd rather you acted naturally and stopped trying to charm everyone."

"I wasn't aware that I was," I said, dropping the smile.

"James Barrie said that if you had charm, it didn't matter if you didn't have anything else, and if you didn't have charm, it didn't matter whatever else you might have. You have an overdose."

"I'll try to curb it," I said flatly.

"My spies tell me you haven't unpacked yet. Planning on leaving?"

"No."

"Well, *do* let us know. There're about three hundred people out there dying to take your place."

I felt like saying, "Boy, *you* sure got out of the wrong side of somebody's bed this morning!" But of course I didn't. You didn't kid around with Jerry. We liked and respected Jerry, but we were also afraid of her, afraid of her displeasure. Also, we thought our fate was in her hands as to whether and when we would graduate and get out of this place.

She looked down at the folder. "Apparently you did poorly on the test."

I felt a constriction in my chest.

"I was afraid of that."

"Any idea why you didn't do better?"

"I never was good at puzzles and problems and word games."

"And yet you graduated from Yale with honors."

"They didn't ask me to unscramble words like RAYLEY and NESSIC. But I'm a whiz at Trivial Pursuit. Go ahead, try me. I beat *Information Please* when I was nineteen."

"You don't seem very worried."

"I am, though. How badly?"

"They're evaluating the test in depth now. You apparently came in here in worse shape than we thought. I see your hands are still shaking."

"Not as much," I said, automatically tucking them under my thighs.

"You'd have had to have had palsy for them to have shaken any more."

I essayed a little humor. "Yes, this last year I've become a pointillist painter without meaning to."

"Another joke!" she said. "Humor's great but you have a way of avoiding hard truths with a quip, and I suspect that's the way you've gone through life—on a smile and a shoeshine, like Willy Loman. Life getting tough? Hey, make a joke, have a little drinkie-poo and things'll look better. Big crisis coming up? Face it like a man—go down to the corner bar and tell a few jokes with the boys. That's what the tests indicate."

"You mean, those little puzzles and problems show that?" I asked incredulously.

"And the personality questions."

"The last section? I thought most of those were pretty simplistic and juvenile."

"And extremely revealing. It's a universally accepted test across the country and usually very reliable."

"And I did poorly?"

"Worse than that."

"You mean"—I swallowed—"Korsakoff's syndrome?"

"They just glanced at the test. They're grading it now."

"Who's they?"

"The psychiatrists."

"You're a—"

"I'm a psychologist. This test is administered and evaluated by experts in the field."

I felt a little queasy. "My brain—it isn't damaged, is it?"

"I hope not," she said. "But how does one know, how does a drinker know? Haven't you ever sat at a bar after two or three drinks with that warm all-knowing feeling, everything rosy-like, caressing the glass, and suddenly you see the great plan of the world spread out in front of you like a blueprint, understood God's entire scheme of things, seen all of life wonderfully clearly? And then the next morning not being able to remember a damn thing and asking yourself what the hell was *that* all about? Or half smashed in the middle of the night written down page after page of deathless prose, absolutely the best since Tolstoy, marvelous stuff, revelations, and earth-shaking ideas—and then read it sober the next day and seen it all change into gibberish?"

"I've done that," I murmured. "Yes, I've done that."

69

"So how does a drunk like you know when he's in his right mind or not?" She looked me in the eyes. "You don't like that word much, do you?"

"I'm afraid I still think of a drunk as a guy in rags in the gutter."

"I've seen as many drunks in tuxedos as in rags. And, I might add, in hospital gowns and cowboy boots and minister's robes and pilot's uniforms. And I've seen one in a mirror. Anyway, I'm hoping that maybe the test was given to you a few days too soon, that you're still confused by the booze in your system. I think you lied about your intake when you came in here. All us alcoholics are liars. It goes with the territory."

"I feel I'm honest," I said hotly.

"Oh, come on! You mean you didn't lie to your wife for years when she asked how many drinks you had? Or to the women you must have picked up at the bar when they asked if you were married? Or when you didn't get your work done on time? Or why the work wasn't up to snuff when it was done? The list goes on and on. Amazing how one lie leads to another when we're drinking, isn't it? They just seem to metastasize like cancer until we're proliferated with them. 'Oh, what a tangled web we weave, when first we practice to deceive,' eh? But the critical part is when we drunks start lying to *ourselves*. Anyway, I'm hoping it'll turn out you're just suffering from alcoholic depression, the medication they've given you for withdrawal, and confusion, and that you'll do better later when you take the test again."

"And what"—I cleared my throat—"what if it turns out to be Korsakoff's?"

"We'll face that if and when we have to."

"Dr. West said it was irreversible."

She didn't answer, but closed my manila folder. She slapped her knees. "Now! I hope you're working on your assignments. See you at Tim's graduation in twenty minutes."

When I was at the door she added, "And remember, sobriety begins with honesty."

"Honesty," I repeated.

"*Rigorous* honesty," she said. "Oh, know where that 'tangled web' quote comes from, Mr. Quiz Kid?"

"Shakespeare," I said. "*Macbeth.*"

"Sir Walter Scott," she corrected. "*Marmion.*"

I went back to my room. My first reaction was to forget I'd ever heard of Mr. Korsakoff and his syndrome. Then I tried to make believe that it was very unlikely that I should have it. Then my second reaction was fear. Then anger. Then rage.

Dave had slipped the clipping by Elizabeth Taylor under the door. I picked it up and crumpled it. To hell with Elizabeth Taylor. I sat down at the desk and yanked open my notebook. I'll show them who has brain damage.

I grabbed the pen and wrote angrily at the top of the page, "A Humiliating Happening Brought on by Excessive Intake of Ethanol."

I'll write an essay that will knock their socks off, hand it in, and tell the psychiatrists to shove it up their collective Krafft-Ebings.

But which shameful happening should I choose? There were so many, going back so far. What about the time I arrived at the girl's apartment, loaded, having to urinate terribly, and didn't make it to her bathroom? How about the time in Spain when I went to the private bullfight and, not thinking I might have to perform, got sloshed and was invited down into the arena by a great matador, and subsequently almost got killed and made an uncoordinated fool of myself? (But not as bad as a drunken friend who tripped and fell on the dead bull and was dragged out by the mules on top of the carcass!)

Or how about the time when I'd been finally admitted to membership in the prestigious Bohemian Club in San Francisco, an honor some applicants wait twenty years for, and the night I was scheduled to greet the assembled club at the big dinner for neophytes, I had been plied with liquor by a "friend" and was too drunk to stand on the dais?

Or should I write up the time, going way back to the time I was fifteen, that my older brother had a big fancy lawn party and I chose that day to get drunk for the first time in my life and make a fool out of myself in front of the college-age guests, climaxing the performance by jumping into the swimming pool with all my clothes on? "Look at that young fool!" said my embarrassed brother to the guest of honor, the new best-selling author William Saroyan. "Not at all," said the flamboyant writer. "He did what he wanted to do at the time that he wanted to do it." Whereupon Saroyan jumped in fully clothed also.

I could write that incident up—it might amuse Jerry. I wanted to amuse her very much. It was back to grammar school and little Binney Conrad was trying desperately to please strict, attractive Miss Graham.

The list went on and on. Which to choose?

I finally decided upon jail. I was an expert on being jailed for drunkenness and drunken driving. Thank God none had involved an injury to anyone. ("All of us drunks are murderers," a friend once said. "Potential murderers. That car we drive is a thousand-pound bomb. The ignition key in our pocket is a concealed weapon.")

I chose the most recent jail experience, just two years before. At that time I was ordered to the Santa Barbara County Jail by a genial judge. The district attorney was less genial and wanted me to get six months, but the judge said he knew all about alcoholics; it was a disease—his son was one—and they were more to be pitied than censured.

But still he sentenced me to the slammer; none of this driver education stuff, drunk-driving school, or AA meetings. Fourteen days in durance vile, Buster.

Here was a first for me. I'd spent quite a few one-night

sobering-up-type of stands in jail, but never actually had been sentenced before God and my wife and young daughter and everybody to *a term!* I felt like Charles Manson or somebody.

Also, this time I'd been arrested for, and was found guilty of, *drunken sitting,* another first.

I'd been picked up once in Tijuana for *drunken walking.* ("Señor Officer, I often walk with one foot in the gutter. Somethin' wrong with tha'?")

And once, after a bibulous lunch with Bing Crosby, whose portrait I was doing, I was arrested for *drunken standing* while swaying in line at the San Francisco airport. ("Jus' getting a ticket home, Officer, live right here, only 300 miles away, wife meeting me. Hey, is this really necessary?")

And, of course, over the last two hard-drinking decades I had a few 502's. No matter how many times it happens, you never get over the sudden fright, the rush of adrenaline when you see that red light flash on behind your car. The heart stops, then sort of fibrillates. ("Good evening, sir, see your driver's license, been drinking?" "Who me, Ossifer?" Once I heard myself—like a cartoon character—actually say "Ossifer." Another time I kept calling the cop "Operator" without meaning to. "M'license's right here—jus' a minute, I'll find it. Picture of my grandson—cute little boy, see, Operator? Hey, are those handcuffs absolutely necessary? I found my license, didn't I, Operator?")

It is all so unfunny when it's happening.

Now in Carpinteria, California, here was a first: arrest for *drunken sitting.*

I'd been to a winy luncheon with a dozen other members of the Santa Barbara writers' group and, on the way home, finding myself nodding at the wheel, I pulled over onto a side road, as I thought one was supposed to do in such cases, and went to sleep. A couple of hours later the car door was jerked open and two cops were peering at me solicitously.

("Been drinkin'?" "Yes, sir, that's why I pulled over. Hey! Are those cuffs absolutely . . . Listen, sir, I live two miles from here, only two miles; wife's waiting for dinner, six kids. Jesus, those cuffs are tight!")

So I was sentenced to fourteen days in the county jail. That's what I would write about. What could be more shameful and humiliating than those days in jail, especially at my age?

It would be the best damn piece I'd ever written! I snatched up the pen.

S I X

I started to write furiously, and only put the pen down reluctantly when the loudspeaker in the hall announced, "Tim's graduation in five minutes."

I took that time to shave. I'd been here how long? Two days? And hadn't even had time to shave yet.

We gathered in an oblong circle in the lounge—all twenty of us patients plus three or four counselors. Tim was dressed in a blue suit and looked bright-eyed and happy and ready for the world.

Jack Davis, one of the counselors, took out a medal the size of a fifty-cent piece from a velvet box and held it up to Tim, who was across the room. It was bronze and had the Serenity Prayer on it.

"Here it is," he said with a good smile. Finally! He was a great big wrangler type, wore cowboy boots and shirts, and spoke with an Oklahoma drawl. But his accent and assaults on the English language camouflaged an acute analytical mind, great compassion, and an abiding aura of serenity. As someone said, "Jack wears life like a loose garment."

"Well, Tim, this little gizmo isn't easily come by, is it?" He gave a chuckle. It was pure Will Rogers, but genuine and uncontrived.

"Who'da thunk it four weeks ago, eh? You was in bad shape, no doubt about it. Ornery. If you'da been a horse, I'da put a twitch on your nose before I'da rode you. Worse shape than even I was in when I quit. If you'd have kept on drinking, you'd have drank yourself to death. Now you have a whole new life in front of you. I didn't much care for the Tim who first came in here, but I've sure got to like the one who sits before me today. You've earned this medallion. You're an inspiration to all of us, and I know you'll do great on the outside."

He kissed the medallion and handed it on to the patient next to him, who said a few words about admiring Tim, and then passed the medal on. It came around the room to me, and I simply said that I barely had had a chance to know him, regretted that, but wished him well.

His counselor, Jerry, spoke feelingly of him, and finally Tim himself, moved to misty eyes, said several husky words of gratitude to the group, the counselors, and the clinic.

Everyone clapped, people hugged him and shook his hand, and asked him to autograph their copy of the Big Book, *Alcoholics Anonymous.*

Then someone said, "Tim, your taxi's here," and, tearily, he left to get his suitcase.

It was time for group. I wondered if it was going to be my turn for the "hot seat," but as we pulled our chairs in a tight circle, I noticed a new face. Essex, from Waco, Texas, had taken Tim's place, and I gathered that things had been said by him in the morning session (which I had missed because of the IQ test) that had irked Jerry; she had come to expect lies from addicts but had never grown to accept them and would not let them go unchallenged.

"Essex, you stated this morning that you took cocaine regularly along with your booze, but said you never dealt, right?"

"That's correct, Ma'am," he said proudly. "Never dealt." He nodded in affirmation.

He was a handsome raw-boned man of about forty, and though he had a perpetual Teddy Roosevelt grin, his bloodshot eyes didn't smile.

"And you say you spent about two thousand dollars a month on the habit?"

"Correct, ma'am." He had a blond guardsman's mustache, and when he spoke, it sounded as though it grew on the inside of his lip as well. "And I'm not proud of my habit."

"And you say you only used about two or three times a week." Jerry was scribbling figures on her scratch pad. "What did you do with the rest of the two thousand dollars' worth?"

"Ma'am?" He gave her his genial little-boy expression.

"At the going price per line and you yourself only snorting a few times a week, I figure you must have ended up with a lot of that white powder at the end of the month. What did you do with it all if you weren't dealing?"

He seemed nonplussed for a second, then answered brightly, "I got a lot of friends in Waco." He nodded; he was a nodder, doing it after speaking to confirm the veracity of his every statement.

"And you gave them all this cocaine every month?"

"Sure—to my buddies." Puzzled, nodding. "Sure, why not?"

"Just gave it to them? Never let them pay for it? With the limited amount of money you make?"

"I make a good salary," he said defensively.

"Not enough to afford twenty-four thousand dollars a year in cocaine, or your mistress, or your plane. Are you sure you didn't let your friends pay you for the dope?"

"Well, to some of them I gave it free," he said uncomfortably. "Others I didn't know so well, I'd let them pay me. I'd let 'em have it at cost."

"Or a little above cost?" said Jerry. "And if they weren't friends at all, a *lot* above cost?" She sighed. "I think you were dealing, Essex, and dealing pretty big. Your salary doesn't begin to cover payments to an ex-wife plus trips to Vegas and Bora-Bora with your girlfriend. Essex, may I ask why the hell are you here?"

He tugged at his mustache. "Because I want to get over my addiction to coke and booze and they say this place is best." He nodded for emphasis.

"What are you hearing, group?" said Jerry, looking around at us.

"Bullshit!" Terry was the first to say it.

Jerry nodded. "Isn't the real reason that your partner said he'd kick you out of the firm if you didn't shape up?"

The mask of geniality vanished. "Let him just try!" he said between clenched teeth, and he twisted his right fist into the palm of his left hand.

"Didn't he put up the money and you agreed to go?"

After a reluctant moment, he nodded.

"Now, this morning you said you were happy and docile when you drank and used, right?"

His Roosevelt smile was back. "Yeah, I'm a pussycat. Some of my buddies like to wreck bars and stuff when they get loaded and pissed, but I just got sleepy and dumb and sometimes sexy." He nodded.

"Never rough up women when you're drunk?"

"Me?" Incredulous. "I'm a lover, not a fighter."

"What are you hearing, group?" Jerry asked.

Terry was first again. "Bullshit!" It was echoed by some others in the group, and Essex glared at them with his cold eyes.

"This morning you said you had an amicable divorce, that you'd never fought with your wife," said Jerry.

"That's right."

"I telephoned her a little while ago and we had a long talk."

Essex, stricken: "You phoned Dolores? Where do you get off phoning Dolores?"

"When you registered, you signed a paper saying it was all right for us to talk to any relatives about your problem."

"So, didn't Dolores tell you I treated her right, that I always make my payments?"

"She said you broke her jaw the day after the divorce when you were stoned out of your mind and violent."

"We had a little argument and I gave her a shove. But it wasn't hard. It was just the angle—you know, the way she hit the wall."

Jerry sighed again. "Essex, we are not going to be able to do a damn thing for you unless you make up your mind about two things: One, that you truly want to be in here, for your own sake, your own health, your own self-respect, not just because your partner wants you to be here. Two, and I'm not even sure that you're capable of doing it at this stage of your life, you've got to learn to tell the truth. Otherwise you're not going to get a blessed thing out of this place and you're just wasting your time and my time and your partner's money. Make up your mind or leave."

He sat, head lowered, silent, his fingers working and feeling over each other like ants' antennae when the insects encounter each other.

She turned to me. "Barny, did you ever do cocaine or any drugs?"

"No," I said. "Thank God I'm just an alcoholic and not a junkie."

To my amazement, Terry leapt up into battle, her dark face darker with anger. "Hey, just a goddamn minute here! Where does he get off saying that?"

"Tell *him*," said Jerry calmly. "Not me. Look him in the eyes and get it off your chest."

I was bewildered. "What did I say wrong?"

"Your implication," snarled Terry, "and your sneering reference to chemical addiction shows you don't know shit from shinola. You have a holier-than-thou attitude about us!"

"No, honestly, I just meant—"

"You obviously look down on us, probably call us dope fiends behind our backs. Well, we're no worse than you drunks! And for your information, you can't even set a table right!"

I appealed to Jerry. "I simply meant—"

"Tell Terry, not me."

"Terry, I only meant that I've got enough problems trying to handle booze, let alone compounding it with other addictions. I don't look down on people on dope."

Terry was only slightly mollified. "That isn't the way it sounded," she muttered.

"Chico," said Jerry, "this morning you were telling us how your brother used to beat you up."

"Yeah, he sure did." Chico's handsome face went sad. "I'd be afraid to come home from school, so I'd stay there playing basketball, sometimes all alone, until very late, till I was sure my parents would be home and then he couldn't beat me up. Funny thing, I was bigger than him and stronger, but he was older and I wouldn't fight back. He'd beat me up hard almost every day and I wished he was dead. God, how I wished he was dead. I actually prayed that he would get himself killed. I went to church and prayed to God that he would die, and one day they called from the police station and said for my father to come down and see if the guy who'd been shot was my brother. And my father took me down with him to the morgue and they showed us his body and he'd been shot three times—here"—he pointed to his body—"and here and here—by a gang of kids."

"And what were you thinking," said Jerry softly, "as you looked at the body?"

Chico swallowed. "I was thinking first, Well, you son of a bitch, you're not going to beat me up again! My father cried, but I didn't."

"You didn't feel bad at all?" asked Dave.

Chico shook his head. "Just relief. But then, after, I began to get a lot of strange feelings. A kind of delayed reaction. And one day I said, Jesus, I killed him! I prayed that he'd die and, by God, I prayed so well that he ups and dies! Then I felt terrible. I wanted for him to stop beating me up, but not to die."

"I know what you mean," said Jerry and for just a second we got a rare glimpse of the woman behind the counselor. "It's terrible to want someone to die—and then they do." She paused, cleared her throat, and added, "But it sure gives you an excuse to get drunk, doesn't it?"

Chico nodded. "Drink, and then cocaine, and then for the last two years heroin, the Big H."

"And you blame it all on your brother's death?" said Terry. "Bullshit. Sounds too pat and easy."

Chico shrugged and struggled with the words. "I don't know what else to blame it on."

"Heredity?" said Dave. "Your parents drank hard, didn't they?"

He nodded. "Not that badly though."

"Every day?"

"Every day. But not like me. And they never used dope."

"Addiction's addiction."

Jerry looked at her watch. She discussed Chico's reading and writing assignments with him, then dismissed us for athletics. Except me. I was to have an interview with Craig, the minister-psychologist in his office in twenty minutes. She reminded everyone that tonight was the AA meeting instead of a lecture. We said the Serenity Prayer, and I walked down the corridor to my room. I picked up the Elizabeth Taylor article off the desk and flopped on the bed, exhausted.

I wondered what my wife, Mary, was doing now. I hoped she understood I wasn't allowed a call for five—or was it "after five"?—days and that I was thinking about her and missing her. And I hoped my son knew I was here at last, that someone had told him; I hadn't had time to call him in Paris in the rush to get here.

I uncrumpled the newspaper clipping and glared at the photo. Elizabeth Taylor looked great compared to when I had seen her in Mexico. I was doing a magazine article on the making of *Night of the Iguana* and Mary and I spent a week in Mismaloya off and on the set and in and out of bars with Richard and Liz. Burton was the quintessential charming drinking companion—"Call me Rich; Dick sounds like an appendage"—and on the days he wasn't performing, he and I hit the beer rather early in the morning, and Mary and Liz did all right, too, with the margaritas, better than all right. Now, in this photo, she looked slim and as bright of eye as in her teens. And she gave all credit to the BFC.

"In the beginning," she said of the treatment, "I felt like I was giving interviews . . . giving the version I would give to the press and keeping the true version to myself. And then I broke all those barriers down and told the truth. Like an onion, I was peeled down to the absolute core."

I wondered when they would start peeling me. Maybe the minister would start the process. I looked over at my suitcase. I must unpack, I thought. But there's been no time in this bloody place. I must work on my jail epic, too.

I thought of Kendall, my twenty-one-year-old special daughter-friend, and wondered if she knew I was here. I'd be able to call her in three more days! We had always been very close. I wondered if all the drinking at home, the fights, and so forth had bruised her much. But she was tough, humorous, self-reliant, and extroverted, and wonderfully goofy; her nickname had always been The Kook. And she

was tall, with legs up to the armpits and a gorgeous face like
Mary's, and she'd been an off and on model since she was
fifteen. She graduated from Taft and was at UCLA when she
got some offers in New York that she couldn't refuse, and
now she was commuting between Milan and Paris doing big
spreads for *Vogue* and *Harper's Bazaar,* and TV ads for Jor-
dache. But she'd always yearned to be an actress, going back
to her youthful days. She was always a great mimic, her best
imitation being Boris Karloff in one word: "Ahn-ti-pash-toh!"
But her major act was imitating a pencil sharpener. She did it
extraordinarily well, and the guttural, rasping, grinding
noises were perfect and with only a little adjusting worked
equally well for her imitation of a model airplane, a power
mower, and a chain saw, and it would send people into
paroxysms of laughter. But even she saw that it was a limited
field, and lately, besides her modeling, she'd been studying
acting seriously and hard with my great interest and encour-
agement behind her.

And then it came to me! The day before I'd left for Betty
Ford's—what was it? Only two days ago? Two days and an eon
ago?—I remembered a letter had come from The Kook
saying, "Hey, guess what! You're going to die! I'm an actress,
a professional actress! Watch *One Life to Live* on the 20th of
this month, one o'clock your time. Sure, it's just a soap but I
actually say some lines! It's a tiny part, but, Dad, it's my first!
Don't laugh when you see it—it's supposed to be serious, no
pencil sharpeners, I promise!"

I was thrilled for her. She'd worked so hard.

Today was what? The 15th. So . . . the show would be
on . . . this Wednesday! I *had* to watch it. But how? There was
a TV set in the lounge, but no one was allowed to turn it on
until the weekend. I would talk to Jerry about it tomorrow.
Maybe they'd make an exception. They had to!

I picked up the article again, thinking with pleasure, Look
out, Liz, there's another actress on the scene.

It was a good article, candid and sensitive. The last paragraph was from the journal she'd kept while here at BFC. It was an early entry:

"Today is Friday. I've been here since Monday night, one of the most frightening nights of my life. Not to mention lonely. But I am not alone. There are people here just like me, who are suffering just like me, who hurt inside and out, just like me, people I've learned to love. It's an experience unlike any other I've known."

Well, we'd have to see about that, wouldn't we?

I looked at my watch. I just had time to unpack before visiting the preacher man.

SEVEN

As I came into the book-lined office, the minister put me at my ease immediately, motioning me to a leather chair in front of his desk.

"There are three reasons why people drink to excess," said Craig with a disarming smile. "Unfortunately, no one yet has figured out what they are."

About sixty, he had a midwestern Sinclair Lewis accent and face, and he wore a clerical collar, but he was neither a Babbitt nor an Elmer Gantry. An ex-alcoholic and a psychologist, he had seen service as a Navy chaplain in three wars, and he was literate and sharp.

I made many notes afterward, but I'm not sure how; I was still on medication, and besides, I was very, very tired. Whoever had warned that this place was "no country club" had been a genius at understatement.

The minister—"call me Craig"—leafed through my case history as he began the interview. "There's a tendency for all of us to think we invented drunkenness, but its been around for a long time. The Egyptians expected and maybe even encouraged it at parties, and we know all about the Romans, don't we? I like Seneca, way back in A.D. 50 saying, 'Drunkenness is nothing but a condition of insanity purposely assumed.' Can't put it much better than that. It's only in fairly modern times that we've tried to find out *why* some of us actually want and crave that condition of temporary insanity. Which, of course, often leads to permanent insanity. By the way, have you ever seen anyone with a wet brain? We see them all the time in the mental institutions, people who've drunk their brain into a nonfunctioning sponge. The hospitals have to put signs in the corridors saying 'Toilet' and an arrow about every ten feet because patients forget what they got up out of their chairs to do and where it is. Pathetic and horrifying. And death by cirrhosis is a terrible one to watch; the liver will take just so much and then it rebels and says I've decided not to get well this time, and develops a galloping hardening and the patient dies a frightfully painful death in a couple of months. I myself came within a gnat's whisker of it."

He asked me a whole lot of questions that I thought had been already well covered by the doctor when I came in, by the questionnaire I had to fill out, and by my counselor. But given the evasiveness and mendacity of the average alcoholic, they were probably cross-checking the answers. I noticed Craig was taking notes.

He asked me about my parents—if they drank—and I answered that they both had two ritualistic and cherished drinks every evening, never got drunk in their lives, and my mother had recently died at a vigorous ninety-three.

"The liquor industry should have gotten an endorsement from her," Craig said with a smile. "So you had no alcoholics in the family?"

"One drunken, charming uncle."

"Every family in America seems to have had a drunken, charming uncle. How about your grandparents?"

"My maternal grandfather never drank in his ninety-three years, sober as a judge. As a matter of fact, he *was* one— Supreme Court of Montana—first governor of Puerto Rico, and so forth. And his wife never touched it either. Same with my father's mother. My father's father, on the other hand, was a high-flying robber baron and politician from Montana and, after going through millions, died broke and a drunk. But he couldn't have had an influence on me and my drinking because I never met him—he deserted my grandmother and my father when my father was six."

"Ah, but you have his genes in you! More and more we are looking to backgrounds; it's rare that an alcoholic doesn't have an alcoholic in his family even if it skips a generation. Also, the ethnic pattern seems important: We see many more drunks of Irish, German, and Nordic ancestry than we do Jews or Orientals. And of course, it's pathetically true of the American Indian and the Eskimo. The northern Frenchman and northern Spaniard drink more than their southern counterparts, and the Arabs drink not at all."

Then he smiled. "Boy, you've sure shot some theories to hell: Your mother drinks every day of her life and dies at ninety-three, and her father is a teetotaler and also dies at ninety-three." He frowned down at my folder. "It doesn't look as though you would have made ninety-three the way you were going."

He asked me all the routine questions: amount imbibed, frequency of drunks, blackouts, and so forth.

"Get along with your parents?"

"Yes. I admired them both greatly, loved and enjoyed them."

"So we can't blame your wretched and deprived child-hood."

"I had the world's easiest and best growing-up."

"A pampered childhood?"

"Not pampered but certainly privileged: four servants, twenty-four-room house, chauffeur, private school, horses, tutoring in music, painting, lessons in boxing early every morning with our father, theater and opera with our mother, the works."

"And how was their relationship with each other?"

"He adored her and she loved him, though he was ill the last twenty-five years of his life and it turned into a sort of nurse-patient relationship."

"Did they quarrel?"

"Never in their life that we were aware of, and they knew each other since their teens."

"Bit abnormal, wouldn't you say?"

"Unusual, certainly, but I wouldn't say abnormal. It seemed to me and my brother that that was the way married couples should act. Perhaps that's why I wasn't prepared for any sort of discord in my first marriage. I couldn't stand any friction, which I suppose other people take for granted. I reacted badly, childishly."

"Describe the marriage, and did liquor play a part in the divorce?"

"We were married at twenty-seven and twenty-three having known each other slightly since childhood."

"Where was this?"

"In a wealthy enclave south of San Francisco—Hillsborough. I was from a prominent family, though I had no money myself, inherited none, and was a struggling, barely published writer and a would-be portrait painter. She was beautiful, petite, introverted, honors graduate of Stanford, potential heiress."

"Did she drink?"

"No. But then I didn't much either in those days. If guests were coming, I'd have to go out and buy something; we didn't just drink at night as a matter of course. I'd drunk occasionally in college and in the Foreign Service, but once married, if I went a week or a month or so without a drink, I didn't even notice. At a party, I'd drink."

"So, how did it happen, the booze problem?" he asked. "We see people come in here attributing their alcoholism to terrible events in their lives, childhood abuse, poverty, chronic failures one after another in their life. Others say they drink because of the mediocrity of their lives. Others because their life is too harried and pressured. Yet look at the survivors of the Holocaust, the camps and all, who didn't turn to drink after their horrendous ordeal. How did your drinking get into full swing?"

"We had a son after three years of marriage, and I was teaching at night and doing some portraits and writing a novel. A second novel, my first having been published to resounding apathy by Random House. I honestly don't remember much drinking in those days. We had very little money, though a short story of mine won the Collier's Prize for a total of seventeen hundred and fifty dollars and was included in the O. Henry Collection of prize stories, along with such big names as Faulkner and Eudora Welty.

"Then it happened. The novel I'd worked on so hard, *A Day of Fear,* was turned down as unpublishable by Random House."

"That must have given you a good excuse to get good and drunk."

"Did it ever! I'd put a lot into that book, everything I knew about bullfighting, all the emotion I felt for my friend, the matador Manolete, and his tragic death. And here it wasn't even good enough to be published!"

"So, you got drunk and stayed drunk?"

"No. Dale, my first wife, rescued the manuscript from consignment to the trash can, and we sent it to a friend at Houghton Mifflin in Boston." I told Craig abut the series of telegrams framed on our wall, starting with the rejection from Bennett Cerf, then the jubilant acceptance by Houghton Mifflin and suggestion that "we change the title from *A Day of Fear* to *Matador.*" Then the subsequent telegrams: "Reader's Digest Book Club wants *Matador*—your share of advance $40,000," then "Book of the Month Club, $50,000 advance."

"That must have called for champagne," said Craig.

"You can imagine—that much money in those days. Then more telegrams, Dell books offering the highest bid in history at that time for the paperback rights, and John Huston buying the movie rights, and its being on the *New York Times* best-seller list for a year, and the twenty-eight translations and on and on. But the best was when John Steinbeck picked *Matador* as his favorite book of the year in the *Saturday Review*."

"That must have called for *two* bottles of champagne."

"At least. I wrote Mr. Steinbeck and thanked him, and he wrote back this unforgettable letter, which of course I know by heart: 'Dear Conrad, I like bullfighting—to me it is a lonely, formal, anguished microcosm of what happens to every man, even in an office strangled by the glue on the envelopes. In the bullring he manages to survive, for a while—sometimes.' And then imagine, I hadn't even met him and he invited me to go to the Virgin Islands with him and his wife."

"Which you did."

"Of course. For two weeks."

"More champagne?"

"Rum cokes. Lots of them."

"Steinbeck have a booze problem?"

"Not in the same league with some writers I've known—Sinclair Lewis, Irwin Shaw, Capote, and so forth. It's an occupational disease."

"Your life had changed overnight, hadn't it? Pretty heady stuff."

"And that's where it went. To my head."

"And Dale?"

"We broke up for a while, six months or so."

"Nothing fails like success, as Fitzgerald said."

I nodded and told him how my world had suddenly been transformed. Short of winning the lottery or Irish Sweepstakes, few successes can equal for sudden dramatic impact what happens to a writer in America when he hits the literary jackpot with a book. Not only is his economic situation radically changed but also his career, social, and marital situations are subject to scrutiny, criticism, and upheaval. As Maugham wrote in *The Summing Up*, the greatest danger that besets the professional author is one that "unfortunately only a few have to guard against. Success. It is the most difficult thing the writer has to cope with. When, after a long and bitter struggle he has at last achieved it, he finds that it spreads a snare to entangle and destroy him."

After being on talk shows, having the book the subject of the cover story in both the *Saturday Review* and the *New York Times* "Book Review" section, and the entire literary section of *Time,* I couldn't walk into a restaurant without someone coming over and introducing himself. They felt the way I always had in the past about writers: Didn't we have a lot in common? After all, *I'd* read my book and *they'd* read my book, so they figured we had a lot to talk about.

I told Craig how even my friends at the corner cleaners suddenly treated me deferentially; people I hadn't heard from for years phoned me; I was invited to parties by people I'd never met, and, though my book was about Spain and bullfighting, on radio and TV my opinion was earnestly sought on politics, Russia, abortion, strip mining, and other things I knew nothing about. It would seem that my every utterance should be somehow oracular just because I'd written a book considered to be entertaining. And certain women, who never would have looked at me twice, suddenly were calling me or showing up at my studio at odd times of day and night to get a book "autographed for my sister." As G. B. Shaw said, there's no aphrodisiac like fame.

I wrote little and drank more. This is not to say I was idle. Quite the contrary. Being the author of a best-selling book is a full-time job—as long as it lasts on the best-seller lists, and *Matador* was there for over a year. There is the flood of speaking engagements, the traveling, the autograph parties, the magazine interviews. There was no time to write. Except to answer letters, an unceasing deluge of letters from strangers and forgotten friends, and even the kindly old postman treated me differently now: Anyone who got this much mail *must* be pretty important, so he started calling me Mr. Conrad. There were letters from all over the world, since *Matador* went into dozens of foreign languages. There were pleas for money. Every certifiable in the world, it would seem, felt constrained to write to me. One woman wrote, "I hope your conscience has prevailed by this time and you are ready to tell the world that I *really* wrote your book!" And the inevitable: "I've led a fabulous life. I'll tell it to you, you write it, and we'll split 50-50"—usually from someone in the Midwest who'd had a lifetime job as a librarian or had been the first in their town to buy a Packard or had a turtle that lived to be 110.

I had my next book outlined, but it was impossible to get to the solitary act of writing, caught up as I was in this new giddy whirlwind. As Maugham points out:

> Success besides often bears within itself the seed of destruction, for it may very well cut the author off from the material that was its occasion. He enters a new world. He is made much of. He must be almost super-human if he is not captivated by the notice taken of him by the great and remains insensible to the attentions of beautiful women. He grows accustomed to another way of life, probably more luxurious than that to which he has been used, and to people who have more of the social graces than those with whom he has consorted before. They are more intellectual and their superficial bril-

liance is engaging. How difficult it is for him then to move freely still in the circles with which he has been familiar and which have given him his subjects! His success has changed him in the eyes of his old associates and they are no longer at home with him. They may look upon him with envy or with admiration, but no longer as one of themselves. The new world into which his success has brought him excites his imagination and he writes about it; but he sees it from the outside and can never so penetrate it as to become a part of it.

"Don't get me wrong," I said to Craig. "I didn't begrudge or regret my sudden success. After all, this is what writers strive so hard for: money, prestige, and to get laid. It's just that . . . well, so much happened at once and everything became so different and accelerated."

"And you drank to make things seem more normal," said the minister, "which made them become more abnormal."

"I drank to slow things down, and it just speeded them up. I regarded alcohol with disdain. I treated it like water."

"And it ended up treating you like dirt," he said. "And Dale still didn't drink?"

"She might order a drink, and then leave half of it. That always amazed me."

"So guess who finished it."

"Of course. And at the end of a cocktail party at our house any of the glasses left unemptied by our guests I took care of. Couldn't stand waste, I told myself."

"And you didn't much care what they'd been drinking."

"My taste grew more and more eclectic."

"As the disease progressed." He studied the material in the folder. "I see here you had a bad episode relating to alcohol about this time."

My face must have registered pain, for he said, "Still hard to think about?"

"It wasn't good, that's for sure."

"Tell me about it. And Dale's reaction to all this."

I told him about the Rover Boy in Hollywood. In detail.

Tennessee Williams observed somewhere that when a marriage goes on the rocks, the rocks can usually be found under the mattress. This wasn't the case with us. We were simply pulling and tugging in different directions.

Dale's and my marriage had been shaky for some time. Both of us had tempers. And we hadn't learned the little marriage-saving catchphrases: "You may be right," in the midst of an argument; or "I love you but," to precede a criticism.

We were too quick to use those marriage-destroying words "never" and "always." ("You're *always* late" and "You *never* do anything to help.")

The baby and the home were all-important to her. She didn't need or want the excitement of people and the hullabaloo that *Matador* had stirred up in my life. She was grateful for the money that was pouring in, pleased with the new house we rented, but resentful of my having to be away so much, of the constant telephone calls from all sorts of strange types at strange hours, and the unknown people who would suddenly appear at the door to get a book autographed or want me to lecture at such and such a luncheon.

One day *Look* magazine moved into the house with a barrage of lights and cameras to do a big story on the happy home life of the author of the number one book on the bestseller list. But before they could complete the story, Dale had moved out and down to her parents' home with the baby after sad and angry scenes that I'm sure are indigenous, with very little variation in dialogue, to every domestic sundering.

"It never fails," sighed the editor assigned to write the article as they scrapped the project. "Fourth time it's happened to us."

Now I was free, loose of foot and far more shaken by the separation than I would realize for a long time. My first act was to purchase that time-honored badge of success in America, the Car. I knew little about automobiles, but I chose a secondhand custom-built Mark IV Jaguar—gaudy, rare, and frightfully expensive. On the way down to Hollywood to see John Huston I stopped at Santa Barbara and showed my new acquisition to my parents.

My father studied the outsized headlights, the leather upholstery, and the fruitwood paneling and its many gadgets. He shook his head. "Looks like something designed over the telephone by Al Capone for his mistress," he said dryly.

A retired investment banker, he was impressed by writing as a career for the first time now when he saw the financial statements from my publishers, and he endorsed it still further when my mother, doing a *New York Times* crossword puzzle, suddenly exclaimed like the woman of Chaillot, "Sixty-three across, sixty-three across!" brandishing the paper triumphantly. ("Sixty-three across" required my name in the squares in answer to the text "Author of *Matador*.")

With me on the hegira to the south was Niels Mortensen, a fellow writer. We had met in the Café Goya three years before, and with music (he played nine different instruments), books, and tropical fish in common we had soon become great friends. Though Danish and brought up in Denmark, he had trained both as an engineer at MIT and a writer-reporter on various American publications, newspapers, and radio. I was relying heavily on his good judgment to help me through the Hollywood labyrinth, for I had read of many writers' fates in Lotusland and I was determined it wouldn't happen to me.

Niels and I checked in at the Garden of Allah, that fabled cottage hotel on Sunset Boulevard where Parker quipped, Benchley quenched, Flynn wenched, and Fitzgerald lounged. After a swim we went to TBA, the movie agents with whom I had signed a contract. They were housed in Beverly Hills in a pretentious building that tried desperately to resemble Tara. My particular agent was Ted Sheinbaum, who turned out to be a tweedy, pipe-smoking friendly fellow. When we were ushered into his thickly carpeted, book-lined, leathery office, he got up from his desk, took Niels's hand in both of his, and said, "This is one of the great moments of my life."

"Er," said Niels gesturing at me, "*he* wrote the book."

With no loss of poise, Sheinbaum revolved to me, took my hand, and repeated the statement with embellishments. "Now, let's talk a little business. This is the greatest property of the decade and we intend to see that you get a great big old pee-potful of money for it. So, who do we sell it to?"

I looked startled. "I told you on the phone about John Huston and Jose Ferrer's telegram."

"Chicken feed," said Sheinbaum. He had a strange mannerism of seeming to take snuff—the index finger and thumb in conjunction going purposelessly to each nostril in turn at metronome intervals. "We've got some *real* offers!"

He rattled off some names of some big stars and directors who had been bidding for my book, all of them impressive but all of them totally wrong for the film in my opinion. The best team for the project, concluded Sheinbaum, was a popular matinee idol noted for his white teeth and inability to register or elicit any emotion whatsoever, a director whose films were slanted toward teenagers, and an aging ingenue whose bust measurement must have been a higher cipher than her IQ. I'll call them Stolid Mann, Lazlo Puttee, and Debra Balloons, since they're all still around and doing their thing.

He talked for an hour about the virtues of his three favorites for *Matador,* and he seemed so sure and so sincere in his admiration that he had me virtually won over by the time we left his office. After all, what did I know about the picture industry? We left full of brotherly love and with a date to meet the next morning with the stars and the director. Niels hadn't said anything in the office, not a word, but I noticed he was frowning as we drove back to the Garden of Allah.

"Maybe I was wrong about Ferrer and Huston," I said. "What do you think?"

"I think . . ." he said slowly, "I think you are getting royally screwed."

"What?"

"I can't put my finger on what or how or especially why, but I know I wouldn't trust that guy as far as I could punt him."

"But why would he pull anything? He wants me to get the best deal possible. After all, he receives ten percent of everything I get."

"I don't know. I just don't know."

Back at the hotel I ordered a couple of double scotches as Niels nervously paced up and down.

"There's got to be a reason," he kept saying. Suddenly he snapped his fingers. He got the telephone and dialed my agents. Then, "Hello, I'm calling for Dore Schary. . . . That's right, over at MGM. Mr. Schary's planning a big picture for next year and he's wondering if you still handle Stolid Mann, Lazlo Puttee, and Debra Balloons. . . . You do? Thank you. He'll contact you soon."

Niels hung up. "There's the answer! Simple—they don't handle Ferrer and Huston, but they *do* handle this other package. And they probably get much more than ten percent for their actors and directors, so to hell with their novelists!"

"What do I do now? I'm under contract to them!"

"You've got to be protected from them."

"Fine thing. From my own agent I need protection."

I suddenly thought of Lou Blau, the air attaché I'd known in the Lima embassy. I remembered he'd left Lima to return to his law practice in Beverly Hills. I looked him up in the telephone book and to my relief he was listed. He remembered me and congratulated me on the success of *Matador*. We reminisced for a while and he asked us for dinner at his house that night. After catching up on mutual friends, I explained my predicament.

"First thing is to get you away from your agents," he said.

"But I signed a contract," I said.

"Standard contract?"

"Yes."

"I know that contract pretty well and I'll break it in five minutes," Lou said, adding with a chuckle, "I drew it up for them five years ago. Next thing is to get you together with Huston and Ferrer."

Huston and Ferrer flew in from Paris that day, and Lou set up an appointment at Huston's Bel Air Hotel cottage for the next day. I was anxious about the meeting and had several drinks that evening to try to relax enough to go to sleep. I still had to take two sleeping pills and felt nervous and tired the next morning. To get myself aroused for the appointment I had a tall scotch and soda and was a little startled to find myself putting my hangover Alka-Seltzer into the drink.

"Let's do the drinking afterwards," said Niels. "Never celebrate before the deed."

"Just upholding literary tradition," I said. "Name me one great American writer from Edgar Allan Poe to Faulkner who didn't drink too much."

"Mary Baker Eddy," said Niels, taking the glass out of my hand.

We picked Blau up at his office and drove up Sunset to the hotel.

Huston's cottage was already full of people when we got there at ten o'clock. Actors, lawyers, agents. A bar was being operated briskly in one corner by Huston's constant companion, the jockey Billy Pearson, the subsequent winner of *The $64,000 Question* and *The $64,000 Challenge*. A glamorous French actress was appropriately draped across the chaise lounge next to a jeroboam of champagne. Soon a tall man, a brown cigarette jutting from his big tan face and dressed in a paisley dressing gown, emerged from a bedroom.

"I'm John Huston," he said with a great smile, "and I hope to hell you sell us that fine book of yours."

Huston's charm has been written of many times and none of the writings have exaggerated it. We drank and talked for several hours, not of terms ("Let the lawyers handle it—there'll be no problems"), but of how we would translate my novel into the film medium. The only point we differed on was that Huston thought we should start with the protagonist in the arena and flash back to the events of the day ("After all, it's Greek tragedy you've written"). I felt that we would lose some suspense since there is some doubt throughout the first part of the story as to whether he'll even get to the arena. But John was reasonable, articulate, and skilled, and I enjoyed our meeting immensely. Jose Ferrer joined us after lunch; he, too, was charming and a pleasure to deal with. They invited me to the premiere of *Moulin Rouge* that night and set a date for the next day for more talks. The liquor did not stop flowing all day, but no one appeared to be particularly affected by it.

Too much had happened all at once. I found I could not sleep at all unless I took vast quantities of alcohol, and then to quiet my nerves the next day I took more alcohol and sleeping pills. Soon I found I was getting dizzy spells and could not sleep no matter what I took. I had to get away from Hollywood for a few days. My brother, Hunt, had married a fine girl whom we'd grown up with, and he and his wife had a ranch three hours from San Francisco. I invited myself there for the weekend; their little house on the river at Knight's Ferry was just what I needed, I was sure. But still I was so wound up I kept up the drinking and pill taking.

After I'd been there one day I started to crack up. Hunt was up at the barn when this awful sensation started coming over me. I moved from the kitchen to the living room as a murky numbness came over me.

"Something terrible is happening to me," I muttered to my brother's wife, Marion.

"What is it?" she asked, after a look at the weird expression on my face.

"I feel—I feel as though I were going down a drain," I said. "I feel unless I break something I'll go crazy. Can't help it. . . ."

I picked up a phonograph record from their old 78 collection and broke it with my fist, and felt temporarily better. I broke several records as Marion looked at me in terror. When the records ran out, I started breaking the windows.

"I'm sorry," I remember saying as calmly as I could. "I'll replace all the records and the windows—but I'll go mad otherwise."

She fled out the door to get my brother, while I broke every window in the house with my fist. I cut myself on the last pane, and that seemed to bring me to my senses. Just then Hunt charged in the door. "You bastard, you've wrecked my house!" he said and knocked me down.

I apologized and tried to explain as best I could what had been happening to me. I suddenly felt infinitely better. After a long cold shower, I dressed, made arrangements with a glazier to repair the windows, and returned to San Francisco, where I spent the night with Niels and his wife. I was convinced that if I could just get one good night's sleep, I would be all right. But again I tossed and turned in spite of—or probably because of—several glasses of scotch and a sleeping pill. I took endless cold showers, but nothing helped. Around five in the morning I felt it coming on me again— that horrible maelstrom whirling me around at an ever-increasing speed, a sickening vortex threatening to suck me down a giant drain. I dressed and, without waking the Mortensens, drove toward the nearest hospital. I knew I was going mad, knew I had to get help and get it very fast. Yet it was similar to when you have to go to the bathroom very urgently: You don't dare run too quickly. I had to keep myself under strict control, just hold out till I got there—I

didn't dare drive too fast. As calmly as I could I walked up
the hospital steps, holding myself rigidly. The only doctor I
knew in the place was Dale's pediatrician and luckily I
bumped into him in the lobby.

"Dr. Marsh," I said in measured tones, "I am very, very
sick. I am losing my mind. I need to sleep desperately."

He smiled reassuringly and ushered me into an elevator.
That's the last I remember. I was told later I went berserk,
was given a massive hypo, and was taken in a straitjacket to a
sanitarium thirty miles from San Francisco. There I spent a
week manacled to a bed and raving while the doctors argued
about what to do with me.

The distinguished neurologist that my brother and mother
engaged recommended that I be given shock treatments
immediately. But Dale, as my legal wife, had to give her
consent. She had her psychiatrist examine me. Afterward he
said he was against the shock treatments.

"He needs deep analysis," he reported to my brother.

"How can you analyze somebody who's so far gone he
doesn't even know who he is or where he is?"

"The last case I saw like this," the analyst said gloomily, "sat
in a darkened room for two years playing with himself.
Analysis brought him around."

Of course, I was unaware of the conflict going on about my
condition. On some days I had some brief, fluttering moments of lucidity when I wondered where I was and why I
was manacled to the bed. But then I would drift off into the
milky void and hallucinations of the insane. When the male
nurses would unshackle me to feed me, I would accuse them
of trying to poison me and would throw the food at them.

Finally, the neurologist threatened to pull off the case. "It's
a clear-cut case of alcohol and barbiturate poisoning," he
said, "and shock will get him out of it."

Dale gave her consent at last. I was wheeled into the treatment area, the cathodes were attached to my head, and the

current turned on. I went into the room a maniac and half an hour later came out rational, asking the conventional "Where am I?" and "How'd I get here?"

The minister shook his head sympathetically. "What an experience. How long were you in the clinic?"

"I stayed two more weeks in the sanitarium, then returned to Malibu in good shape. But it was over a year before I could take a drink, and I have never taken a pill since. It must have been a more ghastly experience than I am able to convey now, but time has conveniently drawn a film over most of it for me."

"What started you drinking again?"

"I took some of the money that was pouring in and opened a nightclub."

"Just the thing for an incipient alcoholic!" He looked at his watch. "Time for dinner, but I want to hear about it. Also, we haven't even touched on religion. Come in tomorrow, same time."

He stood up and we shook hands.

"Oh, and I forgot to ask you, ever try to commit suicide?"

"No."

"Ever consider it, threaten to do it?"

"Not really, why?"

"Just that booze, pills, and suicide are usually a happy family. Interesting syndrome: though not all people who threaten suicide do it, all people who do it have threatened to at one point. See you tomorrow."

I liked him and felt I could tell him anything without fear of disapproval or of shocking him.

As I was leaving, he added, "Like most alcoholics, you have a very low opinion of yourself. I wonder why?"

Usually I sat with Dave and Chico and Beth, but tonight we were joined by a pneumatic, pretty young platinum blonde from the women's hall. Charlene rarely ever spoke to any-one, just batted her mascaraed eyes, always opened wide like a Peter Arno cartoon floozie. We figured that, like the pros-titute in a tale of Steinbeck's, she mistrusted language as a means of communication. But tonight after the others had left the table she actually spoke. "You remind me of some-one," she said with a suggestive little smile.

"Really?" I perked up.

"Someone I really like and admire," she murmured in her husky voice.

Had she read *Matador?* Or any of my other books?

"Yes?" I said, edging my chair closer. Was she going to ask how it felt to fight a bull and what was Manolete really like and would I do a sketch of her?

"Someone wonderful," she said dreamily.

"Yes?" I said. "Who?"

"My grandfather," she said.

And so it goes. So much for Charlene.

In retelling youthful adventures in Hollywood to Craig, I had for a few moments basked once more in its golden if conflicted glow. Youth! Charm! Dreams to be fulfilled! Time had passed so fast amid the roar of clinking glasses and popping corks. Charlene had brought me up short with sober reality, and I felt old.

I needed a drink. Make that a double.

After dinner, and the Serenity Prayer, Dave, Chico, Beth, and I went back to Firestone with the rest of our "peers" (the word "patients" was seldom used by the staff).

The Friday Alcoholics Anonymous meeting at the Betty Ford Center's little auditorium is "open," and outsiders, that is, people not in the BFC, are allowed to attend (as opposed to the "closed" Wednesday meeting in the cafeteria).

This evening the room was jammed with peers and with visitors from the Palm Springs area sitting and standing in the back. Some people were attending their first meeting; others had been going to meetings at least once a week for some twenty years. People all over the state and country and the world were attending similar meetings at this same moment. I was told that AA today numbers 62,860 *known* groups in 112 countries. Probably there are tens of thousands more, because no group is required to register with any central office. (I found out much later that there are fifty-five meetings a week in Santa Barbara, my town of 78,000 people, alone.)

Before the meeting, I asked Dave, who had been trying AA for a month before coming to the BFC, what there is about AA that attracts and fulfills so many desperate people. This program, founded fifty years ago by two men, one a drunken, failed stockbrocker, called by Aldoux Huxley "the greatest social architect of the century," and the other a drunken Ohio proctologist, has worked where the collective brains of medicine and psychiatry have failed.

How? I wanted to know.

The answer is simple, ridiculously simple, he said. "By holding meetings that are attended by alcoholics who wish to stop drinking and who discuss their successes and failures in trying to reach that goal."

I asked, what can these meetings possibly do for an alcoholic and his shattered life that family, clergymen, friends, and doctors have failed to do?

His answer was, "Everything." Then he added, "Or, conversely, if the alcoholic isn't ready or willing or honest with himself, nothing."

But what goes on at these meetings, I wanted to know, what kind of hypnosis or hocus pocus do they do in that one short hour?

"You'll see," he said and explained that all AA meetings are exactly alike and, at the same time, are totally different from one another. The format is as ritualistic as a bullfight, but each has as many facets as there are individuals taking part in the ritual.

Tonight at the BFC it seemed almost folksy, Rotarian. If I'd had any trepidation about the outsiders, it was quickly dispelled by the easy, relaxed, cheerful, serene, and even jocular atmosphere created by most of those attending. Exactly at the appointed time people sat down, became quiet, and the meeting began. I would learn that, with little variation, it is what goes on at every meeting.

A woman took the podium. "Good evening. My name is Marilyn, and I'm *still* an alcoholic!"

"Hi, Marilyn!" came the chorus.

The secretary in charge for this evening, a once-glamorous middle-aged blonde with a huge smile, lots of teeth, lots of gums, welcomed us and gave the usual preamble taken from the Big Book *(Alcoholics Anonymous)*. This is the unvarying opening to every AA meeting all over the world and in any language. This is the way it appears in the book and this is the way she read it.

" 'Alcoholics Anonymous is a fellowship of men and women who share their experience, strength and hope with each other that they may solve their common problem and help others to recover from alcoholism. The only requirement for membership is a desire to stop drinking. There are no dues or fees for A.A. membership; we are self-supporting through our own contributions. A.A. is not allied with any sect, denomination, politics, organization or institution; does not wish to engage in any controversy, neither endorses nor opposes any causes. Our primary purpose is to stay sober and help other alcoholics to achieve sobriety. . . .

" '*How it works:* Rarely have we seen a person fail who has thoroughly followed our path. Those who do not recover are people who cannot or will not completely give themselves to this simple program, usually men and women who are constitutionally incapable of being honest with themselves. There are such unfortunates. They are not at fault; they seem to have been born that way. They are naturally incapable of grasping and developing a manner of living which demands rigorous honesty. Their chances are less than average. There are those, too, who suffer from grave emotional and mental disorders, but many of them do recover if they have the capacity to be honest.

" 'Our stories disclose in a general way what we used to be like, what happened, and what we are like now. If you have decided you want what we have and are willing to go to any length to get it—then you are ready to take certain steps.

" 'At some of these we balked. We thought we could find an easier, softer way. But we could not. With all the earnestness at our command, we beg of you to be fearless and thorough from the very start. Some of us have tried to hold on to our old ideas and the result was nil until we let go absolutely.

" 'Remember, that we deal with alcohol—cunning, baffling, powerful!' "

Here she departed from the text and said, "And—I might add—*patient.* I was sober ten years, but it was out there waiting for me. I made one little slip and it got me again. But I'm back now for good."

She went back to the text: " 'Without help it is too much for us. But there is One who has all power—that One is God. May you find Him now!

" 'Half measures availed us nothing. We stood at the turning point. We asked His protection and care with complete abandon.

" 'Here are the steps we took, which are suggested as a program of recovery:

" '1. We admitted we were powerless over alcohol—that our lives had become unmanageable.

" '2. Came to believe that a Power greater than ourselves could restore us to sanity.

" '3. Made a decision to turn our will and our lives over to the care of God *as we understood Him.*

" '4. Made a searching and fearless moral inventory of ourselves.

" '5. Admitted to God, to ourselves, and to another human being the exact nature of our wrongs.' "

Again she departed from the book. "Now you people here at the BFC are only going as far as this, but we'll read the other seven steps anyway.

" '6. Were entirely ready to have God remove all these defects of character.

" '7. Humbly asked Him to remove our shortcomings.

"'8. Made a list of all persons we had harmed, and became willing to make amends to them all.

"'9. Made direct amends to such people wherever possible, except when to do so would injure them or others.

"'10. Continued to take personal inventory and when we were wrong promptly admitted it.

"'11. Sought through prayer and meditation to improve our conscious contact with God *as we understood Him,* praying only for knowledge of His will for us and the power to carry that out.

"'12. Having had a spiritual awakening as the result of these steps, we tried to carry this message to alcoholics, and to practice these principles in all our affairs.

"'Many of us exclaimed, "What an order! I can't go through with it." Do not be discouraged. No one among us has been able to maintain anything like perfect adherence to these principles. We are not saints. The point is, that we are willing to grow along spiritual lines. The principles we have set down are guides to progress. We claim spiritual progress rather than spiritual perfection.

"'Our description of the alcoholic, the chapter to the agnostic, and our personal adventures before and after make clear three pertinent ideas:

"'(a) That we were alcoholic and could not manage our own lives.

"'(b) That probably no human power could have relieved our alcoholism.

"'(c) That God could and would if He were sought.'

"Now there it is," Marilyn said, "and we can take it or leave it. We can take it and find serenity and peace of mind in sobriety, or we can reject it, try to do it on our own, and probably end up again messing up our lives and those of other people around us. Tonight we have three people who decided to listen to what AA has to offer, and they're going to tell us about it."

Behind Marilyn on the dais sat two women and a man, healthy-looking people under thirty, all graduates of BFC. She introduced the woman at her left first.

"Hi, I'm Betty, an alcoholic," she said as she arose. She looked like the most wholesome PTA, car-pooling, tennis-playing mother on the block, any block in any city. "I can hardly believe that less than a year ago I was sitting out there where you are, a shaky, bloated mess with yellow eyes and a bad liver, wondering if this place really was going to work and if I ever was going to kick my addiction and get out of here and get my husband back. Well, the BFC cured my craving for what W. C. Fields used to call 'spiritus fermentae,' and I got out of here, but I discovered that I really didn't want that two-timing bum back, and I'm happy as hell!"

She laughed along with the audience.

"Seriously, if you want to know my story, just read Mery-man's *Broken Promises, Mended Dreams.* It's the best book on what it's like to be a drinking wife and mother and then to go through rehab that I've ever read. I didn't know anyone else knew what it's like to keep bottles in the piano and sneak drinks and have your kids despise you and then to get well. The book gave me the courage to come here and I thank my Higher Power and the BFC."

She went on briefly and then sat down to applause. The man next to her stood up saying, "My name's Ted. Alcohol, pills, coke—you name it, I've ingested it."

He was slender and drawn and he told his story in a halting, pained way. "I had all the symptoms the books tell you about—anger, worry, self-pity, a preoccupation with death and dying, general depression. I started doing all the things alcoholics do: drink before the party, hide booze, sneak drinks, lied about my drinking, drank alone, drank in the morning, but I never had a real blackout. And then one day"—he gulped—"it happened. Oh, God, did it happen. I came home one evening after a hard happy hour, started to pass out on the sofa. Then my wife shakes me awake and points out the window and says, 'Jeff, look where you left your car,' and so I stagger out to move it closer to the curb, and I see our seven-year-old son is lying underneath the car, unconscious, his leg twisted under him. The wheel was on his leg."

The audience gasped.

"My own son. I'd hit him and it didn't even register, didn't penetrate the fog. We called the paramedics and they saved him, but he'll limp for the rest of his life." He cleared his throat. "Wouldn't you think any sane person would quit drinking and using after that? 'Course, I wasn't sane, no one is that does things like that. I didn't quit. I didn't even slow up. Not till I somehow found myself in here. It was an intervention—my family, friends, our doctor—they all zeroed in on me, 'tough love' they call it. Don't remember how I actually got here. But I sure thank God or my Higher Power or whoever did it for me that I finally saw the light. I've been straight a year, I have a good job now, go to AA three times a week, trying to make things up to my son and to my wife, and life looks awfully good compared to the way it did. You people can make it, too, if I did."

He gave a brief smile and sat down. The next woman, Rosa, stood up. She was a plump, pretty woman of about twenty-five. "I had my first beer when I was twelve. I loved the taste, I loved the feeling. The other kids gagged on it or threw up. I never tasted anything so good in my life. I managed to get some every day. By the time I was thirteen I was drunk most of the time, though no one knew it since nobody'd seen me sober. When I was fourteen I decided to have my first sex and, I don't mean to be vulgar, but one night in the car I said to the guy in the backseat of the car, let's do it, and he said we just did. Hell, I was so drunk how was I to know?"

She laughed as though she were talking about someone else, and we joined her.

"I guess I never did have sex sober, 'cause I didn't do anything else sober. Believe it or not, my husband never knew. I had a good job in a bank and never came up short in my money count. I got away with my drinking for years till the day I bought a new car. I paid cash for it, got in it, and drove it right through the showroom window. Cut myself all up. Police couldn't believe my alcoholic content—they ran it through the blood test three times. I could give you a dozen more stories about my drinking but, what the heck, you've all got your own or you wouldn't be here. I hate to think, when I quit, of what happened to the stock of the Visine company, Listerine, Alka-Seltzer, Tylenol, and Anheuser-Busch. Poor guys! All I've got to say is stay with AA, it works, and good luck here at BFC! Just turn it all over to your Higher Power."

"Thank you, Rosa!" the blond woman at the podium said. "Now, tonight is a speaker's meeting, and we are fortunate to have Meryl C. with us from New York. A graduate of Smith College, she is a playwright and a free-lance writer for such publications as the *Village Voice*. Each of our three graduates tonight has mentioned a Higher Power as regards their recovery. Just what is this God stuff all about and what specifically has it got to do with alcohol? Maybe Meryl, who has been sober several years, can enlighten us."

A dark-haired attractive young woman came up from the front row and stood in front of the podium. "Hi. I'm Meryl and, boy, am I an alcoholic!" She smiled and began talking about her life. "From kindergarten through the fourth grade I went to a yeshiva and learned to pray. I imagined that God had a lion's head on a thin human body, and wore horn-rimmed glasses like my father's. Every night before sleep I prayed for the safety of my family 'just in case.' And I thought that if I told anyone about it, like a wish made over a birthday candle, it wouldn't work.

"In my teens I collected, or rather, stole, library books about runaways, alcoholism, drug addiction, suicide, and sex. Talking about masturbation was much safer than talking about spiritual matters. In my college dorm I became the resident sex and pregnancy expert and accompanied everyone to the local Bill Baird abortion center.

"I admired Anne Sexton and Sylvia Plath, and became the in-house suicidal would-be writer–alcoholic. My reputation for breaking furniture and crawling around the bathroom floor pretending to have been shot, while blacked out, extended much further than my name as a writer, but I laughed at the idea that people whispered about my 'alcohol problem.'

"In the summer of 1981 I went to a writing conference and tried not to have blackouts. I met a woman who was a recovering alcoholic, sober through her involvement in Alcoholics Anonymous. She seemed to have a good time anyway.

"I went to a few AA meetings with her. I decided that AA was a cult to which I did not wish to belong. Some people just talked about drinking, but others talked about dependency on a Higher Power (which I was pretty sure meant God). I knew that belief in God was for the weak or unintelligent and that dependency on alcohol was much cooler than dependency on God. I drank for another year.

"The next summer I arrived half packed and quite bewildered at the writing conference, since I had not planned to return. My sober friend asked me about my drinking. I surprised myself by telling her that I didn't want to drink anymore.

"I went to a meeting that night and looked at the twelve suggested steps of recovery, which we just heard and which hang on the wall of every AA meeting. Seven of the steps alluded to God or praying. A drunk Texan talked too long and called the speaker of the meeting an asshole. Another man talked excitedly about his spiritual awakening, which I imagined in Technicolor. I didn't want one. I wasn't even sure I wanted to stay sober. But if I did decide to stay sober, I was sure I could just go to meetings and not drink.

"I picked a sponsor who didn't talk about God. At meetings, I complained about the stupidity of the slogans, such as 'Keep It Simple' or 'One Day at a Time.' I compared AA to brainwashing organizations. No one tried to change my mind. I was surprised and a little disappointed when no one asked me to leave.

"I didn't know that sobriety was important to me until I was in AA for nearly a year. I was at my cousin's wedding, musing once again about whether or not I was really an alcoholic, because if I wasn't, I could drink. I called my sponsor, but still felt like drinking. An uncle handed me a glass and said, "Club soda." It was gin. Panicked and enraged, I threw the glass on the floor. I left the wedding with a new awareness: I didn't want to drink.

"I originally joined AA to get out of trouble, get rid of my symptoms, not to stop drinking. Realizing that I had come to *want* to be sober was quite powerful. I started feeling more connected with people, and less alone and afraid.

"Soon after the gin incident, I talked at a meeting about how grateful I was that the accidental taste saved me from drinking. The chairwoman smiled at me. 'You're not going to like this,' she told me, 'but it sounds like your Higher Power is working for you.' I made a face, considered what she said, and then mentally ran through all the notions of God I had rejected. I knew I didn't believe in God the lion, God our father, God the punisher of sins, or Jesus Christ as God.

"I considered other definitions of a Higher Power. I heard a few people say that their AA group was their Higher Power. One woman described God as a loving force, or the kindness generated by people. I knew that Jung had said that a spiritual experience might be the only hope for an alcoholic's recovery. AA's Big Book says that an alcoholic's sobriety is a 'daily reprieve contingent upon the maintenance of his or her spiritual condition.' 'Spiritual condition' sounded mysterious, and I wasn't sure how to assess whether mine was healthy or not. I didn't even know what 'healthy' meant, though I was pretty sure I wasn't, nor did I know how to get there.

"'How do you go about having a spiritual awakening?' I asked the people I thought might know. I had already looked for messages from God in bathroom graffiti and fortune cookies. A soft-spoken woman who had been watching me struggle pointed to the twelve steps hanging on the wall. 'The twelfth step is last for a reason,' she told me. 'It talks about having had a spiritual awakening as *the result* of the steps.'

"I took her suggestion and started reading the AA book that describes the steps, particularly Step Two. 'Came to believe that a Power greater than ourselves could restore us to sanity.' One evening, feeling alone and afraid of the dark, I experimented; I prayed to feel the presence of God and to not feel afraid. I went to bed cynical. But when I awoke at about three A.M., my room, which is usually black, was not dark. Feeling safe and happy, I went back to sleep. The next day, I was mixed up. Maybe the moon was brighter, or wishful thinking had temporarily improved my vision. Or maybe I had really felt the impact of a Higher Power as an experience or presence. *Why* the room was light didn't matter. What mattered was that I had felt unafraid.

"I have been sober for three years, and still feel confused and embarrassed about God. I want to sound cynical and smart, rather than vulnerable and unsure. Logic and predictability offer the illusion of protection, so letting go, even partially—in pursuit of something less known—is scary. Even hopefulness—that a Higher Power can make a difference in my life—is often hidden. But part of the understanding of God I have involves willingness and openness. This means experiencing without imposing intellect as an obstacle.

"Several months ago, in pain over a relationship I thought was ending, I called a spiritually sound friend for help. She told me to pray on my knees. (Her idea, not AA's.) I felt betrayed. Couldn't she come up with a more practical, less dramatic suggestion? 'Besides, I'm Jewish' I told her. 'Jews don't pray on their knees.' 'Where does it say that?' she asked me. I said, 'I don't know, the Bible or somewhere.' She laughed. 'Since when are you so familiar with the Bible?'

"I said her suggestion had nothing to do with AA. She said she knew that, and appealed to my intellect by telling me that it was an ancient posture that could trigger some collective unconscious memory. I said, 'Fuck it,' and tried it.

"Praying on my knees twice a day made me feel silly and vulnerable. I pulled down the shades and locked my bedroom door, even when no one was around. When I started feeling less afraid of losing the relationship, I knew it wasn't from the position. The spirit of willingness that accompanied that gesture, the willingness to risk feeling uncomfortable, was reflective of my emotional stance. Humility no longer felt like groveling.

"Higher Power experiences are subjectively felt and understood. Like nightmares, they're hard to explain to someone who wasn't there. The changes I've felt have been just that, changes in feelings. I don't believe that intellectual and spiritual gains are separate. If alcoholism is a physical, emotional, and spiritual disease, recovery is also threefold. My fascination with damaging behavior has greatly decreased.

"I'm still reluctant to say that I have had a spiritual awakening. It might be more accurate to say that I'm waking by degrees. It's not always easy, or even possible, to believe in and trust a Higher Power. I still have reservations and fear. I'm still caught between the eight-year-old me that believes 'just in case' and the scared me that seeks to locate and explain God before being willing to risk cracking the door. But practicing helps. I know that I've come a long way from the angry, lonely feelings I had when I romanticized self-destruction. My fear is baggage I don't want to carry. When I remember to set it down, I feel more honest, vulnerable, and loving than before. Sometimes I even feel open, hopeful, and committed to my spiritual growth."

She sat down to great applause.

"Thank you, Meryl," said the moderator. "Now I should like to give out some hard-earned chips. Who has been sober thirty days?" She went through the audience and hands went up. She passed out some plastic medallions to pleased people. "Maybe those first thirty days are the hardest. Who's been sober six months?" More hands. "One whole year?" Three medallions awarded. "Great going. Keep coming back. It works!"

She took the podium again.

"I'd like to conclude the meeting by reading something from William Madsen, the distinguished anthropologist.

My exposure to the culture of Alcoholics Anonymous left me with a quiet hope for mankind. We live in an age when we have transferred our guidance from leadership by God to a faith in scientific infallibility. But science has proved to be all too inadequate to solve the world's needs. We still have warfare, poverty, insanity and massive anxiety. As science blocked the threat of infantile paralysis, it also left us with the terror of a nuclear doomsday. I think we are slowly finding that science is not in fact a deity out there guiding us, but rather a man-made tool. And like all human products it is not perfect. However, throughout history man has come up with alternate answers and survived despite the death of gods or the failure of scientific techniques. Science has failed to cure alcoholism, and the alcoholics, despite their seeming inadequacy, came up with an answer. It is not a perfect answer, but nothing on this earth ever is. A.A. has demonstrated that man has within himself the resources to survive handicap and disaster. A major part of that resource is the ability to cooperate with others to solve a common problem. A.A., to me, is a demonstration of the words of Camus, "Man's greatness . . . lies in his decision to be stronger than his condition."

Then the moderator said, "After a moment of silence, Meryl will lead us in the prayer of her choice."

We all joined hands with our neighbors, observed the silence, and then said the Serenity Prayer in unison, and the meeting was over. It was one hour exactly after it had started.

Impressed and filled with different reactions and thoughts about what we'd heard, we walked back to McCallum Hall across the moonlit grass and talked quietly about the meeting. Meryl C.'s remarks about God had especially moved me. I didn't know anyone else thought so much like me about religion. I was beginning to see why AA and the BFC worked: It was the discovery, over and over, that none of us alcoholics was unique, that we all shared the pain, shame, restless questing and self-loathing that nearly all drinking persons, ipso facto, have.

Later that evening, one word came to me to help explain the success of the treatment and AA.

We were all in the lounge, all twenty of us—eating pizza, drinking hot chocolate, some playing gin rummy, others in a boisterous game of charades, others working on the next day's assignments, others in serious discussions. There was a nurse, a businessman, a policeman, a rock star, a psychiatrist, a professor, a playboy, a factory worker, a pharmacist, a diamond merchant, a surgeon, an entrepreneur, a secretary, a carpenter, a model, a housewife, a farmer, a truck driver, and a writer. One was a lesbian, one an architect, a homosexual; there were four Catholics, one Jew, thirteen Protestants, one black Baptist, and one Mormon. One had arrived in an ambulance, another in his fifteen-year-old pick-up truck, another in his Lear jet. The oldest was sixty-eight; the youngest, twenty. The only thing they had in common was addiction to a chemical substance and a desire to get rid of it. And here they all were on a Friday night, a day of the week when by this time most of them in their past life would have been stoned or drunk, and instead they were sharing a—and the simple and unremarkable word came to me—"fellowship." It was something most of us had never in our lives known to such a degree—a deep and meaningful *fellowship*. I'd heard people who had been in the Army or Navy or Marine Corps in wartime talk about unlikely and extraordinary fellowships created by sharing life or death situations.

This, too, I reflected, was a life or death situation.

NINE

I woke up thinking, "How strange—I'm not waking up thinking how lousy I feel and where did I leave the car last night and where am I going to get my first drink. I feel pretty good and almost looking forward to what the day might bring. And only two more days and I'll be allowed to call Mary!

And what would she be doing right now? Rolling over in bed and getting ready to get up and feed "the monsters"—six dogs and seven cats and Macomber, the African gray parrot, who was probably already whistling "Some Enchanted Evening" or "Colonel Bogey March." What a bird that was! When the refrigerator door was opened, like the true pet of an alcoholic he would say chidingly, "Glug, glug, glug!" And when a friend brought the writer Colleen McCullough to the house, Macomber exclaimed gleefully, "What a pretty pussy"!—and she loved it. I missed him.

Saturday at BFC started out like the other days, but there

were some differences that were unimportant except to us, the inmates.

We got up at the same time, six-fifteen, went to breakfast, did our "therapeutic chores," and took the mile-long walk.

The sky was crystalline, the mountains spectacular as their snow-capped peaks caught the first sun, and the desert air, which would soon become hot, was still crisp. Most of us walked and talked, while some of the younger peers jogged by in sweat suits, logging three or four laps to our leisurely one. It was good to be out here in the early morning, and I felt better physically than I had for a long time. Not perfect—it would take many weeks and months to undo the damage the booze had done—but certainly better. It almost felt good to be alive on such a morning. I became aware that I was *becoming aware,* noticing things more: the cloud formations, the orange glaze of the mountain top, its cool gray-violet base, the lizard skittering along the sand by the road, a kestrel hovering high above waiting for the first shrew to appear, then spotting the lizard and dive-bombing it successfully. It *was* good to be alive, hangover-free, and with congenial companions.

As we walked along, Dave and I discussed the AA meeting of the night before.

"That girl really nailed me on the religion bit," I said. "I've had trouble with that Higher Power stuff the way she did, never having been a churchgoer. I can't swallow that God as Santa Claus concept or Michelangelo's airborne old man or his-eye-is-on-the-sparrow business, if that's what they want me to think of as my Higher Power."

"Your Higher Power doesn't have to have anything to do with formalized religion," Dave said. "Your Higher Power is as you perceive it or her or him. Something must be more powerful than you to have made you, to have created the world, the cosmos, right?"

"Some*thing,*" I said. "Not some*body.*"

"Okay, call your Higher Power Nature or Energy, if that will make you feel better, if the word 'God' makes you nervous. Or for starters, for your immediate purposes right now, call it your conscience. You do have a conscience, don't you?"

"What are you doing in here?" I asked. "You sound like another damn counselor."

"I got a head start on you, remember."

"I'll admit all this God talk makes me uncomfortable. The way that girl said last night, at home sex was talked about more freely than religion when I was growing up. Yet my parents were the most Christian-acting people I knew. Were the founders of AA religious nuts or ministers?"

"They were just two desperate drunks who found out they could help keep each other sober."

Dave sketched the story of AA's founder, Bill Wilson. In 1934, Bill was a Wall Street stockbroker who had crashed with the stock market, had been detoxed from booze four times, and was now into three bottles of gin a day. He was supported by his wife, who had a job at Macy's. He was too broke to afford a private facility, but he was a likable man and had so many friends that a group chipped in and sent him to Towns Hospital. Here he learned from the revolutionary chief of staff, Dr. William Silkworth, new ideas about alcoholism: The doctor believed that alcoholism was a disease characterized by a mental obsession coupled with a physical compulsion triggered by the first drink of alcohol, that the alcoholic was allergic to alcohol and was powerless to stop drinking once he started. He told Wilson that alcoholics were not morally degenerate but sick people caught up in a disease process that was hopeless and fatal and irreversible if drinking continued.

Bill left the hospital convinced he would never drink another drop. But a month later he was drinking worse than ever. He sobered up again only to fall off the wagon once more and went back to Towns Hospital. A reformed drunk friend known only as Ebby came to visit him and said he'd found a solution to his drunkenness in the religious movement then in vogue, the Oxford Group, also called Moral Rearmament. Ebby said he'd learned to admit he was licked, take stock of himself, recognize his character faults, confide in another person his shortcomings, make restitution to those people he had harmed—and to live a life of giving with no thought of return.

Bill fought the formula, balked at the idea of a Higher Power, said he only believed in what he could see and touch and measure. That very evening Bill's depression became unbearable and later he would write:

> All at once I found myself crying out, "If there is a God, let Him show Himself! I am ready to do anything, anything!"
>
> Suddenly the room lit up with a great white light. I was caught up into an ecstasy which there are no words to describe. It seemed to me, in the mind's eye, that I was on a mountain and that a wind not of air but of spirit was blowing. And then it burst upon me that I was a free man. Slowly the ecstasy subsided. I lay on the bed, but now for a time I was in another world, a new world of consciousness. All about me and through me there was a wonderful feeling of Presence, and I thought to myself, "So this is the God of the preachers!" A great peace stole over me and I thought, "No matter how wrong things seem to be, they are still all right. Things are all right with God and His world."

Bill was frightened.

Was it just a hallucination? Many alcoholics undergoing withdrawal experience visions both benign and malevolent. Was that all this was? Was he crazy? No, Dr. Silkworth assured him. Silkworth had heard of such spiritually-transforming experiences and was convinced Bill had undergone one.

Bill Wilson never drank again. From those two men he got the combination of spiritual and medical concepts that would form the nucleus of AA. But it remained for him to meet a suicidal doctor, Robert H. Smith, an "incurable drunk," on a visit to Akron, Ohio, for AA to be born. Bill sat up one night with the desperate doctor and outlined his story of how to begin to recover through the steps of deflation, surrender, confession, restitution, and giving. The treatment began to work, just by Dr. Bob's being able to share the saga of his wretched existence with a fellow alcoholic. Two weeks later the two of them sat up all night with a desperate Akron lawyer who would then quit drinking forever and become AA member number three.

"The rest is history," said Dave. "In 1937 there were forty members; by 1939 there were one hundred. An article in the *Saturday Evening Post* in 1941 brought six thousand responses to the little AA office. Now nobody knows the number of millions AA has helped and is helping."

"I'm not a joiner," I said. "In Johnson's words—a most unclubbable man."

"You don't *join* anything! You just walk in when you feel like it and walk out when you feel like it. Hell, it isn't Kiwanis or the Elks."

A sweat-suited man puffed up to us. About fifty, tanned, and with an outrageous orangutan-colored toupee, Morrie was a real estate tycoon from Florida and never failed to tell a terrible joke.

"Must be awful to be old," he jibbed. "I been around the track twice awreddy. Hey, know why girls don't like gang bangs? They hate writing all those thank you notes, that's why!"

Morrie cackled and trotted off.

"He looks on top of the world," I said.

"To quote Terry, 'bullshit.' I hear he's still in total denial after two weeks here, claims he was just a social drinker, only here to please his daughter, who's 'mistakenly' worried about his health. But Dan said that Morrie almost cracked yesterday in his group session, almost let people see a little of what's beneath the jokes and under the tan and the toupee."

We were sternly admonished not to discuss what went on in group session with peers of other groups, but everyone did.

Beth loped up in a chic sweat suit and a towel tucked in around her neck. "My husband married a Rubens," she panted, "but I swear by my Higher Power that he's going to end up with a wire-thin Giacometti by the time I get out of here!"

"You're an artist!" I said.

"Trying to be," she said. "Going to commercial art school at night."

"I teach portraiture," I said. "I'll give you a lesson if you want."

"I'd like that!" she said over her shoulder as she trotted off.

Coming back into McCallum, I ran into Jerry heading for her office.

"Can I talk to you a moment?" I said.

"Sure, Barny."

"It's not about addiction."

"Thank goodness."

"I hate to ask for special privileges, but . . ."

I told her about Kendall's upcoming appearance on the soap opera, how much it meant to her, how much it meant to me.

"TV is strictly for weekends." She frowned. "Rules."

"It would only be for a very short time," I said. "She'll never be able to understand why I couldn't watch her first professional acting job."

Jerry shook her head. "I think people have been bending rules for you all your life, Barny. But not in here."

She walked off.

I was stunned.

I felt my face get red with fury. One lousy hour out of their stupid routine. What possible difference could it make in anything? Didn't Jerry realize how important this was to me? Maybe I should go directly to Mrs. Ford herself. She had kids, she'd understand. Or, better still, just walk out the front door of Firestone—they didn't have guards or anything like that—just walk out the day of the TV program, hitchhike to town, find a bar, watch the program,—and maybe have a drink just to show them that I could damn well take or leave the stuff anytime I felt like it—and be back before anyone missed me.

But I began to think it through. If I got caught, I'd be bounced; Kendall wouldn't want me to risk that. Maybe they were right—nothing, absolutely nothing, should distract us patients from thinking about our recovery. And the idea of one drink—what good did one drink ever do anyone?

Depressed, I went to the cafeteria and picked at breakfast. Afterward, I worked on my essay on the prison experience, subtitling it, "Git a Little Drunk and You Lands in Jail."

I was absorbed until Dave came by my room at ten for Alcohol Awareness. Beth joined us, and after the circle and the Serenity Prayer, we headed out across the grassy field, past the pond, toward Eisenhower Hospital, a quarter of a mile away. With us were all the rest of the BFC clientele, all sixty of us, plus most of the staff. Milling around in front of the spectacular circular Annenberg auditorium were dozens of townspeople who were interested in alcohol and drug addiction and came for the weekly programs.

"I've heard this guy speak before," someone said, "and he's fantastic."

In the plush, modernistic lobby were several giant reproductions of famous paintings on medical themes. Beth was fascinated by the Rembrandt scene of the Dutch doctor lecturing as he dissects a cadaver. She didn't know much about Thomas Eakins and I could show off by expounding on his highly realistic painting of an operation.

At ten-thirty we were in our seats, sticking close to fellow

125

McCallum members as we were told to do, along with an audience of about 300.

A handsome older man stood at the podium, ran his hand through a shock of bottle-red hair, and spoke in a trained voice. (He was a famous radio and TV announcer—and a recovering alcoholic.)

"Dr. Max A. Schneider is a member of the faculties at the Harvard and University of Buffalo Schools of Medicine and, since 1966, the University of California/Irvine College of Medicine, past president of the California Society for the Treatment of Alcoholism and Other Drug Dependencies, president of the American Medical Society on Alcoholism and Other Drug Dependence, et cetera, et cetera. *But:*"— here the introducer grinned—"he'll be very familiar to a lot of you—he probably made the films that you were forced by the judge to see after your drunk driving arrests!"

The moment the dark-haired energetic man stood up I recognized him from his films. Much younger than his years, sixty-three, he exuded a dynamic charm and sincerity. Speaking rapidly and informally, he launched into his talk, punctuating the sentences with incisive hand and arm gestures as exclamation points.

"As a physician, I am interested in the alcohol problem because it is now a leading cause of death. With all of the problems that booze causes, it is now the third leading cause of death in the United States. It is considered the number one medical problem by the United States Public Health Service and the fourth leading medical problem in the world by the World Health Organization. The number of people who are sick and disabled physically, from alcohol, the huge number who are psychologically affected either directly or indirectly, the amount of money that is lost because of the inability of people to function properly or who become economically dependent, are of such tremendous import that I, as a physician, must become interested.

"I am a drinker; I do not have a drinking problem. I am not a prohibitionist. I believe in having children, but I certainly feel that uncontrolled nymphomania becomes a medical problem that must be dealt with. I take an occasional drink because I enjoy the taste of it and the sociability associated with it. I do not use booze for its 'tranquilizing' effect. For some unknown reason, I am not addicted.

"What we are going to talk about basically is chemistry and physiology. We are going to talk about C_2H_5OH—the chemical alcohol. It doesn't make a bit of difference if this alcohol is tequila, scotch, beer, bourbon, wine—alcohol is alcohol. One twelve-ounce can of beer has the same effect as four or five ounces of wine or a shot of whiskey. Booze is booze! And it doesn't make any difference if it is on the rocks, in the rocks, or under the rocks.

"This is not a moral lecture. I am not involved with the morals of this. I am involved with the physics of it, the chemistry of it, and the medicine of it. I don't care if you have sex with a giraffe, but when you develop giraffitis, then I must worry about it medically.

"We are going to find that booze has two basic effects: One, it is an irritant, and two, it is a sedative.

"Booze goes down the esophagus—the food pipe—into the stomach, and like any other food, it gets mixed with saliva as it goes down. It is easy to understand that there is an irritant here because you can feel it burn as it goes into the mouth and down the food pipe. And then it enters the stomach. I like to compare the stomach with the armpit; they both have a great deal in common. The armpit sweats sodium chloride. What do we call it? . . . Salt! Plain old salt. And the stomach sweats. It sweats hydrogen chloride, which we call hydrochloric acid. We know that there must be something protecting our skin from the effects of this salt; otherwise we would have a constant heat rash. The substance that is sweated out by the skin in addition to the salt, which protects the skin from the action of the salt, is an oil. The stomach also sweats out a protective chemical called mucin. This protects the lining of the stomach from its own secretions—the acid.

"If you put out more acid than you do mucin, you then get to the point where the mucin will not protect your stomach against its own acids, and you get an inflamed lining of the stomach, which we call gastritis. The irritating effect of alcohol is to cause the sweat glands of the stomach to produce this hydrochloric acid in its maximum amounts within twenty minutes after ingestion of a single drink of booze. As a matter of fact, alcohol is probably the greatest single irritant that we can ingest.

"All other foods are prepared for digestion in the stomach and then pass down through the intestinal tract to be absorbed from the intestinal tract into the bloodstream. This is not true with alcohol. Ninety-five percent of the alcohol is absorbed directly into the bloodstream through the lining of the stomach and the first part of the intestine—the duodenum. Within twenty minutes from the time of taking a glass of booze on an empty stomach, it is absorbed into the bloodstream. If this alcohol is diluted with a meal, then the rapidity of the rate with which the alcohol gets into the bloodstream and the rapidity with which it builds up a level in the bloodstream are slowed down by the dilution factor. So you can see that drinking alcohol on an empty stomach will have a stronger and more rapid effect than drinking with or after a meal. And so the alcohol gets absorbed into the bloodstream.

"Alcohol affects the small intestine directly by causing a condition called malabsorption syndrome. Not only does this keep food from getting into our body, but there is also an increase in the excretion of many important minerals from our body. Alcohol washes zinc, magnesium, and other trace minerals affecting taste and smell out of the body. Of great importance is the unfortunate fact that booze also washes calcium out of the bones.

"Once the alcohol is in the bloodstream, it goes quickly *to every single cell and tissue in the body!* Every one! Those cells and tissues that have a large amount of moisture absorb the alcohol more readily than those with a higher density and less moisture. One of the organs that picks up the alcohol in large amounts is the pancreas.

"The pancreas lies underneath the stomach and next to the intestine. The pancreas is an interesting organ because it manufactures two major groups of chemicals. The one group is digestive enzymes—very potent chemicals that are secreted by the individual cells and gradually collect into little tiny canals, which finally empty into the small intestine through a tube about the size of a lead pencil. These chemicals, including amylases and lipases, are extremely strong and help us digest the proteins and fats in our intestinal tract. When the alcohol reaches the cells of the pancreas, it irritates the cells, causing them to swell, blocking off the passage of these chemicals. The chemicals then begin to accumulate and digest the pancreas itself and begin then to break out through the lining of the pancreas. We call this condition acute hemorrhagic pancreatitis. This is an extremely painful disease. It is so painful that we never have any trouble getting the patient to the doctor. It requires huge amounts of pain reliever to alleviate the pain. In essence, we find that the patient's enzymes are now beginning to digest the lining of his abdominal wall. One out of ten patients who develop this disease dies in the first attack. Of those who survive and never drink again, one will develop chronic recurring pancreatitis and the others will get well. If those who get well begin drinking again, even just an occasional 'binge,' many will again develop pancreatitis and again have the risk of death."

The doctor then gave a long dissertation on what alcohol does to the liver, a chilling series of facts, much as Dr. West had done a few days before, ending with: "There are other functions that are interfered with when the liver is sick. The levels of cholesterol, fatty acids, and triglycerides are increased in the bloodstream when a person drinks over three drinks a day. This means that the circulating fats in our bloodstream are elevated. And these fats are deposited into two interesting places. One is back into the liver, so that we get fatty infiltration or a fatty liver. After all, they do this to geese—don't they?—to make their liver fat for paté de foie gras. The excess fats caused by the sick liver harm the heart and blood vessels, as well as the liver itself. Two other metabolic problems can be caused or aggravated by alcoholic liver disease. The liver's ability to deal with sugar—to store sugar and to transform foods into energy—becomes impaired, creating abnormal highs and lows in blood sugar levels. A chemical called uric acid is produced in abnormally large amounts in alcoholic liver disease. This frequently causes attacks of gout, a very painful form of arthritis.

"One other thing happens with the liver. All blood circulating through the body going back to the heart must circulate through the liver. When the liver becomes swollen, either through the inflammation or the scarring resulting from the cirrhosis, it narrows down the blood vessels going through it. This causes an increase in the back pressure of these veins and we begin to get swelling of veins in various parts of our body. We call these swollen veins varicose veins. We see them in the legs, in the rectum, where we call them hemorrhoids, or piles, and we get them along the sides of our abdomen. Upon examining a patient, one of the telltale signs that he or she has been drinking too much is the appearance of the veins around the sides of the abdomen. This means that the circulation through the liver is backing up.

"Let's talk a little bit about the heart. Yes, it is true that many doctors have prescribed alcohol as a tranquilizer for the ticker. And it is true that some studies show that one or two—not more—drinks of alcohol a day *may* protect males from coronary artery disease. In the early days alcohol was the only kind of tranquilizer we had, and even today some physicians will still utilize booze as a sedative for people who have heart trouble. Modern evidence advises against this. Today's knowledge dictates that even small amounts of alcohol may be harmful to a person with any kind of heart disease. Alcohol increases the amount of fat—cholesterol and triglycerides—in the body and bloodstream. In addition, it increases the work load of the heart. Alcohol also inflames the heart muscle, causing myocarditis. This is a serious disease unto itself and will certainly aggravate any previously existing cardiovascular condition. Particularly vulnerable are young people who exercise strenuously following binge drinking. And alcohol is a very common cause of high blood pressure.

"Let's talk about the kidneys. There is no evidence that booze damages the kidneys themselves. Alcohol, however, does affect one's fluid balance. Most people who have had a few drinks know that they have had to get up and head for the head. I can usually tell at this point in my talk who has had a few snorts by who wanders off to the head while I am talking! As long as the alcohol content is going up in the bloodstream, there will be a diuretic or urinating effect. As soon as the alcohol content has reached its maximum, there is an outpouring of antidiuretic hormone from the brain, which then causes retention of fluids in the body and is another cause of swelling of tissues following drinking.

"In the urinary bladder we get inflammation of the lining from the alcohol. This causes an inability of the urinary bladder to stretch properly and creates a condition of frequent urination of small amounts. Surrounding the opening of the urinary tract before it goes to the penis of the male there is a gland called the prostate gland. This gland is irritated by alcohol and begins to swell. This is called prostatitis. This gland is one of the organs that is involved with the sexual act in the male.

"Two things result from this swelling. The first is that there is a narrowing down of the urine flow from the bladder and, therefore, frequently will create difficulty in emptying the bladder. The other effect will be interference with the ability to be able to obtain an erection or maintain an erection. It may also interfere with the ability to climax during sexual intercourse. Three drinks a day will sedate the testicles and decrease male hormone and sperm count. Prolonged abuse of alcohol causes atrophy or shrinking of the testicles. The failure of the sick liver to detoxify and remove the female hormones that every man has causes a buildup of these hormones. This also interferes with a man's sexual ability, and may even enlarge his breasts. A combination of the above factors certainly can harm a man's sex life.

"And what happens to the sex life of a woman? Alcoholic women have a higher incidence of menstrual irregularities. Sexual potency can be decreased by alcohol. Alcohol decreases vaginal lubrication. Should pregnant women drink? Emphatically no! The evidence is very clear that drinking causes a much higher incidence of premature births. The mother's alcohol affects the unborn child—the fetus. The baby may be smaller, have a smaller than normal head, have a deformed head, or be mentally deficient or develop other severe abnormalities due to momma's drinking during pregnancy. The fetal alcoholic syndrome and fetal alcohol effects, horrible realities, are now the third leading cause of mental retardation in the United States and *the only one that can be prevented!*"

He talked about alcohol's effect on the brain much as Dr. West had. I winced when he mentioned Korsakoff's syndrome. I hadn't heard any more about that possibility. Perhaps if I didn't think about it and not mention it to anyone, it would just go away.

Dr. Schneider went on, "Some people have developed a hypersensitivity to alcohol. And no matter how good their intent—that is, to just relax and feel better—once they have developed this hypersensitivity to alcohol, there is nothing that can change it. I have patients who say, 'Doc, I don't want to get drunk. I don't want to get bombed and make a fool of myself, I just want to drink like you can. You take one, or maybe you take two, and that's enough. Why not me? As soon as I take one or two, I can't stop and I'm off to the races. What is wrong with my willpower?' My answer is that there is nothing wrong with your willpower. It is purely chemical. The thing that says to you, 'I'm only going to take one or two,' is your judgment, your inhibitions. And what is the first thing that is put to sleep by alcohol? It is your judgment and your inhibitions! If a person has developed this hypersensitivity, so that the judgment is quickly put to sleep by one or two or three drinks, then he or she must recognize this sensitivity just as the doctor must recognize the hypersensitivy to penicillin or any other drug. The willpower comes with the recognition of facts as they are—do you or do you not have a hypersensitivity to a drug? If you do and choose to ignore it, then of course this is a matter of denial, lack of use of judgment, or pure emotional blocking. One of the things that must be realized is that this disease of hypersensitivity is a progressive disease. It never gets better but always gets worse. You can't lose it. Once hypersensitive, always hypersensitive. You may go twenty years without a drink and finally say, 'Well, let's try it again and have one or two or three drinks,' and history will repeat itself.

"What a person does is up to him. He can go down the tube or he can use this as an opportunity to stop and ask, 'What am I doing to myself? What is the kick out of living in the drug and alcohol scene?' The young people frown on the old people using booze and getting drunk. The old people frown on the young people using drugs and getting high. And those of us in the healing fields stand back and see that there is really no difference: We see a portion of each generation destroying itself by depending upon a chemical to solve its problems. How far does a person have to go before he recognizes what he is doing with his own life? This is a disease, a progressive, fatal disease, and can be interrupted only by recognition and proper treatment."

He sat down to enthusiastic applause. It had been a long talk, and it was late. I left the others and hurried back to the cafeteria to help set the table with Terry. As we worked, I asked what she thought of the talk.

"Bullshit," she replied quietly.

I noticed her hands were shaky and her lips were trembling.

"Something the matter?"

"Tomorrow," she said.

"What's wrong with tomorrow?"

"Sunday. Visitors' day."

I thought of her husband and her daughter—his stepdaughter—and the relationship she'd told me about.

"They're coming," she said.

"Together?"

She nodded, biting her lip.

"Maybe it won't be so bad," I said, putting my hand on her shoulder.

She shrugged it off brusquely. "Bullshit," she said as she walked out of the cafeteria.

TEN

At lunch, Morrie, the real estate salesman from Florida, via Brooklyn, wasn't his usual bouncy self, in spite of his red and yellow aloha shirt and two-toned shoes.

"Ahh, that counselor of mine!" he growled over dessert. "Really on my case, drivin' me nuts. A state of the art asshole. Looks like Captain Kangaroo, doesn't he? Keeps tryin' to get me to say I drank more'n I actually did! I tell him listen, buster, I been handlin' my booze A-okay for forty years— never more than one Stolie-over before lunch, two Cutty-and-Sevens before dinner, and maybe, just maybe, mind you, a thimble of Fundador after. I don't call that real drinkin'. Most of my clients spill more'n that at luncheon."

"So," asked Dave, "why are you here?"

"Hell, my daughter, she's paranoid, exaggerates everything, thinks my health is bad because of drinking. Like her mother, she hates booze and men. I'm thinking of gettin' out of here. I'm no fuggin' alcoholic. I can quit anytime I feel like it."

"But apparently you've never felt like it," said Beth quietly.

"What the hell is that supposed to mean, Tubby?" he snapped. He glared at her. "For your info, Lardy, I got my bag packed and I'm ready to say ah-dee-yoss ah-meego to this dump."

"But, Morrie," protested Dave, "you've only got two weeks to go!"

"Four!" Morrie ran his hand over his reddish toupee. "Captain Kangaroo upped my sentence this morning."

"Can they just do that whenever they feel like it?" I asked apprehensively.

"If they think it's justified," said Dave. "The Committee, whoever they are—I guess all the counselors and clergymen and doctors—they can recommend extending your time. Liza Minnelli did eight weeks."

"Yeah," said Morrie. "If you don't give the right answers when they push their little buttons, they can slap on weeks . . . or even months. Well, that's one way of looking at it, as the fly said as he walked across the mirror."

I wondered if I would draw any extra time and, if so, how much. Thirty days was going to be hard enough. I would try to do everything right. But what did "right" mean exactly?

"Rigorous honesty," Jerry had said.

"That fascist Captain Kangaroo hates my guts," Morrie said, brooding. Then he suddenly brightened. "Hey, hear about the guy meets this other guy, says, 'Hi, boobie, how're those kids of yours—those twins?' An' the first guy says, 'Triplets,' an' the other guy says, '*Triplets?* Jeez, how time flies!'"

He gave his loud laugh and stood up, his face suddenly tense again. "Well, pilgrims, see you in church." Then he added, "You guys are lucky—you got Jerry. As they say in Chinatown, my counselor is a plick. I'm going over the wall

and back to sunny Sarasota." But he could never just leave—
he always had to make an exit. "T'was a woman who drove
me to drink," he said in a W. C. Fields twang. "And I never
even wrote to thank her!"

When he had gone, Dave said, "Poor Morrie, he really
hasn't got the message yet, hasn't put his full weight down
here. Lots of anger and denial and still trying to con people."

"Do you really think he'll leave?" Beth asked. "After logging two whole weeks here?"

"Who's to know?" Dave shrugged. "Last week a woman
took off after being here twenty-nine days—the day before
her medallion ceremony! Just walked out and down the
road. Even left her suitcase in her room."

"You alcoholics are a strange lot," said Beth with her pretty
little-girl smile. "Sure glad I'm not one."

Chico came into the cafeteria and headed for our table.
"Hey, you guys!" he said. "Get off your duffs! Mrs. Ford is
really furious about all the cigarette butts around the place,
especially McCallum, and Laverne says we got to clean it all
up before the lecture."

"Why the big rush?" I asked.

"I think Mr. Firestone and some other big shots are coming over."

Chico was talking to me, but his gaze never left Beth, and
his moist Latin eyes were full of tenderness. I'd noticed that
before.

We got up, left the dining room, and went out into the
bright sunlight.

"Hell, I don't even smoke," I groused as Chico handed us
each a plastic bag. Free time was so rare I didn't want to
squander it this way.

Dave and Beth bent over and started picking up the many
cigarette remnants as they walked along the path back to
McCallum Hall, and Chico and I worked our way across the
grass down toward the pond.

After a while I straightened up, a small number of butts in my bag, and my back screaming.

"You Mexicans are better at this stoop work than us gringos," I said. "You were born to it."

"Chinga tu madre," he said amiably, and kept working.

There were some migrant ducks on the pond paddling around the three plastic swans. One of the birds was going around in circles, a wing angled out unnaturally. I pointed it out to Chico.

"Broken," he said putting down his bag.

He strode down to the pond and waded out into the water up to his knees. He herded the wounded duck away from the others, crowded it into a little inlet, and then leapt forward and made a diving catch in both his big hands as though it were a low pass in a football game.

Dripping wet, he sloshed up to me holding the bird gently but firmly, the wounded wing clamped to its side.

"Teal," he gasped. "Hen." His black hair was plastered down over his forehead.

"Will you have to wring its neck?"

"I hope not."

We went back to his room in McCallum, and Chico gave me the duck to hold while he quickly changed into dry clothes, then left "to see what I can scrounge up from the nurse's office."

The duck made a few half hearted pecks at my fingers and then stayed quiet. I sat on the bed and studied the frightened bird's plumage: the intricate patterns in the feathers would make a wonderful acrylic painting. I'd never seen a picture of a duck from directly above; I resolved to do one when I got out of the BFC.

I looked around Chico's room, which he shared with Willy. Stuck in the mirror was a photo of his dog and another of his parents standing woodenly in front of the barn on their farm—a Latin American Gothic.

Thumbtacked on the wall was a two-foot piece of parchment and written on it in superb calligraphy was this quotation:

For this is the journey that men make: to find themselves.

If they fail in this, it doesn't matter much what else they find.

Money, position, fame, many loves, revenge are all of little consequence, and when the tickets are collected at the end of the ride they are tossed into the bin marked FAILURE.

But if a man happens to find himself—if he knows what he can be depended upon to do, the limits of his courage, the positions from which he will no longer retreat, the degree to which he can surrender his inner life to some woman, the secret reservoirs of his determination, the extent of his dedication, the depth of his feeling for beauty, his honest and unpostured goals—then he has found a mansion which he can inhabit with dignity all the days of his life.

> James Michener from *The Fires of Spring*
> Love and luck from Beth!

Fires of Spring—wasn't that from Omar Khayyam? How did it go—"Come fill the cup and into the fires of spring the winter garment of repentance fling." Omar was always filling or lifting a cup or a jug of wine—I wondered how they dealt with alcoholics in those days.

The door opened, and Chico came in carrying a cardboard box. He saw me reading the parchment and said proudly with his sad smile, "Beth made that for me."

He put the box on the desk and took out various objects: scissors, a hemostat, gauge, adhesive tape, tweezers, cotton, and two tongue depressors.

"They wouldn't give me any alcohol," he said apologetically.

While I held the bird, Chico gently straightened the wing, took out several shotgun pellets with the tweezers, and cut back the feathers from the wing itself. He deftly set the bones, and bandaged and taped them between the wooden tongue depressors. Then he taped the wing to the teal's body.

"I'll get her some food and water later and turn her over to the SPCA tomorrow."

"I'm pretty impressed, Doctor," I said as Chico poked holes in the box and carefully put the bird inside.

Chico shrugged, but he was happier than I had yet seen him. "I was studying to be a vet there for a while. Then the heroin got to me and I had to go into a factory and make some big bucks to support the habit. But I love animals. We keep forgetting we humans are animals, too, great apes. Chimps, orangutans, gorillas, gibbons, and us."

"I like animals a lot, too," I said. "Especially wild ones."

I told him about Zorro, the fox we had in San Francisco.

"Great animal, perfectly tame. Children could pick him up by the tail and he wouldn't bite. Best friends with the dog, clean, newspaper-trained, even sometimes when you were reading it!"

Chico laughed. He laughed so rarely, this fine sad young man, and it was good to hear it. "And what happened to El Zorro?"

"He got away one day and didn't come back as usual and we were all very sad—the children, the dog. After all, how could a fox survive in a city? But Michael, our ten-year-old, wouldn't give up. He went to a disc jockey and Herb Caen, the columnist, and asked them to announce the fact that we'd lost our fox, and sure enough, after seventeen days, someone called from the cable-car barn and said they had seen a fox there. Michael and I sped down there, the boy called the animal, and it suddenly appeared and jumped into his arms."

"And there wasn't a dry eye in the house."

"Correct."

"Ah, animals are wonderful. I'd like to get back to vet school."

"Why don't you?"

"Maybe," he said dubiously. "If I complete the program here, maybe I'll go back."

"What do you mean *if*," I said. "When!"

He frowned. "I don't know. I don't know." He shook his head. "I can't sleep."

He stood up and paced, driving his fist into the palm of his other hand as he walked up and down.

"You don't know what it is, the Big H. Just count yourself lucky you didn't fall into that mess. I can't sleep."

He stopped abruptly in front of the parchment and read the words, his lips moving, as though reading it for the first time.

"Beautiful, isn't it?" he murmured.

"I want to copy it," I said.

"I meant her writing, all the flourishes and things."

"Yes," I said. "I never could do calligraphy."

Then he said abruptly, "I love her."

"Well, who doesn't?" I said lightly. Then I saw the look on his face and in those eyes, which were two moist olives.

"Oh, Lord," I said when I saw how he meant it. Then after a few moments I added lamely, "She's married."

"Yes," he said, barely audibly.

"Does she know how you feel?"

He shook his head. "I can't sleep," he whispered. "I love her."

I couldn't think of anything to say. I looked at my watch. "We'll be late for the lecture," I said.

The one o'clock session featured the guest speaker Dr. Schneider again, but it was restricted to BFC patients, unlike the morning program. In the lecture room he spoke on nutrition and alcohol and was 100 percent more forceful and informative than the previous speaker on the same subject had been.

I made notes on some of his ideas, which he delivered with the rapidity of an Uzi gun. "Alcohol as a food contains only calories. There are practically no vitamins, minerals, or needed proteins in booze. A few trace minerals and vitamins are found in some alcoholic beverages but the amounts are insignificant. There has been the suggestion that vitamins should be added to beverage alcohol. This would *not* be an effective answer to the multiple problems of malnutrition in alcohol consumption.

"One half pint of bourbon has six hundred and seventy-five calories and no other nutrients. The amount of weight gain or weight loss a person has depends upon the number of calories that is taken in and the number of calories that is used up. If you take in more calories than you use, then, of course, energy is stored and you gain weight. If you take in fewer calories than you use, you will lose weight.

"Alcohol replaces our good calories and needed nu-trients—proteins, carbohydrates, fats, vitamins, and miner-als—with the 'empty' calories, which contain none of the substances we need to develop cells and to grow. We satiate our appetite with booze. Taking in less food, we become deficient in needed minerals, such as zinc and magnesium. Among other things, zinc is necessary for normal senses of taste and smell. When we don't have enough zinc, we begin to lose our senses of smell and taste and thus our appetite decreases. There is also evidence that there is a direct effect of alcohol on the brain centers of smell, taste, and appetite itself. When we lose our appetite, we take in less food. We develop morning nausea and then tend to stop having break-fast and skip other meals, again decreasing nutrient intake. It's a vicious circle.

"It has been estimated by researchers at the University of California at Los Angeles that if a person's intake of alcohol is

20 percent or more of his or her daily calories—that is, two drinks at lunch, a before-dinner drink, wine or other drink with dinner, and an after-dinner drink—he or she probably is suffering from the disease of alcoholism.

"Brain protein (cell) development is impaired in the presence of alcohol. Visual disturbances occur because alcohol blocks the interaction of zinc, vitamin A, and vitamin B-12 in the retina, and night vision becomes impaired. When the liver is digesting alcohol, it is prevented from oxidizing or digesting other nutrients, adding to the ineffectiveness of those needed chemicals even though they are present.

"Hyperexcretion is another way in which alcohol affects nutrition. Alcohol increases the loss of nutrients both via urine and stool. In addition to the night blindness and taste and smell problems that have already been described, changes occur in sexual hormone production. Loss of magnesium, calcium, and potassium will increase heart irregularities and spasms of the coronary arteries.

"It appears that one or two drinks a day may protect men against coronary artery disease. It also appears that *more* than two drinks a day alters this and that heart disease can be made worse by drinking more than two drinks daily. The alcoholic patient cannot afford the luxury of that possible protection of even one or two drinks. The alcoholic must not drink at all. All other kinds of heart disease are made worse by alcohol.

"The evidence points to a definite role of alcohol in the cause of some cancers. Cancers of the head, neck, esophagus, and liver are seen more frequently in heavy drinkers than in non- or light drinkers. Selenium excretion is increased in heavy drinkers, and at least one author suggests this may be a nutritional factor in cancer formation.

"Alcohol does appear to decrease one's immunity factors. This decreased immunity may effect tumor formation as well as resistance to common and not so common infections.

"Carbohydrate metabolism—the way our body handles

sugars and starches—is severely affected by alcohol consumption.

"The heavy drinker has wide swings in blood sugar levels. High blood sugar may cause lethargy and fatigue. Low blood sugar, or hypoglycemia, causes irritability, decreased alertness, mental confusion (the brain requires adequate sugar supplies to function normally), agitation, convulsions, and even coma. A heavy drinker who goes without food for as little as eight hours may suffer convulsions or coma.

"Loss of calcium from bones, or osteoporosis, occurs as we grow older. The drinking of alcohol increases this process, weakening bone strength and making us more susceptible to fractures, especially of our arms, legs, and hips, a serious problem for senior citizens. Aseptic necrosis of the hip is most often seen in senior citizens who drink heavily.

"Alcoholism is a complex disease. We don't fully understand its cause. We have no cure for it. It strikes about one out of ten who drink alcoholic beverages regardless of age, sex, religion, intelligence, education, morals, social position, or sexual orientation. We have a good understanding of its effect upon family, work, social and economic survival, and medical, mental, and nutritional health. We know it is a primary disease—not just 'the outward manifestation of an underlying psychiatric disorder.' We also know that it is a treatable disease, requiring the efforts of knowledgeable, experienced, concerned people, the patient's family, and, most important, the patient himself/herself. It must be a team effort!"

After the lecture, we had an entire half hour of free time, thirty precious and cherished minutes. I used the first five minutes to put my dirty clothes in the machine in the laundry. Then I went to the bathroom and simultaneously read the short paragraph for this date in February in the little *Twenty-four Hour Book*. (One never knew when one was going to be quizzed on it.)

*   *   *

144

If alcoholism were just a physical allergy, like asthma or hay fever, it would be easy for us, by taking a skin test with alcohol, to find out whether or not we're alcoholics. But alcoholism is not just a physical allergy. It is also a mental allergy or obsession. After we've become alcoholics, we can still tolerate alcohol physically for quite a while, although we suffer a little more after each binge, and each time it takes a little longer to get over the hangovers. *Do I realize that since I have become an alcoholic, I cannot tolerate alcohol mentally at all?*

Then I went to my desk, opened my notebook, and managed to write two paragraphs on my jail essay before the loudspeaker in the hall crackled and summoned us to the lounge for the weekly Saturday Afternoon Hall Meeting.

We arranged our chairs in a circle, all twenty of us, plus three counselors, and the meeting was presided over by a counselor named Laverne. She had grayish blond hair and looked like a pretty small-town librarian with her horn-rimmed glasses. Until she spoke, that is; she had a voice, as we used to say in Montana, that could worm a dog.

"I wish to comment negatively upon certain aspects of our daily life here in McCallum!"

It sounded like a calliope as she rattled off some grievances and offenses.

Housekeeping problems first: People were leaving coffee cups around (we each had our own with our name on it) instead of putting them in the sink, someone left the laundry room a mess, someone wore shorts in the cafeteria, two people were caught smoking in their rooms, whoever had the vacuuming detail of the hall was doing a rotten job, and rooms 13, 18, and 20 had poorly made beds. (Mine was one—shades of summer camp: "Conrad, I've seen sloppily made bed rolls in my day but yours always takes the cake!")

Laverne glowered, took her glasses off, hooked a stem in her mouth, and looked around the room slowly. "Healthy people keep themselves and their environment clean. Sick people don't."

She put the glasses back on and said sternly, "It has come to my attention that one of you has offered the housekeeper fifty dollars a week to make his bed. This will not be tolerated. I know it's a first for some of you, as it was with Elizabeth Taylor, but here we make our own beds. And we make them neatly."

Dave and I glanced at Essex, and his guardsman's mustache was twitching, but other than that there was no sign of culpability.

Next Laverne took up the matter of a flasher: Report if we saw a swarthy man in a Burberry coat and nothing else, who'd been displaying his shortcomings in the vicinity of the Jacuzzi lately.

I was again impressed when the counselor said that Mrs. Ford had been inspecting the premises the day before and had noted with displeasure that the garbage bag had not been removed by eight o'clock from in front of our building as it was supposed to be; Mrs. Ford was certainly not a figurehead or merely a fund-raiser around this place.

Laverne appointed a new "granny." He or she would have the thankless duty of seeing that his peers got to medical appointments on time, didn't skip the circle, and did his or her chores. For the coming week it would be Peter, the doctor with the great sense of humor.

Then it was announced that we would play a game. One person was sent out of the room—in the first case, Beth. Then Laverne pointed to someone in the circle, in this case, Roy, Morrie's hated counselor. A huge water-bed of a man, he had bangs and a walrus mustache.

Beth was told to come back in and was supposed to ask everyone in turn such questions as, "If he or she were a car, what kind would it be?" in order to determine the designated one's identity. The car was an Edsel, the animal a bear. When it came to Morrie and he was asked what historical character

the subject would be, Morrie barely hesitated before grimac-
ing and saying in measured tones, "Dr. Mengele." When
Beth asked me what TV show the subject might be on, I
replied, *"Captain Kangaroo,"* and she quickly guessed "Roy."

We had started reluctantly, but as the game was repeated a
few more times, there was mounting enthusiasm and laughter. I suppose it had its therapeutic purpose—everything did
at BFC: Deflation of egos? Learn to laugh at yourself? Or just
fun and camaraderie?

After the game the meeting took a more serious turn. It
focused on one woman. Reena, a beautiful dark-haired Latin
"model" of thirty, had always worn layers of pancake
makeup, mascara, and lipstick. She generally dressed, as
someone said, in what looked like the flag of a Central American country. Today her counselor had ordered her to go
three days with no makeup at all in order to help her "get in
touch with the real Reena." Rumor had her a high-priced call
girl.

When I'd seen Reena in the lounge or sauntering into the
cafeteria, undulating in her pink slacks and green blouse, she
always acted very ladylike—aloof and almost haughty. Still, I
used to be reminded of the verses of the old "Wild Party"
poem about a dancer:

> Her body was marvelous:
> A miracle had fused it.
> The whole world had seen it—
> And a good part had used it. . . .

and:

> She was swell to sleep with.
> Her toe-nails were scarlet.
> She looked like—and had been—
> A Mexican harlot.

*   *   *

147

Now, without makeup, Reena was a different person. I wouldn't have known who she was if Laverne hadn't said her name. Her skin was gray, washed out, and she looked like the angry, plain, frightened alcoholic that she was.

"Reena, how are you doing today?" Laverne made the mistake of asking her.

Reena told her how she was doing. Reena told us all. And she phrased it in the language of a Marine drill sergeant.

To put it mildly, she didn't like or trust us. She didn't like or trust the counselors, and Betty Ford could take her Center and perform an impossible physical act with it. She said she had delivered herself, body and soul, to this place and what had happened? People talked badly about her behind her back, accused her of being a falling down drunk and doper, and the women hated her and were jealous of her and her life-style. "Hypocrites!" she screamed at all of us, and burst into sobs.

When she finally quieted and cringed in her chair, weeping silently, Laverne said in a surprisingly soft voice, "I think you're mistaken, Reena. No one hates you." She looked around the circle. "Does anyone hate Reena here?"

"No!"

"I think, on the contrary, Reena, they love and understand you. I think this is part of your problem—your failure to trust people. I know you had a rotten childhood—I know you were raped by your uncle and so forth. But that's over. This is *now* and you must learn to trust people! You must start today. Let us begin by trusting your peers. Let's try a little experiment. Everyone stand up."

Then Laverne led Reena to the center of the room. She told the woman to close her eyes tightly. Lavern motioned for all of us to come closer, and pointed at several people, waving them in behind Reena.

She took both of Reena's hands and she spoke quietly and soothingly, almost hypnotically: "Reena, you've never liked yourself, but you are basically a fine, fine person. Look how you've taken care of your old mother and your daughter, for example, through thick and thin. We recognize your fine qualities, and your bad points are no worse than ours and we love you and want to help you. Everyone here wants to help you, don't we?"

"Yes!" we chorused.

"We love you, Reena," said someone, and others echoed it. "We love you."

"Do you love them, Reena?"

The woman, tears flowing over her high cheekbones, whispered, "I don't know."

"Do you trust them?"

She caught a sob. "I—I—don't know!"

"Are you willing to try to trust them?"

Reena shook her head, her eyes still shut.

"If you should fall, do you think they would catch you?"

Reena hesitated.

"They love you, they want to help you. They would catch you, wouldn't they?"

She murmured, "I don't know."

"Reena," said Laverne, "when I count to three, I want you to fall straight backward. Do you hear me?"

The woman barely nodded.

"One," Laverne started, "two . . ." She let go of Reena's hands.

Reena stood rigidly, her eyes shut, her hands clenched at her side, her mouth working silently.

"Three!" Laverne commanded.

Reena swayed, then like a tree sawed through in a forest, she fell slowly backward, her body straight. Twelve inches before she would have hit the floor a dozen hands caught her. Then, slowly they lifted her up and put her on her feet.

And now she was laughing and crying and hugging the people crowding around her who were touching her and saying, "We love you," and she was kissing Laverne and gasping to everyone, "Thank you, thank you, I do love you, I do, oh, I do!"

As I started to go back to my room, Peter, the new granny, performed his first official act. "Don't forget," he said, tapping his watch, "you have an appointment with Craig in seven minutes."

ELEVEN

"Yesterday you told me you'd never thought of committing suicide," the minister said as I sat down in his office. He shuffled through some papers in a manila folder on his desk. "What'd you think you were doing when you were pouring all that gasoline into your body every day? You're not stupid. Didn't you realize that was a slow death?"

"Maybe I wasn't in a hurry," I quipped.

He glanced up and said sharply, "Your counselor warned me that you were inclined to use a joke to avoid a truth."

Aha. A little cross-checking going on here.

"Seriously, didn't you realize that a quart of booze a day would kill you?"

"A quart a . . ." I exclaimed indignantly. "I never drank *that* much!"

Only hopeless drunks drank that much.

"Well, let's just do some figuring here." Craig picked up a pencil and poised it over a scratch pad. "You usually had your

151

first drink of gin and grapefruit juice about eleven o'clock, right?"

A *lot* of cross-checking going on here! I nodded.

"Double?"

I nodded again.

"Sure you did. As Joe Pursch says, that's so the first shot can keep the liver occupied and off guard so that his friend, the second shot, can sneak around up to the brain and start making the drinker feel good. Okay, so now you've had two ounces. Did you have a second?"

"Sometimes."

He looked at me skeptically. "Most times? Especially if the bartender or another guy at the bar was buying?"

"Sometimes," I said.

"Okay, we're up to four ounces. Now, we still have drinks before dinner and wine with. You and your wife could polish off a bottle of wine each, couldn't you?"

"Well . . ." I remembered how on our cruise trips the steward would automatically place a bottle in front of each of us at the start of the dinner and usually they were empty after the dessert. "Not all the time."

"And at parties, maybe a drink or two after, and/or a brandy? Oh, and let's not forget our old pal the dressing drink that we had to get us in the mood for the party."

I nodded and watched uncomfortably as his pencil moved up and down on the paper.

"Well, what d'you know! We're up to a fifth and maybe even a quart."

I felt my face flush. "I wasn't intentionally lying," I said lamely.

"I know you weren't. Most heavy drinkers consume a lot more than they think over the average week. Now, at the rate you were going you were on a collision course, but you probably only were semiaware of it. But, intellectually, you knew that too much alcohol is a poison, so it was, indeed, a suicide process. And speaking of a death wish"—he glanced down at my file—"what about this bullfighting?"

"I don't think it has to do with a death wish any more than going off a high diving board or downhill racing or mountain climbing or football."

"Is it exciting to do?"

"The greatest thrill I've ever had is to make a bull go from point A to point B without going through you. And then, of course, at the same time to execute a beautiful maneuver."

He took a pipe out of a drawer and began filling it. "You must be very brave."

"On the contrary, I was scared most of the time. Very scared, until the actual fight began. Then you're too busy to be afraid."

"Why did you do it?"

"As Thomas Fuller wrote, 'Many would be cowards, if they had courage enough.'"

"I still think you were brave."

"Will Rogers said, 'Everybody is ignorant, only on different subjects.' I say we're all cowards, but afraid of different things. I was terrified of cattle when we spent our summers as children in Montana. I was scared to ride the calves and steers the way the other boys did in our little rodeos."

"So bullfighting was a question of overcoming terror? That-which-I-once-feared-I-no-longer-fear sort of thing?"

I nodded. "Plus the excitement of doing it and learning to do it well. I've never dived off a high platform but it must be similar, the emphasis on technique, grace, feet position, and so forth—plus the danger. You can't have thrills without some danger."

"I was reading the famous Otto Fenichel about that subject last night." He opened a tome to a page marked by an index card and read: "'When the organism discovers that it is now able to overcome without fear a situation which would formerly have overwhelmed it with anxiety, it experiences a certain kind of pleasure. This pleasure has the character of 'I need not feel anxiety any more. . . .

"The counter-phobic attitude may really be regarded as a never-ending attempt at the belated conquest of an unmastered infantile anxiety. . . .

" 'The most outstanding example is probably the entire field of sport, which may in general be designated as a counter-phobic phenomenon. No doubt there are erotic and aggressive gratifications in sports, just as they are present in all the other functional pleasures of adults. Certainly not everyone who engages in sport is suffering from an unconscious insoluble fear of castration; nor does it follow that the particular sport for which he shows a later preference must once have been feared. But it will generally hold true that the essential joy in sport is that one actively brings about in play certain tensions which were formerly feared, so that one may enjoy the fact that now one can overcome them without fearing them.'

"So"—Craig lit his pipe—"It's like the thrill we got when Daddy threw us up in the air: We were afraid we'd fall, but then Daddy would catch us."

It all sounded like a load of Freudian overthink, but if it made Father Craig happy . . .

"I forgot to say that fighting bulls under the right conditions, such as having a cooperative animal, can be a lot of fun, quite apart from overcoming fear."

"Fun?" He shook his head. "I saw some bullfights. Hardly my idea of fun. I must say I always root for the bull."

"I was afraid you were going to say that."

"Why?"

"Because it's such a cliché. And it means you like animals better than people."

He frowned and lit his pipe. "I happen to like animals," he said defensively.

"So do I. We have six dogs and seven cats and a parrot.

And in the past I've had ocelots, foxes, and a gibbon ape. The bulls in the arena die as quickly as that hamburger you had for lunch today, and a lot more nobly. Bulls that are selected for the ring live a whole year longer—a third of their lives—than the ones chosen for McDonald's."

"But their death is cruel."

"Sure, it's cruel—indefensible but irresistible, they say. But it's not as cruel as zoos and circuses and rodeos and fox hunting. And the trapping of fur-bearing animals for the vanity of the women of this world."

"How'd you get into such a strange field?"

"Well, alcohol played a part. A small part. I was full of youth and tequila one day—eighteen in Mexico City, studying painting at the university—a friend took me to a bull-fight. I said it looked unfair; the bull always went for the cape. The guy explained that it attacked the cape because the man was so skilled he made it go at the cloth instead of his body."

"Not because it's red?"

"Bulls are color-blind. Anyway, I said it looked easy and my friend said why don't you try it and I took another swig and jumped down in the arena with my raincoat as a cape. When I saw half a ton of black fury with huge horns bearing down on me, I learned more about bullfighting than I'd ever got from Hemingway's *Death in the Afternoon.* I made a couple of clumsy passes, then jumped head first over the fence, white of face and wet of pants."

Craig smiled. "So you retired as a bullfighter?"

"No. The matador—who, incidentally, was killed a year later—invited me to come to the ranches to learn something about the science. And believe me, it is a science. In ballet you just have to learn the steps. In bullfighting, you not only learn the maneuvers, dozens of them, but you have to key them in to the vagaries of your unpredictable and lethal partner, the bull. You learn first by practicing with a boy who pushes a bicycle wheel with sharp horns mounted on it. He imitates the bull exactly. I was knocked down a lot."

"It must be embarrassing to say you got gored by a Schwinn."

"Eventually you advance to calves, but calves from the strain of *toros bravos,* the wild bulls bred for centuries solely for the arena. After a while I graduated to bulls and got my knee busted up by one of them. So I went back to the States and went to Yale on a cane. When I was graduated, I tried to get in the Navy, but I couldn't because of the injury, so I went into the State Department."

"And that was the end of your bullfighting career?"

"No, the beginning. I was sent to Spain as a vice-consul."

"Weren't you awfully young?"

"Twenty-one. I guess one of the youngest they'd had. But remember, this was during the war and there was a shortage of qualified men around. I felt guilty about that—about being in beautiful Spain in a cushy job with servants and a chauffeur while my friends were off fighting the war for me. And then I felt really guilty when my three best friends were killed and a fourth had his leg blown off. When I think of them, I still feel guilty as hell for being alive."

"You tried to join. If you'd been accepted into the Navy, they still would have been killed."

I didn't say anything and he went on, "Did you drink when you were in the diplomatic service? Weren't there lots of social functions?"

"I don't remember much drinking. In Sevilla and Málaga—southern Spain—any sign of drunkenness was a social disgrace. In Pamplona and Bilbao and other parts north of Madrid they drank a lot more. I remember getting drunk with the naval attaché at the San Fermín fiestas, where the whole town was drunk for a week."

"That supports our theory about alcoholism being more prevalent in northern, colder climes."

"In those days it was not the norm for me to drink much. A bit of sherry and maybe a cognac and soda. I remember being so surprised to see Manolete drink hard the last year of his life. And not wine but scotch. A southern Spaniard, he was the exception that proved the rule."

"Why was he drinking? Wasn't he the idol of Spain?"

"He was thirty. That's over the hill in bullfighting, and he was tired and he wanted to get out. He'd had his gorings, he'd made millions, still, he hated to step down from being the number one. He was having problems with his mistress, too. He was drinking a lot. I remember drinking with him, not so much that I wanted to get drunk, but to be so lucky as to be able to do it with this great man, this great figure, this international star."

"And how was he when he was drunk?"

"When he was sober he was so regal, so cool, so commanding."

"And drunk?" Craig pursued.

I shrugged. "I guess you'd call him sloppy. It was quite a shock. Like when I saw Sinclair Lewis drunk some years later."

"How'd you feel about them when you saw them drunk?"

"I guess you'd say . . . disappointed. Disillusioned."

"How do you think people around you felt when you were drunk?"

"But I wasn't a big star with an image."

"I bet you were to your kids. Ever see your father drunk?"

"Never."

"How would you have felt?"

"Horrified."

"And you, how were you when you were drunk? How'd you behave?"

"I hate to think."

"You've *got* to think. That's what you're at the Center for."

"Probably like any other drunk."

Craig nodded. "Probably started out jovial and went down hill. Like all of us. My own progression was like a nasty little poem. I'd go from jocose to amorous and then to bellicose and then lachrymose and finally comatose."

"Might I ask, sir," I began hesitantly, "why you drank? With your religion and all? It's none of my business, but . . ."

"You're right, it's none of your business," he said gruffly. Then, "Who knows?" He went on quietly, introspectively, looking out the window. "The struggle between the layman in me versus the clergyman that my family wanted me to be? Looking at the world as it was and not as it should be? A confirmed idealist in a less than perfect world? Seeing all my friends killed in battle while all I could do was cry helplessly and say a few prayers and figure out some cheap phrases to console their families?"

He puffed on his pipe. "I never found out the exact reason for my drinking and you might not either. The important thing is that I got alcohol out of my life, the way you must get it out of yours."

He turned away from the window, cleared his throat, and said, "So, Manolete was on his way to drinking himself to death and you were a witness to the decline. What happened finally?"

"He was goaded into a final series of fights by a young new star, and in trying to prove he was the greatest, he got himself killed. That's what my novel *Matador* was about."

"And you found this admirable—to throw away this one and only precious life of ours in a last display of bravado for an insatiable and thrill-seeking crowd?"

"He went out in a burst of glory," I protested.

"*Vain*glory is perhaps a more apt word. Meanwhile, you were emulating him—continuing to fight bulls?"

"I fought many times in those three years in Spain under the coaching of the great Juan Belmonte and Arruza."

"And you enjoyed torturing those animals?"

"It isn't torture, and that certainly isn't the point of bull-fighting. One of the reasons Manolete was so popular is that he dispatched the bulls so quickly and cleanly as well as caping them so artistically. And I honestly don't think the bulls feel any pain in a bullfight. I've never had a sword stuck in me or a banderilla, but I've had a horn go in me—had it go nine inches right through my leg—and I barely felt it. It was just as though someone had punched me hard there. An hour later in the hospital it began to hurt like hell. But you see, for the bull, there is no hour later. He's dead in a matter of minutes, and it's in hot blood and the adrenaline is pumping. And, though it's no consolation to the bull, we eat the meat."

"You just toss that off—you were gored. Most people go all through life without that particular experience. It couldn't have been as casual a happening as you make it sound."

"Let's just say it got my attention at the time, and it smarted quite a bit."

"There you go with the jokes! I want you to tell me about it sincerely—all about it—what you felt about it then and now. *Feelings!* As you've probably been told, alcoholics lose touch with their feelings. How did it happen?"

I told him. It was when I was thirty-six, married father of three, living near San Francisco, writing and painting and running a nightclub on the side. I went to Spain leading a group of bullfight aficionados. My wife stayed home because she didn't like bullfights and was studying higher mathematics at the University of California. In Madrid I met a man I knew who was organizing a bullfighting exhibition to be held in El Escorial in two days. There were several older bullfighters on the program—wouldn't I like to round out the card? Seemed like a logical idea at the time, even though I hadn't fought even a calf for several years.

"Had you been drinking when you agreed to do it?" Craig interjected.

"Somewhat."

"Have you ever fought when drunk?"

"Spaniards say never fight a bull when drunk because drunken bulls are the most dangerous."

"Another joke!"

"Sorry."

"The next day when you were sober, why didn't you back out of it? Tell them you had a family? Why did you do it?"

It was a losing battle; there was no way I could explain it. I said simply: "It goes back to not having the guts to be a coward."

Picasso would have understood. Once, in answer to a woman interviewer's asking him if there had been anything in life he had missed, he replied: "I would like to have been a hero. I missed having the experience of proving my manhood through physically testing myself. To be young and a warrior, to feel the exaltation of being a hero . . . to know I was one, to prove it to myself, to face fear and defy it. Proximity to death brings heightened life. But it must be a youthful confrontation when there is everything to lose.

Picasso went on: "I didn't fight in wars. I didn't even fight the bull. It is with men as it is with bulls. There are brave bulls and the others. This is a very important thing to a man . . . to know that you can measure up. You think you would. You tell yourself you would act with heroism, but you can never really know for certain. To have excelled in combat, to have been a brave gladiator . . . I will never know for certain. Not being a man, you could not understand what I mean. Every man knows."

Now it was Craig who was saying: "Didn't you really want to see if you could still do it? Facing middle age and all? Go on, please, in detail."

I sighed and tried to set the scene for him—the brown rolling countryside outside of Madrid, the ranch of Pedro Gandárias. I began to relive the painful experience of almost thirty years ago.

As we drove up the dirt driveway we saw that everyone was already down at the little bullring. It was a hundred yards from the main ranch house, a dazzling whitewashed white against the green fields, and there were about 150 guests in the stands chatting and drinking Manzanilla. We parked and climbed up the steps.

A picador on a padded horse was in the ring. This was to be a *tienta,* where the young cows are tested for bravery. It is an important phase of bull raising, because while a bull may get his size from his father, they say his fighting heart comes from mama.

"Just in time!" Pedro called up to us. Then he motioned to the man on the wall and said, "All right, turn in the big one."

The man jerked the rope that went down to the latch on the *toril,* and the gate clanged open. Into the ring dashed a three-year-old heifer, sleek and greenish black, surrounded by a haze of dust.

People unfamiliar with fighting stock have a hard time telling a young fighting bull from a fighting cow: Fighting cows have long, sharp horns, virtually no udder, and a conformation totally unlike that of a dairy cow. Besides that, they are crafty, speedy, and can turn like revolving doors.

This cow of Gandárias's charged the picador hard, nearly spilling the horse as the man shot the small point of the lance into her withers. If she took the pic several times bravely and willingly, she would be marked for breeding; if not, for the abattoir. This one's back legs were driving her into the padded side of the horse, and she kept hooking into the mattress hard until she was lured away with a cape. The cow had probably been caped many times before and tended to head for a man's body instead of going at the cape. Usually for affairs like this an inch or two of horn is sawed off, because there is no infirmary and if you get hit in the femoral artery you can bleed to death in five minutes. But for some reason they had left the murderous horns intact on this cow.

I went down the steps and was let into the arena. I was

handed the small muleta, and I noticed my hands were trembling as I took it. I draped it over the wooden sword and stepped out from behind the *burladero*. The cow was about thirty feet away, looking lethal and a lot bigger than she had from the stands. She pawed, wagging her wicked horns.

I planted my feet, arched my back, and shook the muleta. The wise cow dropped her head and lunged forward. She covered the 30 feet faster than a racehorse, her neck stretched out to kill.

I didn't step back, and the animal hurtled past me. Its near horn sliced by only a couple of inches away from my leg, and I heard a sharp "Olé!" from the spectators. I knew then why I had gone down into the ring, why, I guess, I'll always go down until I'm too old to swing a cape at all. It wasn't the applause. It is purely and simply that no other thrill in the world can compete with the exquisite, unique elation that comes from making an attacking animal pass by your legs.

I should have quit when I was ahead, because after that first pass everything was downhill. I suppose I gave it ten more passes, but I was lousy and the cow was lousy. The cow crowded, hooked, swerved, and was generally uncooperative. On the last pass she slammed straight into me and knocked me into the air. Remotely, vaguely, I was aware that the horn seared my left leg, but I was too busy trying to get away from the animal to worry about how deep it might have gone. Unfortunately, I can't tell you how it feels to be gored, because I honestly did not feel the horn go in and out of my flesh, so very sharp was it and so quickly did it happen.

After someone lured the animal away, I lurched over to the fence, disgusted with the cow and myself. And then I felt something wet on my left leg. There was a growing dark stain on the upper inside of my pants, and when I looked down, I saw that I had one black boot and one shiny red one. I felt a sickening jolt in my stomach.

Pale and wobbly, I was led out behind the ring. The blood

was pumping out like water from a garden hose. Solanito, a professional matador who had also performed that day, quickly tied a length of rubber tube high up on the leg, and the bleeding—through a hole about the size of a fifty-cent piece—stopped. Then we drove off fast to the nearby town of El Escorial. After forty-five minutes we located a doctor, a toothless, colorful old devil with dirty fingernails. He examined the wound superficially and whistled silently but said, "It's no _cornada_, just a _puntazo_, a little puncture. But then"— he laughed a wheezy laugh—"I've never seen a horn wound before."

Since the bleeding had stopped and the leg really didn't hurt much, I began to relax, but Solanito looked worried. "There's only one person who knows—go see Giménez-Guinea, and quick."

It was fitting that this advice, which probably saved my life, came from a matador, for if the Virgin of the Macarena is the patron saint of _toreros_, Luis Giménez-Guinea is their savior. The bullfighter's most fervent prayer is, "If I'm to get it, let Giménez-Guinea be nearby."

We drove back to Madrid in a hurry. They put me in a big drab room that smelled like all the hospital rooms of the world. The orderly took off my pants and cleaned up the leg while we waited for the doctor to come from his house. The wound didn't look so ugly now, and I began to feel pretty silly about dragging Giménez-Guinea to the hospital to look at me. After all, he was unqualifiedly the greatest horn-wound specialist in the world, handling as he did over one hundred gorings a season. But the leg was beginning to hurt like the devil, and I was suddenly pleased and relieved when the door banged open and Giménez-Guinea stalked in, followed by an assistant wheeling a tray of instruments.

He was an awesome sight. Tall and broad, he was a cross between a scowling Douglas MacArthur and a Sioux chieftain. He had a hawklike crag of a nose, patent-leather ungrayed hair, and at the age of sixty-eight he looked hardly fifty.

"What do you have?" he growled without bothering with salutations.

"No *cornada*, Don Luis," I said. "The other doctor said it was just a little *puntazo*."

I propped myself on my elbows and watched apprehensively as he leaned over my leg and spread the wound with his fingers.

"A little *puntazo*?" he snorted, and I didn't like that snort. "Just a little *puntazo*, eh? Watch!"

From the table he took a foot-long instrument that had a handle like the ones on the little mirrors dentists use. Deftly he inserted the handle in the mouth of my wound, and with no hesitation, no guesswork as to which direction the horn had taken, he put nine inches of it into the hole without hitting the sides of the wound.

Then, bending over with his face close to mine, he bellowed as though terribly angry with me, "You don't have a little *puntazo*. You have a horse-killing *cornada!*"

For the first time in my life I fell back in a complete faint.

When I came to, I heard him saying a million miles away, "I should be operating on him right now, but I have to go to the bullring. Get him ready, tetanus antitoxin, penicillin." Then to me, "I didn't hurt you. You fainted out of fear. When did you last eat?"

I told him groggily and he nodded. "You'll be all right. I won't be back for three hours and that will make six hours since your last meal. We will operate then."

Then he was gone. I still don't know whether I fainted because he hit bottom with his nutpick or because he himself seemed so alarmed. He had treated some 2,500 bullfight gorings and had watched the legendary Manolete's life ooze away from a wound that was almost in the same place as mine and no deeper.

A great depression settled over me as I waited hour after hour. The pain was building up, and I wanted to get on with the show. I had visions of four or five toreros being gored and, since Giménez-Guinea is the plaza's official doctor, they would come first. Here was a time I really could have used a drink.

Finally, he burst into the room, sweaty and tense, and I was wheeled into the operating room with a smile of relief on my face. "Once Giménez-Guinea gets you on the table," say the toreros, "death can never elbow him aside."

I was in the operating room for over an hour, and then spent two days in a groggy, feverish, swirling jumble. I heard his voice as though from a great distance.

"You're pretty bad off," he said with his usual bedside finesse. "Better tell your wife to come."

I murmured, "She's in California."

"*Dígale que venga*—tell her to come!" Then he asked, "How long will it take her to get here?"

"Two days."

"*Dígale que no venga*," he said. "Tell her not to come. In two days you'll either be well or dead."

By the third day my fever had dropped, and Don Luis strode briskly into the room.

"*Por poco la diñó usted*," he said cheerfully, in Madrid slang. "You nearly kicked the bucket. But you're all right now, and fifteen days from today you'll walk out of here under your own power."

"And you did?" asked the minister, here in his BFC office.

I nodded. "Just barely."

"And what did your wife think of your bullfighting and getting gored?"

"She thought I was crazy," I said. "But she came to Europe and got me."

"And you were all right? You'd come very close to dying."

"I limped for a few months. And at least I got one laugh

out of the experience. The day the news item broke in the *Times,* Eva Gabor ran into Noel Coward in Sardi's and said, 'Dahling, did you hear about poor Bahnaby? He vass gored in Spain!' and Noel exclaimed, 'He was what?' and she said, 'Gored,' and he said, 'Thank heavens. I thought you said bored.' At least that's the way the gossip columnist Leonard Lyons reported it."

Craig smiled. "Good epitaph—gored but never bored. So, end of bullfighting?"

"I cut the pigtail off, as the matadors say. But I'm still paying for my youthful follies. Three months ago I had my other leg reoperated upon—the knee that was injured in Mexico."

"You were almost gored to death," he mused. He puffed on his pipe for a while. "Isn't it just possible that you started drinking heavily in order to finish up the job that bullfighting failed to do?"

"Come on," I said.

"You reject that idea?"

"Summarily."

"Yesterday you talked briefly about your blissful childhood." He looked down at the file in front of him. "Your brother—your only sibling—didn't he get badly hurt when you were about eleven?"

"He was sixteen, was riding in a rodeo in Livingston, Montana, and he got his leg clobbered. It became infected and he was fourteen months in the hospital, then home in bed for many more months. Then they cut it off."

"That doesn't sound so blissful. Were you close?"

"Very. Still are. He shaped my life more than anyone. And in a way I lived the life he couldn't because he was lying in bed with weights on his leg. A good athlete, he wanted to be a boxer, but he couldn't. That was the only reason I became captain of the boxing team at college. Probably the reason I fought bulls. He wanted to write and play the piano and go out with glamorous girls, so I did all those things for him."

"And I bet you never did those things quite well enough to suit him."

I laughed. "I still don't."

"The older brother syndrome."

"Compounded!"

"Ike Eisenhower told me he couldn't impress his older brother even when he became president," Craig said. "You say he shaped your life. Where was your father all this time?"

"He had an accident—was riding with my mother, turned to talk to her, and was knocked off his horse. He was never exactly the same again, though he lived another twenty-five years. He remained a humorous, wonderful man, but lost the drive and quickness he'd had mentally, and physically he could barely shuffle."

"And what did he think of your brother's rodeo career and your bullfighting?"

"I think he understood. After all, he'd boxed at Yale and had gone adventuring in Alaska and Montana."

"I don't think your childhood was as blissful as you'd like to remember. Do you know the writings of Max Beerbohm?"

Ah, a reader. "Slightly."

"He wrote somewhere, 'The past is a work of art, free of irrelevancies and loose ends.'"

"That's good." I very much wanted to show I could keep up with him. "Like that opening sentence 'The past is a foreign country: they do things differently there,' in the novel written by . . . by . . ." I stammered. Who wrote it?

Damn! I could not think of the author. Or the title of the book. Korsakoff's syndrome?

"I know it! Give me a minute!"

"That's all right. You'll think of it."

"Maybe I *have* got brain damage," I said, suddenly panicky.

"I doubt it." He changed the topic abruptly. "You mentioned seeing Sinclair Lewis drunk. How'd that come about? I'm from his neck of the woods—Minnesota. Read all his books and all that. My father could have been the model for

Babbitt, and my mother was a ringer for Carol from *Main Street.* I hope I never become an Elmer Gantry, however. Sinclair Lewis was a great writer, all right."

"I was Lewis's secretary for five months back when I was twenty-five. I'd quit the State Department and gone to Lima for a year following the bull circuit. I was trying to write a novel, so when I came back to California to visit my parents and heard that Sinclair Lewis was in town, I wrote him a note suggesting that we meet. After all, I figured we had a lot in common: *I'd* read all his books and *he'd* read all his books, so we should have a little chat about them."

"Ah, the confidence and ingenuous arrogance of youth!"

"To my amazement, he invited me to tea. I hadn't really expected he'd answer me. After all, he was the most famous American novelist, our first Nobel prize winner for literature, bigger than Hemingway then, multimillionaire, and all that."

"Tea? Wasn't he a legendary boozer?"

"He had that reputation, a horrendous record. But at this time in his life he was on the wagon and had been for eight years. He was very old and on the decline and he was"—I stopped and realized—"Lord, he was the same age I am now—sixty-three!"

Craig shrugged. "And the president of the United States is ten years older than that. To a twenty-five-year-old, everyone over forty is doddering. Go on."

"Well, he asked me what I was doing, and I said writing a novel, and he said let me see the first seventy-five pages, and I did. And the next day he told me to throw away the first seventy-two. But, 'There was some great stuff on the last three pages; let me see some more.' He called the next night at two A.M. and said he liked this part of the book a lot, and if I'd learn to play chess, I could come to his home in Williamstown, Massachusetts, and be his secretary. And I did and it was a fascinating time. Just the servants and the two of us in this great mansion and writers and publishers and producers streaming in and out all the time."

"What was he like? He looked like Ichabod Crane in photos."

"Worse than that. 'Red' Lewis was frightening looking, pocked and skeletal. But he had the keenest intellect and sharpest sense of humor and wildest imagination. He was extremely volatile, moody, and difficult, but I worshiped him and learned a lot about many things in my time with him."

"Did he think you had talent?"

"Apparently. At least he encouraged me—helped get my first novel, *The Innocent Villa,* published by Bennett Cerf. Not a good novel, I'm afraid."

"Do *you* think you have talent?"

"Do I?" I shrugged. "Not much. You quoted Beerbohm earlier. I like what he replied when someone asked him the same question: 'My gifts are small. I've used them very well and discreetly, never straining them; and the result is that I've made a charming little reputation.'"

Craig gave a laugh. "I've met all sorts of alcoholics in this job and one thing I've learned is that we may be pompous or arrogant or full of grandiosity and false pride, but way down deep the one unshakable thing we alcoholics are convinced of is that we are no damn good."

He banged out his pipe in the ashtray. "Why did you leave the job with Lewis?"

"It all started with a girl. One day I went down to the town to get a book for Mr. Lewis. In the bookstore was a pretty, vivacious girl of twenty-seven named Ida. I was captivated, and I whiled away so much time talking to her that I realized I'd be late for lunch, an unforgivable sin in the Lewis mansion. I dashed out of the store, jumped in the convertible sedan, and found the keys wouldn't work. What a time for the ignition to jam! I released the brake and coasted down the inclined street to the garage. As the men began to dismantle the ignition, one called out, 'Whose car is this, anyway?' 'Sinclair Lewis's!' I said. 'Hurry!' 'Mr. Lewis drives a Buick,' the man replied. I had got the wrong car. I ran back up the street and left word that if they saw a distraught person looking for a car, it was in the garage, and sped off to face Mr. Lewis's wrath. But there's a happy epilogue. I told Mr. Lewis about the girl. He said bring her to lunch; and he fell in love with her. But unfortunately, I liked her, too . . . so he fired me."

"That's a happy ending?"

"I had a letter last week from Ida just before I came in here. Imagine, after all these years! She's dying of cancer and wanted to tell me about what had happened so long ago. After he fired me and I went back to California, he proposed to her, offered her millions. But she wouldn't marry him, though she kept seeing him—she was fascinated by his personality, and his mind. 'I loved him,' she wrote me, 'but I wasn't in love with him.' Imagine, not until this last week did I know why I was fired way back in 1947!"

"If he wasn't drinking then, when did you see him drunk?"

"Two years later."

I told the minister about going to France on my honeymoon. I'd always wanted Dale to meet this fabulous character, and when I read on the front page of the *Paris Soir* that America's *"plus grand romancier"* was in town, I telephoned Red. He insisted that we have dinner with him. We picked him up in our Citroën at his hotel. He'd only been in Paris a day, but he seemed jubilant, frenetically so. He was stimulated by the city he'd come to know during his early triumphs.

"First time I've really been in Paris for twenty years," he said. "I'm going to take you to a marvelous little place on the Left Bank where we all used to go. You'll love it—gay, stimulating. All the good artists, writers go there, the top newspapermen, the thinkers."

We crossed the river and, after asking a few people, ar-

rived at the address. It was a miserable and dirty little café
with only one customer, a student who was studying a book
by the light of a candle in a bottle.

"This can't be the place!" Red exclaimed.

Dale checked the address and the name, and it was correct.

"But where is Madame Blanc?" he asked of the bored-
looking waiter.

"Dead," yawned the man, "these fifteen years."

"Sixteen," said the student, who might have been Madame
Blanc's grandson.

We sat down at a table and Red ordered a drink. I had
never seen him drink before. It was astonishing to watch him
down a brandy: It disappeared in a single sucking sound. He
had three to our one and kept looking around the dusty café,
frowning.

"This is simply not the place," he repeated irritably. "That's
all there is to it. The other place was far bigger, brightly lit,
music, full of people. Not it at all."

As we ate our depressing meal, the waiter routinely
brought an old ledger that served as a guest book. It was full
of names of the past. On almost the first yellowed page I saw
the signatures: John Dos Passos, Dorothy Thompson, Sinclair
Lewis. I tried to show the page to Red, but he wouldn't look
at it.

"Matter of fact," he said as he motioned the waiter for
another brandy, "I remember now, wasn't even on this street.
Different part of town."

Somehow we got into a discussion with the student. Red
invited him over and asked him a great many questions about
his life and studies. The student didn't introduce himself and
neither did we. He spoke English well but with a thick accent.
He was a literature major and was very serious behind his
thick glasses.

"And what American writers do you read?" Red asked, too
casually.

The student thought for a moment, then said, "My favorites are Fitzgerald, Hemingway, Steinbeck, and Sinclair . . ."

Red's face lit up pathetically. "Ah . . . Sinclair . . ."

"Upton Sinclair," continued the youth.

Red frowned and cleared his throat uncomfortably. "Any others?"

The youth shrugged. "I've read them all. But those are the ones I most admire."

We left. In the taxi Red mimicked the student's accent and manner to perfection: "My fahvoreets ahr Feetzgerohl, Emeenwhy, Stynabecque, an'"—here he departed slightly from the original—"an' thees Seenclair, thees Seenclair Loowees."

I found it hard to believe that he had actually convinced himself that the youth had listed his name among his favorites. Yet when we joined Red's brother, Claude, at the Café du Dôme later that evening, Red recounted the story, the accent honed and the story embellished. ("My fahvoreet nohvel off thees Seenclair Loowees ees, how you call heem, *Ahrohsmeet*.")

He had several more brandies. I looked around the café at the interesting characters. "Isn't this where you and Fitzgerald and Joyce and Hemingway used to come?" I asked.

"We all used to come here," he said with a snort. "But I was always at a different table. Never belonged in their group, never belonged to any group. Never belonged to anybody." He put his arm around Dale awkwardly. "Now, if I'd only had a beautiful little sweet wife like this, the whole story'd be different. I might have been a great writer."

We helped Claude get him home, helped him up the stairs to the lobby of the hotel.

"If he keeps drinking like this, he'll be dead in a year," said Claude mournfully as we said good-night at the elevator.

We had a date for dinner with them the next night, but upon arriving at their hotel at six o'clock, we found that Red was in a drunken stupor. He left Paris for Italy soon after, and we never saw him again. Claude did not miss by much in his sad prediction, for Sinclair Lewis died in Rome of alcoholism.

"I heard of a final macabre irony," I told the minister. "A friend of mine went into the United States embassy at Rome and saw a consular official down on her knees with a broom and pan. 'What are you doing?' he asked her. 'Sweeping up Sinclair Lewis,' was the answer. Red's ashes had been put in a safe pending final disposal and the urn had fallen out, its contents spilled."

"A sad end indeed," Craig agreed. "How'd you feel when you saw him lurching around ludicrously, this great mind practically reduced to baby talk?"

"I cringed for him. The way I cringed when I saw Faulkner and Thurber staggering around together in the lobby of the Algonquin Hotel, the blind literally leading the blind."

"Anybody ever cringe for your behavior?"

"I'm sure."

"Who?"

"Kids."

"Who else?"

"Wife."

"Who else?"

"Friends."

"And didn't you ever wake up in the morning and cringe for yourself? When you get out of here are you going to continue to be an embarrassment to your family, your friends, and yourself?"

"I hope to God not," I said.

"Ah, there's the first mention of that dreaded word! God! Do you believe in Him?"

"I'm afraid I'm like that woman who spoke last night—I don't believe in an old gent with whiskers sitting on a cloud watching our every move."

173

"Now who's talking in clichés? Who here has been asking you to believe in the guy with the whiskers? Nobody's asked you to believe in anything except a power or force higher or greater than you yourself. Is that such a big deal? Surely you don't believe in *nothingness*. Norman Cousins said recently that 'nothingness surrounds us, but it cannot claim us. The proof of God is in the rejection of nothingness. Pure nothingness nowhere exists.' Does that make sense?"

"I suppose so."

"When you were gored and thought you were dying, did you call on God?"

"I probably blamed Him. How could you do this to me, damn it, get me out of this mess, that sort of thing."

"Ah, there's nothing better than a good dying to bring a boy back to the church and make a believer out of him! Everyday life is not so dramatic. Now, you've only been here a few days. I predict, if you're like nearly all the others, that you will experience a spiritual change along about the end of your second week. That's the way it seems to happen."

"You mean," I said skeptically, "a spiritual awakening?" My voice put quotes around the phrase.

He answered, "A spiritual *awareness* certainly."

"A great white light suddenly filling the room? The way it did with the founder of Alcoholics Anonymous?"

"It takes different forms."

He glanced at his watch. "Before we quit, tell me about them."

"Who?"

"Your friends who were killed. . . . Where'd they get it?"

"Well," I began tentatively. "There was Nion Tucker. He was my very best friend since childhood. A born leader. I bet he was a great Marine."

But I didn't visualize him as a soldier. I had a flash of his stocky frame, about twelve years old, hunched over the 14-foot sailboat we built from scratch as he squeezed caulking into the seams. The boat took us six months to build and then it sank the first day on the lake. I could see us both looking at each other in horror as it settled in the water, and then we dissolved into hysterical laughter and kept it up for the rest of the afternoon.

"He got it in Iwo. First off the landing craft, of course. Like Jerry Baker in Normandy."

I felt tears in my eyes as I went back in time. Jerry, gentle Jerry, handsome Jerry, with the wonderful way with horses and the fierce love of his family that made him the most homesick boy at boarding school.

"First of our group to enlist, first killed. They found the poems of Robert Frost in his pack. And then there was Dick Westdahl. Dashing Dick, older than I—he was a counselor at the summer camp I went to and we became lifelong friends. Only about six years, actually. He was amazingly talented. Captain of his college boxing team, he taught me to box and play the piano and to appreciate literature and art. Battle of the Bulge."

I wiped my eyes with the back of my fingers and went on. "And Dick Young, my best friend at Yale, who never bought textbooks and spent most of his time in the bar and still got straight A's and was convinced he was going to be a coward in the war. But in Germany he went out to save a wounded friend and stepped on a mine. When they found him, he was reading a book—he was in shock and his leg was off at the hip and ten feet away." Damn, I was crying. Craig saw I was very moved and asked quietly, "And how did you feel when you heard of their deaths?"

"I told you, I felt terrible, awful."

"No, you didn't," Craig said in a steely voice. "You felt glad. We saw that syndrome all the time in the war. It's what most of your so-called battle-fatigue cases were."

I looked at him dumbly. *"Glad?"*

"Soldiers cracked up all the time over it. They were intensely sorry about their buddies, but they were also intensely glad, and that's what they couldn't handle."

"Glad?" I whispered again.

He reached across the desk and grabbed me firmly by the shoulder for emphasis. "You were glad it was *them*," he said fiercely, "and not *you!* That's why you felt guilty!"

A sob burst from me. I covered my face with my hands and cried as I hadn't cried in years. He didn't say anything for a while, just let me cry, and then when I had got hold of myself, he said quietly, "Why don't you go wash up for dinner, Barny? It's Saturday night at Betty Ford's."

TWELVE

Like Saturday night at boarding school, there was a festive atmosphere in the cafeteria; as in boarding school, we were looking forward to a special dinner, a movie afterward—and tomorrow was Sunday!

I found out quickly that I wasn't the only one who'd had an emotional afternoon; as we pushed our trays along the counter in line for roast beef, mashed potatoes, and peas, Dave Dixon, behind me, said in a low voice, "Hear about Morrie? He cracked in a session with his counselor today."

"No!"

"Broke down completely, apparently. Admitted he was drinking more than a quart of vodka a day, straight. And that was the only straight thing about his life—he's gay. There's no wife or daughter. He's here because his employer says he's out of a job if he didn't come for treatment. He's not in real estate; he's what you call a pre-need cemetery-lot salesman."

"That's sort of real estate," I said. "On a small scale."

"And he tried to commit suicide three times last year before the intervention that got him here."

"Poor bastard. Is he still planning on leaving?"

"I don't know. He's alone over at that table there."

We took our trays and wended our way through the tables of laughing and chatting people.

I almost didn't recognize Morrie. He wasn't wearing his reddish wig and his head glistened, only a few wisps of white hair at the sides marring its perfect baldness. Strange to say, he seemed younger without it, more like a real person, anyway. He was not a bad-looking man, I realized.

"Hi, Morrie," I said as I set my tray down. My gaze couldn't help but travel to his pate, and he noticed it.

"Toupee, or not toupee," he murmured with a weak smile. "That is no longer the question. Actually, the wonderful thing about being bald is that you can hear the snowflakes."

It was not his only attempt at his usual brash jauntiness during the meal; he essayed a few jibes at his counselor, "Captain Kangaroo": "Well—whatta you expect from a guy with teeth marks on his pencil?" And later: "I hope he jumps on his bicycle and finds that someone's stolen the seat!"

But mostly he stared dully at the untouched food in front of him, totally subdued. He was pale and drained, but on the other hand he seemed far more tranquil than we'd ever seen him. After coffee we stood up to leave and he blurted out, "All's I want to say is I'm sorry!"

"What for, Morrie?" said Dave.

"Sorry I told you guys so much shit that wasn't true," he said huskily.

"It doesn't matter," I said.

"I was conning you," he said. He was close to tears. "Conning everybody."

"That's okay," Dave said, putting a hand on his shoulder. "None of us is an angel. We love you as you are, Morrie."

He hugged both of us and the tears ran down his cheeks.

"I'm gonna stay awhile, give this place a real shot. All my life I've conned people, but I don't seem to be able to get away with it here. I love all you guys. I even love Captain Kangaroo."

We left Firestone and headed back to McCallum Hall for coffee. That line from the forgotten novel was still bugging the hell out of me. I wanted to be able to tell Craig the next time I saw him that I'd remembered it. Then I wouldn't have Korsakoff's syndrome, would I?

"Dave, you're encyclopedic," I said. " 'The past is a foreign country: they do things differently there.' "

"They do?"

Apparently he misread the signals and thought I wanted to play a round of Interesting Esoterica, for he countered brightly, "A starving octopus will eat its own tentacles!"

"Riveting," I said. "But this quote that's bothering me—it's the first sentence of a well-known novel. I just can't remember it."

"Sorry," he said. "Dixon's m'name and science's m'game."

At McCallum, several people were exercising the Saturday prerogative of watching TV—a giveaway program—and I thought with a pang that in four days my daughter Kendall's soap opera would be on, and I wouldn't be able to watch it.

Maybe if I did especially well on my jail essay on Monday, I could try asking Jerry again for special permission.

If only it were on a weekend! And there was no VCR unit to tape it here. I wondered if Mary had made arrangements with a friend to record it so I could see it when I got sprung.

I wanted to talk to her about that. About a lot of things. About how she was doing and how she was feeling without me. Maybe great, maybe terrific; I didn't like *that* thought too much. She said she was going on the wagon when I left, to back me up empathetically, and I wondered how that was progressing. Could she do it cold turkey where I could not? And I wondered how all the animals were, and if Kendall had snagged the modeling job in Paris, and what mail I'd received, and what people were saying about my being here in the looney bin, and if my agent had sold any writing so I could start paying my son back for this place's tuition, and all sorts of things that husbands and wives have to talk about. And right there was the pay phone, ten feet away, but I wasn't allowed to use it, not till Monday, day after tomorrow! A long, long time away.

I asked several people if they knew where that quote was from. It had assumed irrational importance to me. I asked where Tex was. We called him the Lone Ranger; he was laconic, reclusive, and extremely well read. He did crosswords as fast as he could read the clues. I found him in his room working on an assignment for Monday, chair tipped back, cowboy boots on the bed.

"Heard it, read it, and saw it," he drawled when I asked him about the line.

About fifty, he looked like a grizzled version of Gary Cooper, but in spite of his drawl, his big silver buckle, and his fancy rodeo shirt, he was a Ph.D. and an English teacher at Cornell.

"*Saw* it?" I asked.

"Yep. They made a movie of it. British, I believe. Flashed that sentence on the screen over the opening scene."

"What was the name of the movie?"

"Same as the book."

"What was the name of the book?"

"Danged if I know."

"Who wrote it?"

"Danged if I can remember. Why are you so all fired up to find out?"

I told him of my fears that my brain cells were permanently destroyed.

"Hell, man, how long you been dry? Just a few days! You don't have Korsakoff's. Listen here."

His long arm reached out and took a book from the pile on his desk. "Listen to what old Doc Pursch says." He read: "'Certain areas of the brain are responsible for how we act, think, and feel. Neuropsychological testing of these cognitive, affective, and motor areas shows the extent and source of the impairment. Actually, it measures the behavioral manifestations of brain disruptions rather than actual brain-cell destruction.

"'The difference here lies between destruction and damage. Impairment because of brain cell destruction, e.g., Korsakoff's psychosis or Wernicke's encephalopathy, is permanent because destroyed brain cells don't regenerate. But impairment because of swelling of the brain or damage to nerve pathways (which is common in alcoholism) *improves when drinking is stopped.* As the swelling subsides, or as the nerve connections regenerate, there is improved function and behavior."

"We are born with about ten billion brain cells, some of which we normally lose as we get older. Alcohol abuse substantially increases the normal rate of brain-cell loss, but it may take three to six months for brain function to return after drinking stops. I have seen improvement of brain function even after one year of not drinking. Undamaged areas of the brain seem to take on some of the functions of other areas of the brain that were destroyed, much like an employee taking on the added tasks of a co-worker who has left. But this never happens in the alcoholic who still drinks. He can only get worse.'

"So you see, buster," said Tex, "you just haven't given the old brain enough time to recoup. I've been dry three weeks and I can't think of that sucker who wrote that line either. I even used that book you're talking about in one of my classes, and I can't think of its name, but you don't see me worried none."

I thanked him and was somewhat relieved.

Tex said: "Heard a good story yesterday. Dorothy Parker and a friend went to see Fitzgerald lying in state in the funeral home. 'Don't he look just beautiful,' oohed the friend. 'Why shouldn't he,' says Dorothy, 'he hasn't had a drink in three days.'"

"Good story, but Fitzgerald was on the wagon when he died."

"Killjoy."

I left the room and went down the hall.

Hartley!

I ran back to Tex's room and stuck my head in the door. "Hartley!" I said. "L. P. Hartley!"

"Hot damn!" said Tex. "And what was the book?"

"The Go-Between!" I shouted jubilantly.

"Right on!" said Tex with a big grin. "Give that man an A for the semester and the cheerleader of his choice!"

I went off to the movie with a lighter step.

I soon found out that the Saturday night movies at the BFC were different from the ones way back in the days at the Taft prep school. No Madeleine Carroll–Ronald Colman or Flynn–de Havilland adventure stuff. But it *was* a romance, sort of. The film was called *Romance to Recovery* we read in the program as we waited for it to begin, and, surprise, it was about alcohol.

I sat in the lecture room with Chico, Beth, and Dave. I noticed that Morrie was sitting with Peter, the gay doctor. Morrie seemed animated and effusive. I could hear him saying, "I do *so* love the cinema, don't you, Petah?" He was Claude Rains. "My dear Rick, what in Heaven's name brought you to Casablanca?" Now he froze his lip to become Bogart. "My health. I came to Casablanca for the waters." And Claude again: "The waters? What waters? We are in the desert." Bogie: "I was misinformed."

Morrie roared at himself. "You and I were misinformed, too, Peter—there are no waters here in this bloody desert!"

Essex, the Texas coke addict, slinked in and sat across from

us. He was wearing an elaborate purple and gilt crown. I
asked Dave what that was for.

"King Baby syndrome," Dave whispered. "Has to wear it
for three days—teach him some humility."

I looked at Essex's frozen smile as he stared straight ahead
at the blank movie screen, his guardsman's mustache twitching ominously. As D. H. Lawrence wrote about an evil
matador, "He looked at me with his yellow eyes, and that
pleasant look which was really hate undreaming."

He looked ludicrous, embarrassed and furious, the way
Teddy Roosevelt might have had someone clapped this
crown on his head at a White House reception.

"I give Essex twenty-four hours more here," I said.

"Maximum," said Dave.

"On the other hand," Beth said, "look at Morrie and
Reena—they're still here."

Reena was in the front row and though she still wasn't
wearing any makeup, she looked serene and almost pretty.
Fat Willy and Terry were sitting together, and Moishe, the
Israeli roommate I seldom saw, was next to them. All sixty of
us were here; only a medical reason could excuse one from
any scheduled function, even the Saturday night movie.

Tonight there was a bonus. The man who had made the
film introduced it—none other than Dr. Joseph Pursch, perhaps the best-known expert on alcoholism in the country
because of his syndicated column, his book, and his successful treatment of Billy Carter and Betty Ford herself. He
was not connected directly to the Center, but his influence
was felt constantly throughout the world of alcohol and drug
addiction. He received an ovation as he walked up to the
podium, a quick, sleek, dapper man with a shock of white
hair. He spoke with a slight accent of his native Yugoslavia.
Talking rapidly and often humorously, he touched many
bases in his short introduction. He told of an experiment
working with sons of an alcoholic father mixed in with sons
of nonalcoholics. The boys were given whiskey-laden drinks,

and were then subjected to sway tests. Those with non-alcoholic fathers reacted to the alcohol and swayed quicker and more than the others, reinforcing the increasingly prevalent idea that there is an X factor in certain people that causes them to tolerate at first, and react differently to alcohol than nonalcoholics. Though equally drunk after six or seven drinks, the sons of alcoholic fathers hadn't received the warning signals that the other children had been getting on the way to intoxication.

He talked briefly about the bad news—the enormously high rate of alcoholism among doctors and pilots—but said that the good news was that once in treatment, the recovery rate was 93 percent. "They don't want to lose that precious license!"

He made several amusing derogatory remarks about the average doctor's ignorance of alcohol-related programs, adding, "Doctors often prescribe Valium for alcoholics on the assumption that alcoholics suffer from a Valium deficiency, as a result, the patient tends to smell better but he doesn't function any better."

"Regarding the theme of the film he was going to show, he stated that "no man is a drinking island."

He went to the blackboard and wrote a list:

> Family
> Friends
> Legal (Driving Under Influence citations)
> Money (increased health and
>   car insurance, etc.)
> Health
> Spiritual
> Job

"All of these are generally seriously affected by the alcoholic's drinking, as we shall see in the movie."

The film itself began and there was Dr. Pursch on the screen, standing in front of a large facade of a dollhouse. There were Dick and Jane in the windows of their rooms and the children, Richie and Janie, in theirs. In a lively fashion, Dr. Pursch told the story of Dick's drinking and how Jane "enabled" him, that is, unwittingly helped him continue to drink, covering up for him at the office when he was too hung over to go to work and lying for him in social matters. The wonderfully awful situations he devised for his characters elicited many laughs of recognition from his audience. But he made telling points about how the parents' behavior caused devastating changes in the children's lives, and how sick the whole family becomes as a result of putting up with the alcoholic's disease and hiding it instead of seeking treatment.

The film was a half hour long, but Dr. Pursch's magnetism made it seem half that length. There were questions afterward, deftly answered, and then the program was over.

"We're free!" said Beth. "Until Monday! Do you realize that?"

It felt good not to be racing to anything or hurriedly having to read or write anything. I had lots of homework due Monday, but I'd think about that later. It was only seven-thirty.

The others went back to McCallum to play charades or watch TV. I felt like neither. What I wanted was a book—a book that had nary a mention of ethanol in any form. No weighty thoughts, no message, just a good exciting story that I could lose myself in. No Robertson Davies, Herman Melville, or Saul Bellow tonight. It was Saturday! I could kill for a Robert Ludlum or my favorite suspense writer, Elmore Leonard.

I went into the little bookshop across from the cafeteria knowing I was licked, that every one of the dozens and dozens of books and booklets and pamphlets on the shelves is about alcohol, but I idled through them anyway. Mrs. Ford's book was prominently displayed and Dr. Pursch's "Dear Doc" and *Broken Promises, Mended Dreams* and that old faithful in a new edition, *The Lost Weekend*. ("You loved the movie, now enjoy the book!")

Then I saw a book entitled *The Courage to Change* by Dennis Wholey. On the cover it said "Personal conversations about alcoholism" with such famous people as Billy Carter, Sid Caesar, Jerry Falwell, Jason Robards, Rod Steiger, Wilbur Mills, and . . .

Elmore Leonard!

My favorite writer a drunk?

Well, I'd learned a long time ago that virtually all writers have or have had a booze problem, so it was no big surprise. And my prayers had been answered—I had something by Elmore Leonard to read, a Saturday night treat. I'd earned it, by God; after three whole days in this place I deserved it.

I bought the book and took it back to McCallum. When I came into the kitchen area, Beth and some others were peeling slices of pizza off the bottom of a cardboard container.

"Hey, Geezer," she called. "Have a slice! When are we going to do that portrait you promised?"

"Tomorrow," I said. "For sure."

"Charades in ten minutes," she said. "That's an order."

I went into my room, flopped down on my bed, and started leafing through the book. It all looked interesting. I sampled bits and pieces, phrases, and pages of the stories of these famous people who weren't afraid to come out and tell terrible things about themselves and about what they did when they were drunk or stoned. And there was wisdom and good advice from unlikely sources.

Grace Slick said, "If you think you have a problem with alcohol, you probably do. Because people who don't have a problem with alcohol don't think they have a problem with alcohol."

And Sid Caesar: "You know you're going to have a hangover in the morning. You know that. And in spite of that, you go on. That's punishment. Admit that nobody is pushing you to do it. It's happening because you let it happen. You want it to happen. 'Look at the drunk I am. Look how I fall down. Look how I vomit. Look at the foul language I use. Look at the fights I get into. Look how I punish myself. Look at what I'm doing.' This is calling attention to yourself in a negative way. Do you want to go through this? Do you want to debase yourself like this? For what? Is it worth what you're doing? Who are you getting even with?"

There were gripping accounts of alcoholic battles by the actor-writer Tom Tryon and by Jason Robards. I remember seeing Jason drunk with Lauren Bacall—we had lunch once in San Francisco at Enrico's sidewalk café, over twenty years ago—and I can remember thinking, Lord, how can he get that way out here in front of everyone, making everyone cringe with embarrassment.

And now here I was in the BFC reading about his miraculous rehabilitation after a near-fatal car accident.

There was an interview with Billy Carter, and I remembered Sterling Hayden, the actor-writer and recovering alcoholic, telling me once how upon reading that Billy was going into a rehabilitation center, he sent a telegram saying, "Congratulations—we haven't met, but as one who's been where you are now, I send my respect and good wishes." Then later that day, after several drinks and after mulling it over and realizing he had no particular reason to respect Carter, he wired again: "Disregard previous telegram. Forget the respect but keep the good wishes."

I flipped the pages to Elmore Leonard, author of the hard-hitting books *Stick, LaBrava,* and *Glitz.* His interview was totally candid and sounded like something from one of his books:

When I think back to my twenties, social events always had to involve drinking. If someone came by, I'd always offer him a drink. I would be happy to see people drop in because then I could have a drink. I didn't realize, until later, that I welcomed this excuse. Now I am amazed at how little people drink and that they leave a drink when dinner is ready.

I was getting more noticeably drunk. I wasn't handling it the way I used to be able to. In fact, I was two different people. There was a definite personality change, like talking louder, acting wackier, which I thought was a lot of fun. I'm being funny, I thought. This is really funny stuff. It wasn't funny at all. But everyone was always laughing. Most of the people were not too far behind me, but I had to admit that I drank more than almost anybody I knew. There were a few guys who would keep up with me, but the majority of our friends didn't drink half as much.

I tried to hide my drinking from myself. I would sit in my office—actually I had three offices. I had a refrigerator in the front office and in the middle office there was a kind of lounge. I had a bottle of sherry and little glasses there on the table. I would go in there and have a little glass of sherry from the decanter, then I'd have another one. After that, I'd get out the bottle and fill up the decanter to where it had been, in case anyone noticed. Then I'd get a cold bottle of white wine out of the refrigerator and put it in my desk drawer. I'd open the drawer very, very quietly, though no one was in the office, and take the wine out and drink a big, big swig of it and put it back in. Not a soul was near enough to hear anything. I didn't want to hear it.

In 1977 I was divorced. I wonder if the booze gave me the courage to leave home, to leave the situation I was in, having been married for twenty-six years. Now that I know what I know, I'm sure I would have done it in the right way with a clear head. But I did it drinking and got away with it. There were all kinds of reasons. The drinking did enter into it, there is no question about that. My first wife doesn't have a problem that I know of, but we always drank. We always drank together. We always drank before dinner. We always had wine with dinner. Every single night we would get into arguments, with me drunk and her part of the way, with me saying vicious things, which I couldn't believe the next day. I'd be filled with remorse.

I rested the book on my chest for a moment. I shut my eyes and saw the scenes. Boy, that was me and Mary. Get about half way through the dinner and the wine would start to take hold and suddenly I was saying things I didn't mean, words coming out of my mouth as though they had a life of their own, slashing and wounding and having no connection with the real me, or what I thought of as the real me when I was sober. And then maybe something Mary said would trigger a mean response in me and I might dump my plate on the floor or tip over the whole table and lurch out of the house hurling epithets and climb into my car and slam off into the night to the nearest bar, which is probably what I had in mind all along anyway. And then, as Elmore Leonard said, the remorse the next day. Oh, Lord, the *remorse.*

And as Sid Caesar said, why do it to yourself? Who are you getting even with? Who was I drinking *at?*

I wanted to read more in this book, but the ten minutes was up; it was time for charades. My eyes were so heavy. I closed them. I had to get up right away, right now; they were waiting. I used to like charades. I remembered when Mary and I were first married we used to . . .

When I awoke, it was Sunday morning and the sun was streaming in the room.

T H I R T E E N

"Sunday, Sweet Sunday, with nothing to do . . ." as the Rodgers and Hammerstein song begins. I lay in bed luxuriating in the not-having-to-get-upness. My roommate was sacked out, his matutinal devotions overlooked, possibly prayed out from the day before, catatonic in his bed with a pillow over his eyes, and only his hedgehog beard protruding.

How wonderful and refreshing to wake on a Sunday and not have the first thought be, Where the hell do you suppose I left the car?

It was eight-thirty and still time to make breakfast if one wanted to, and I wanted to. With the alcohol out of my system, I could smell and taste as though for the first time. All those false calories liquor had supplied were gone and what I craved was *food*. And sweets!

In the cafeteria this morning both were plentifully supplied by apple juice and oatmeal with brown sugar and waffles with syrup and English muffins and honey—lots of honey.

I walked into the seating area with my laden tray and saw Terry and almost didn't recognize her. She was sitting with Beth and was all fancied up for husband and daughter, the alleged child molester and acquiescent child, due in four hours. Wearing a plaid skirt instead of blue jeans, she had lipstick on and would have looked pretty if she didn't have a tense and worried pinch to her face. I sat down with them, saying, "Beautiful day."

"Bullshit," muttered Terry.

"So, today's the big day. Visitors!"

"If I live through it," Terry said darkly.

"When do they get here?"

"Lolita and Humbert Humbert? Not till one. I just might go over the wall before then. Or up it."

Beth touched her shoulder. "Probably will be better than you think. How about you, Geezer, got anyone coming?"

"No visitors allowed in the gulag on one's first Sunday," I replied.

"That's right. I don't have to worry either—my family's all in the East. Hey, we can do that portrait!"

"I don't have any materials."

"I do—charcoal pencils and paper. You missed some good charades last night! It was really funny. Peter seemed to draw all the dirty ones. He had to act out 'penis envy' and 'Dalkon Shield' and 'menopause,' and it was so funny, since he's gay and all. He almost died of embarrassment."

Essex was at a nearby table with his King Baby crown on, talking with Dave and seemingly more adjusted to the humiliating headpiece. "Just what is that syndrome?" I asked.

"Apparently drunks are particularly susceptible to it. Selfish arrogance. Goes back to infancy, when they get what they want when they want it. Instant gratification, attention *right now* for the little king, bottle *right now*, love *right now*, and to hell with what anyone else needs or wants. Sometimes carries over into maturity, whatever that is."

"André Malraux says he once met a priest who said that in fifteen years of hearing confessions he'd never encountered a grown-up."

"Speaking of that, you going to church? Dave's going."

She explained that there was a nonsectarian service held at ten for anyone who wished to go.

"You may not believe in God," said Terry like the trumpet of doom, "but God believes in you."

It was the only option I'd been offered since my arrival. "I think I'll skip it."

"Me, too," said Beth. "Let's do the portrait instead."

"I've got a great idea," I said. "Let's nobody mention alcohol or pills for the rest of the day. Any other subject but that."

"You're on. Spread the word. Not even an allusion to addiction. Death to all violators!"

But after breakfast when I went back to my room I found Dave had slid under my door some excerpts from a 1966 *Saturday Evening Post* article about Ernest Hemingway by A. E. Hotchner. (Where did Dave *find* these things?) And of course the parts he had bracketed were about alcohol. Dave had written across the top, "If only your hero had had a BFC to turn to! Think of the work he might have produced in his old age! He might even have *had* an old age!"

Hotchner told of Hemingway's decline in Spain in 1958, three years before the author's suicide:

> I hoped that when Ernest overstayed the closing of the bar that first night, it would prove to be an exception, but it wasn't. He drank heavily every night, Scotch or red wine, and he was invariably in bad shape when finally induced to go to his room. He passed up the things that used to attract him—young couples, gay girls, rough cafes, the bullfight people, the fireworks display, the street carnival—preferring to sit for hours in a rooted

position, with one or more listeners, not really caring who they were, sipping his drinks and talking, first coherently, then as the alcohol dissolved all continuity, his talk becoming repetitive, his speech slurred and disheveled.

Ernest's mornings, unassailably vibrant all his life, were now silent newspaper-and-tea convalescences. Ernest would joke it off when I came into his room. "Am a little pooped," he'd say. "Went five rounds with the Demon Rum last night and knocked him on his ass in one-fifty-five of the sixth." The morning drinks of tequila or vodka would partially restore him in time for his lunches with his mob, which he enjoyed, and he was back in full form by the time the bull-ring hour rolled around. . . .We all went on the terrace outside the bar and Ernest sent for a Scotch to ease him through the ordeal [newspaper interview].

From the beginning it was obvious that the reporter had never read anything Ernest had written. In a thick, sausage accent he asked, "Is this your first trip to Spain? Have you seen any bullfights before? Do you write your novels or dictate them?" Ernest was tolerant at first, but when the reporter asked, "How many women have you been in love with?" Ernest opened up.

"Black or white?"

"Well, how many of each?"

"Seventeen black, fourteen white." The reporter was getting it all down in his notebook.

"Which do you prefer?"

"White girls in the winter, black girls in the summer."

Ernest then made several efforts to ease off the questioning and leave, but the young German was wound up and insistent. Without warning, Ernest suddenly wheeled around and threw his whiskey in the face of the photographer.

"I told you no pictures, you son of a bitch!"

. . .That night Ernest got very drunk. He was argumentative with Mary [Hemingway] during dinner, which featured partridges he had bought in Segovia; he did not touch his. Mary left the table as soon as she could, leaving Ernest and me in the deserted dining room (it was offseason). Ernest talked endlessly and not too coherently about the war, while drinking several bottles of wine. His plans had been destroyed and he was taking solace in the past.

When I finally got him up to his room, he stopped in the hallway a few feet from his door and glowered at an electric wall-fixture. He suddenly went into a boxer's crouch, feinted with his left a few times, then hit the light with a neat right hook that broke the bulb and knocked the fixture onto the hall carpet. The metal tore a gash in his knuckle, which started to bleed, but he paid no attention to it. He put his other hand on my shoulder and looked at me intently. "Hotch, I been drunk one thousand five hundred and firty-seven times in my life, but never in the morning." He opened the door of his room and disappeared. . . .Mary and I stayed in the bar of the Palace Hotel while Ernest kept his appointment with Dr. Madinoveitia. I had never seen her so concerned about Ernest. She felt that drink had become something for him that it had never been before and she did not know how to cope with it.

"I try to hold him down, but no matter how tactful I am, Papa resents it as nagging and, as you know, he can't stand policing up. So, if anything, that aggravates the drinking and we wind up quarreling, which I hate, but what can I do? Not say anything? How can you stand by silently while someone you love is destroying himself? The things that used to sustain him—working, reading, planning, writing and receiving letters—they are fading away. He doesn't even have people around to lean on him and bring him their problems—Papa always liked that. Now there's just *his* problems and *his* hurts and a day-after-day depression."

These anecdotes saddened me. I had, of course, known that Hemingway had been a heavy drinker, but I hadn't realized how far the disease had progressed. Then I remembered George Plimpton's writing that the great writer's liver bulged out from his body like "a long fat leech." And, as Dave said, what if there had been a BFC then? Or was he too far gone by then? And was I too far gone by the time I'd arrived here?

That telling picture of Hemingway sitting there holding court, sip-sip-sipping, not caring who the audience was as he wallowed in the past. . . . I saw myself the last time I'd been in Pamplona, saw myself drinking with young people who'd read my books, holding forth on the current state of bullfighting, getting plastered, waking up at six in the morning, incredibly, in a field of sheep on the outskirts of town. The animals were in a circle around me, staring curiously at this strange creature in their midst and looking more concerned than hostile.

After a while Beth brought the drawing pad and charcoal to my room.

"Where do you want to do it?"

Moishe had gone, and it was quieter here and no gawkers, as there would have been in the lounge.

"Why not right here?"

She sat on the bed, and I drew the curtain and arranged the bedside light as best I could to achieve what they call Hollywood lighting—the source coming from slightly above and to the side, which put one side of the face in shadow except for the small traditional triangle of light on the cheek. She looked especially pretty today.

"Nice," I said as I pulled up a chair and began to draw. "Very Elizabeth Taylorish."

I had fun doing what I enjoy most, drawing and teaching.

She could see the sketch pad reflected in the mirror above the bureau and she watched the portrait develop with interest. I liked showing off for her.

"As you probably know, the eyes come halfway between the chin and the top of the head—hard to believe—and they are about an eye-width apart. Unless you're Jackie Onassis, and then they're two eye-widths apart; saw her in a restaurant once and couldn't believe the distance between the tear ducts. The tops of one's ears line up with eyebrows, ear lobes line up with nostrils. Bottom of nose about halfway between eyebrows and chin, mouth about halfway between nose and chin."

Beth talked about her art, mostly design, and her plans to study more and go into commercial art when she'd licked her addiction. She talked about her young husband, who had been so supportive and understanding of her alcoholic problem. She told me about her big Newfoundland dog, Fassbinder, that she missed so.

I thought about mentioning Chico and his confession, but to what end? As it happened she brought up the subject, how worried she was about Chico's restlessness, and how fond she was of him.

After about an hour and with a fairly creditable likeness emerging, the bedroom door was yanked open, and Laverne the tight-mouthed counselor stood there.

"What's going on here!" she demanded, scowling, her nostrils flared like a carousel horse.

I thought she was kidding and said brightly: "Welcome to the Betty Ford school of art, featuring portraiture by numbers, finger painting, and origami—two college credits and—"

The humor was lost.

"You realize," Laverne said ominously, "that you can both be bounced for this. You are in deep shit."

I started to explain, show her the portrait, but she snapped, "You may never go into the room of anyone of the opposite sex! For any reason! You know that!"

She turned and was gone.

Beth was bright red. "I feel as though I were back in high school and the principal's just caught me necking in the locker room."

"I feel like a dirty old man," I said.

Chastened and down in spirits, we left the portrait unfinished and went to make the circle before lunch.

After eating, several of us went to the already crowded swimming pool in bathing suits and luxuriated in the sun and wallowed in the rare privilege of the newspapers. Chico and several others were playing volleyball in the pool, the net stretched over the water; others were reading in the deck chairs, and some were entertaining family and visitors. I drew up a chair next to Dave's and told him about Beth's and my infraction.

"Do you think they'll kick us out?"

"No. But it will go on your record. Too many things like that and they'll withhold the medallion."

"Big deal."

"Just wait. After you've been here awhile you start to covet that thing more than the Croix de Guerre or the Maltese Falcon."

He suddenly looked over at the entrance to the pool area. "Well, glory be, there's Nurse Ratched and her monster we've been hearing about."

I saw Terry and an attractive, distinguished-looking, well-dressed man. Could this be the dreadful husband she'd told us about? The one who beat her regularly like a gong and seduced her fifteen-year-old daughter? It was easier to believe the daughter was as Terry had described her: She was a proper little Lolita, dressed in leopard leotards, with overly made-up eyes and a sulky lip-glossed mouth.

Terry, suddenly and uncharacteristically shy, introduced

us to them. He had an easygoing grin and a firm handshake; it was hard to imagine him as a wife beater and child molester. Had Terry made it all up? Maybe it came down to what the doctor had warned me so many days ago: The way you can tell when an alcoholic is lying is when you see his lips moving.

We made polite conversation for a few moments, and they moved on, and Dave and I went back to reading the *Los Angeles Times* and the San Diego newspaper. We read and talked idly about world affairs and books and films and never a word about alcohol or addiction. But then Dave blew it.

"Interesting stuff," he said, handing me a folded section of the newspaper. It was the ubiquitous Dr. Pursch and his syndicated column "Advice on Alcohol," answering some woman's problem with her husband. I sighed resignedly and read:

Most psychotherapists today agree that one-to-one therapy is not the answer for drinking alcoholics, especially if the focus of therapy is to find out why the alcoholic drinks.

I know a number of recovered alcoholics who are sober for 35 years or more. Most of them never found out why they drank. What they did learn was how not to drink anymore, and that's what kept them sober.

What your husband needs is to be in group therapy with other addicted patients who meet two or three times per week. This is most effective when the treatment emphasis is on current living problems and on how patients experience the world when they are not using alcohol or other mood-altering drugs.

The improvement in their psychosocial functioning is almost immediate because nobody can see through the defenses of an alcoholic/addict as quickly as another alcoholic/addict in a group setting in which the therapist

keeps the process on track by not allowing it to deterio-
rate into horror stories or sea stories. Also intra-group
manipulations have to be confronted immediately, and
psychoanalytic speculations discouraged very strongly.

I would cut that out and show it to the minister, tomorrow.
There was more, but I liked the ending of the column:

A more workable approach is that the alcoholic first
learn to live without alcohol or other drugs for at least a
year before he climbs on the psychoanalytic wagon in
search of why he was drinking. You don't look for the
cause of the fire when the building is ablaze; and you
don't teach navigation from the deck of a sinking ship.

So, the conversation turned once more to alcohol, and
there went the idyllic afternoon of *dolce far niente,* the
planned sweet-do-nothing time.

Like the little girl returning *Moby Dick* to the library because there was more in it about whales than she cared to
know, I was beginning to think that there was more about
alcohol around this place than I cared to know. I decided to
go back to my room to get away from it.

I took a dip in the pool and was just putting on my terry-
cloth robe when I saw Jerry coming across the lawn toward
the pool.

"There's a 'pigeon' in Firestone," she said. "Just arrived. I
want you and Dave to greet him, show him around, and take
him to his room."

"Who is he?"

"A very well-known inventor and businessman from
Boston. His name is Dr. Spenser Mark. Just arrived in his
Lear jet."

I felt honored to be asked to help someone else, being such
a newcomer to the program myself. Dave and I hurried

across the 200 yards of lawn to the central building. Our pigeon was in the main lobby leaning nonchalantly on the counter of the admissions office. I thought of how I'd been there in that position, sick and confused, just a few days before. Dr. Spenser Mark was wearing an English spy raincoat, complete with belt epaulets and shoulder flap, and next to his Gucci shoes was a Louis Vuitton suitcase. He was about fifty, and under his dapper Tyrolean hat, full gray sideburns protruded. He had the type of face and bearing that watery blue eyes should have belonged to, but his were brown with huge pupils, set in puffy flesh.

We introduced ourselves, and he replied in his crisp, refined tones, "Any nooky around here?"

Dave and I looked at each other. "Ah . . . well . . ."

"Where's the elevator?" he demanded. I noticed that he popped something in his mouth. "Elevator?" He gave me a withering look and said as though to a child:

"You know, up-down?"

"I'm afraid there isn't one," I said.

"No elevator?" He belched. "Christ, how do I get to my room?"

"The whole place is only one story, sir," said Dave. "We'll take you over to McCallum and introduce you to your roommate."

"Roommate!" he exclaimed. "I'm not putting up with any roommate! Where the hell is Mrs. Ford? I demand a single room."

"I'm afraid there are no single rooms in the place."

"You're not going to tell me Elizabeth Taylor had a roommate!"

"Three," David said. "She was in what we call the Swamp."

"Shit, she must have loathed every minute of it."

Dave shrugged. "She says she loved her roommates and liked the experience."

"Don't patronize me," he snarled. "None of that stuff, f'Chrissake."

I picked up his suitcase, and as we walked away from the counter, I started some small talk: "I know Boston's a big place, Doctor, but by any chance do you know my great friend, George Andrews?"

"Old Georgie Porgie?" I noticed the man was walking a little unsteadily. "Used to bang his wife! He doesn't quite make it on any level at all, does he? I'd say old Georgie's just one bubble off plumb." He suddenly went white and stopped. His hand went to his forehead. "Think . . . I think . . ." he said barely audibly, "just . . . sit for a minute . . . right here . . ."

He lurched toward a sofa, then spun and sagged backward, and before we could grab him, he crumpled, landing partially on and partially off the sofa.

"Quick," said Dave, lifting the man's legs onto the sofa. "Get a doctor!"

Dr. Mark's eyes were rolled back in his head, his tongue protruded, and he was marble-white. I ran to the elderly woman at the admissions desk. There was no doctor on the premises at this moment, but she called the paramedics at nearby Eisenhower Hospital, and they were there in a matter of minutes. They worked over the unconscious figure for a short while, then quickly lifted him onto a stretcher and rushed him out the door to the ambulance.

Upon later reflection, this incident probably illustrated for me better than anything the saying that alcohol is "cunning, powerful, and baffling." Not so much because the effects of the alcohol and pills the doctor had ingested that day before coming in to register had had such a devastatingly sudden effect, but rather because of how he was when he came back to the Betty Ford Center in six days after a close brush with death. This man, whom I'd perceived as the quintessential obnoxious boor in our first brief meeting, turned out to be, when sober, a gentle, sensitive, creative, and caring human being.

Many people before completing their programmed course

at BFC were convinced that a good part of that mysterious brew that Doctor Jekyll concocted in his laboratory was pure 90 proof ethanol; if not, its effects on a person's conduct and personality were very similar. Dr. Mark was in worse shape than I was when I came in, but, as with all alcoholics, it was a matter of degree.

F O U R T E E N

I woke up as usual to Moishe's muttered Hebraic prayers before the official waker-upper pounded on the door, and my first thought was, It's Monday. I get to call Mary this afternoon!

I realized that this was the longest time in twenty-four years that we'd been out of communication.

I started to plan what I was going to say to her, how I was going to compress all my feelings and all the things that had happened to me in these few days into a short conversation—short of necessity since there'd be the inevitable line of other people waiting impatiently to call on the pay phone.

The second thought was, Oh, Lord, my jail essay is due this morning at group therapy and I still have about three pages to go to finish the already very long saga.

I got up quickly, dressed, and managed to get some fast paragraphs written before the call to breakfast. I squeezed some more writing in before the mile-long walk, and during the walk itself I avoided Dave and Beth and Chico so that I could concentrate on how I'd end the piece.

There was a little time before the nine o'clock lecture and I managed to finish the job. I read it over and actually it seemed to flow pretty well, considering the conditions under which it had been written. It wasn't bad. In fact, I thought it was pretty good. Maybe when I got sprung from here I'd rework it and send it to the *New Yorker* or *Atlantic*. After all, nearly everyone had *almost* been arrested and jailed for drunken driving, hadn't they? Wouldn't they want to know what the experience was like if they'd been nailed as I had been?

I was counting on this article for a lot. I wanted to make a super impression on my counselor, Jerry, for many reasons: I needed to make up for the first assignment I'd done badly. I wanted to prove to her that I didn't have brain damage; I wanted to show her that I was working hard, taking the program seriously, was deserving of the medallion we were all working toward, and that I didn't need any more days added to my thirty-day "sentence." Also as a born ham, I wanted to interest her and entertain her as well as the rest of my peers.

And probably most of all, I wanted to soften her up so that I could ask her again for special permission to watch my daughter's acting debut on TV, which was only two days away.

As I made some last-minute changes and refinements, I felt sure that it would do the job. I was ready.

But first I had to go to the auditorium and sit through the lecture. It was Dr. West again, and as usual, he was fascinating, but I fidgeted as I did my best to concentrate and scribble some notes on the talk.

"Nature or nurture?" he began in his incisive, no-nonsense voice. "What do you people think?"

He paced up and down behind the podium as he spoke, almost musing, running his hand over his dark gray hair, his thick eyebrows frowning as though considering the problem for the first time.

"Is alcoholism hereditary or is it caused by environmental factors? Probably both of these factors play a role in the cause of alcoholism. By 'nature' we imply a genetic predisposition to alcoholism, and by 'nurture' we mean causation associated with environment."

"It is an established fact that alcoholism 'runs in families.' Among male or female alcoholics, studies show that rates of alcoholism among their male relations range from twenty-five to fifty percent and among their female relations, five to eight percent. These rates are at least five times what would be expected in the general population.

"According to Dr. Donald Goodwin, by most estimates at least one quarter of the fathers and brothers of alcoholics are likewise alcoholics. The lifelong expectation rate for alcoholism among men in the general population is from about three to five percent.

"Adoptive studies, wherein male infants with an alcoholic parent were adopted into a nonalcoholic home, show alcoholism occurred at the rate of four times that of the control groups.

"Heavy drinking was distinguished from alcoholism by a set of criteria for alcoholics, which includes social and occupational dysfunctioning, occurrence of withdrawal signs and symptoms, and loss of control. Alcoholism occurred relatively early in life, that is by the twenties or early thirties, and in this seemed to have a genetic predisposition, whereas heavy drinking did not seem to be genetically influenced.

"There is a subtle difference between heavy drinking and alcoholism."

The audience seemed to perk up here; a small voice in most of us was still saying, *"Hell, I'm not an alcoholic, I'm just a heavy drinker."*

"Characteristically, alcoholics are seen to have the behavioral characteristics of compulsion, loss of control, and a continued use in spite of adverse consequences. This is not true of heavy drinkers.

"A study reported by Dr. Goodwin shows that concordance for alcoholism among identical twins is fifty-four percent. Since identical twins have the same genetic makeup, the argument for hereditary predisposition seems to be reinforced.

"There are those who see alcoholism not so much as a result of genetic predisposition to alcoholism, but as a result of 'nurture.' They argue that genetic predisposition to alcoholism is difficult to prove conclusively. They propose that environmental and cultural factors play a major role in the development of alcoholism.

"Research is progressing and one day it may be clear what roles 'nature' and 'nurture' play. In the meanwhile, we see alcoholism as an interplay between susceptibility—genetic predisposition—environment, and exposure to the agent—alcohol. Thank you, and now get on with your recovery!"

At ten-thirty the seven of us in our group gathered in Jerry's office. (We would have been eight if an unexpected event hadn't happened to Dr. Spenser Mark on the way to recovery.) We drew up our chairs in a tight circle. I realized how I was noticing things much more when I saw that Jerry's eyes, which I had thought were blue, were actually hazel, and that the legs under the ultrasuede skirt were very well formed indeed.

"I'm Jerry," she started, "still and forever an alcoholic."

"Hi, Jerry!" we chorused.

"Terry, how'd visitors' day go?"

"Hi. I'm Terry, an addict and alky."

"Hi, Terry."

For once she didn't answer, "Bullshit." She was back in jeans and a denim shirt and no makeup and the usual hurt-angry look in her eyes.

"I'm okay." She squirmed in her seat. "Okay, I guess."

"He seemed like such a nice young man," Dave volunteered. "Different from what we expected."

She shot him a scornful sidelong glance. "Gimme a break! This guy is nice like Jack the Ripper's nice, the greatest bullshit artist since Barnum!"

"I take it you didn't have a good time," said Jerry. "And your daughter?"

Terry's mouth worked and no words came out and her face twisted and she struggled but still she couldn't speak, and Jerry reached over and put her hand on Terry's hand. "Stay after group," she said. "Skip aerobics and we'll talk."

She turned to her left. "And you, Willy? How'd it go with your father?"

"Fine," the architect answered. "Oh, I forgot. I'm Willy, a drug addict."

"Hi, Willy."

Just in the few days I'd been here he seemed thinner, less flushed, and calmer.

"Well, not fine exactly," he said, "but better. We can talk a little. Not much, but a little. Of course, my father doesn't understand anything, really. He figures he paid his six thousand bucks, I've been here almost four weeks, why aren't I cured? I must say I sorta feel that way, too."

"Recovery can take a long time," Jerry said. "True, we live in a microwave society—instant everything: instant coffee, instant sex, instant Cream of Wheat, McDonald's. But you've devoted years, the best years of your life, into making yourself an addict, the very best addict you knew how to create, honed and polished, and you can't just expect to completely undo all those patterns in a few weeks. But, Willy, you've made tremendous strides and I'm proud of you. If you could only see yourself the way you were when you lurched into this office a short time ago."

"Doesn't seem so short," Willy said with a grin. "Seems like a lifetime. But I'm going to make it. I already feel I'm a completely different person, a far better person. There's magic in this place."

"There is indeed," she said. "Tough love it's called." She turned to the perennially grinning young bearded surgeon from Chicago. "Bill?"

"I'm Bill and I'm a junkie."

"Hi, Bill!" chorused the group.

"How are you today?" Jerry asked.

"Depressed."

"Why are you grinning? You haven't said anything funny."

"I don't know." He blushed and grinned wider.

"It's a defense mechanism. Now tell me again how you are but without that, if you'll excuse the expression, that shit-eating grin."

"Okay," he said seriously. "I'm depressed."

"Depression is usually caused by anger turned inward and directed at oneself."

"It was just seeing everyone with visitors yesterday and here I am stuck in this gulag and my girl's two thousand miles away."

"What are you hearing, group?"

"Feeling sorry for himself," said Chico.

"On the pity pot," said Essex. He was beginning to pick up the language at least.

"I thought you'd broken up with your girl," said Jerry. "Sure it's not your mother you miss?"

Bill blushed—he was a blusher—but he didn't grin this time. He discussed the fact that at almost forty he still lived with his mother, his mother picked out his clothes for him, and, of course, liked none of his girlfriends.

"By day after tomorrow," said Jerry, making notes in her binder, "I want you to have discussed with five of your peers the possibility that your addiction might have been encouraged by your overdependency and conflicts with your mother. And I want you to record in detail theirs and your reactions. You know, Bill, as someone said, the most difficult secret for a man to keep is his own opinion of himself, and we all can see that you don't like yourself much. I'll bet the moment a girl shows any serious interest in you the old Groucho Marx syndrome rears its ugly head: 'I don't want to belong to a club that would allow members like me in it.' Right?"

Bill nodded.

"Sure!" she said. "Any girl who'd like a guy like you must have terrible taste or be crazy or slutty, so you find a way, subconsciously or not, to break it up and that's where mama comes in. I've got some stuff for you to read on that tonight."

She turned to me. "Barny, you're grasping something that looks longer than *War and Peace*. Your jail experience?"

I nodded.

"Read it, as much as we have time for."

I cleared my throat. "I'm Barny and I'm an alcoholic."

"Hi, Barny!"

I started to read, my voice high with nervousness.

So I went to the county jail to do my time, driven there by a quietly sniffling and compassionate wife. I waved good-bye, smiling bravely but weakly, at the big door, clutching my suitcase.

"Don't worry," my always optimistic lawyer, had said on the phone. "You'll go right to the honor farm; you'll like it!"

For the money I'd paid him I'd sort of expected him to come down and see me off, as it were.

"Books?" I asked. "Do they have books at the honor farm?"

"Of course. Great library, TV, exercise—just like what the Watergate boys got."

From the outside the great gray building on a hill outside Goleta didn't look any worse than any other administrative building. On the other hand, it didn't look like my idea of an honor farm either. Haldeman and Ehrlichman wouldn't have put up with it. I had no choice.

I presented my papers to a cute girl in a cop uniform at the desk.

"Honor farm," I said.

She smiled broadly. I seem to have made a good joke. She pressed a button, the barred door opened, I stepped in, and the door clanged behind me, making the same sound it had always made for Cagney and Pat O'Brien.

A burly cop—is burliness a prerequisite for copdom?—led me down a hall.

"Honor farm . . . ?" I began.

He smiled amiably and deposited me in front of a window where there was a line for fingerprinting. Another pretty girl—they seemed to be too pretty to be cops—took my fingerprints, another took my wallet, keys, watch, and belt. I was led down another dark corridor and into a brightly lit room with about five other men in various stages of undress, and behind a counter a bald genial man (everyone was so genial in this place) was taking civilian clothes and dispensing prison uniforms and plastic sandals. He pointed at the suitcase, and I put it on the counter.

"When do I get it back?" I asked as he took it and slung it in the back. "Let me get a book out of it!"

"Fuck off," he explained genially.

"No books? No library?"

That got a laugh from everyone.

"Stah-ripp!" the bald genial man snarled, and I stripped. The gray garb with "County Prison" stenciled on the back didn't fit, and I had to clutch it at the waist because they didn't issue belts; with a belt you could kill a guard, hang yourself, or garrote a casual acquaintance.

I began to think that maybe I wasn't at the honor farm. A terrible, terrible mistake had been made, in spite of all the money I had paid the lawyer. This feeling was reinforced when I and three others were herded down a hall and into a cell 15 by 20 feet where about ten other men were standing or lying or vomiting into the hole in the center that served as a latrine.

"What the hell are we doing here?" asked one of our group. A genial guard going by didn't answer.

There was no way of knowing what time it was since there were no clocks or windows. But we were there for many, many hours. The place was too small for everyone to lie down at once, so we took turns stretching out on the bare cement floor and leaning against the bars. The night was enlivened by drunken bellows from other cells and once by the screams of a skinny youth across the way being beaten by two big policemen. ("Oh God, I didn't do it! Stop, for God's sake. I'll never do it again, I didn't do it, oh, please, stop . . .")

By now I was almost positive that this wasn't the honor farm. It was a holding cell, but holding for what and for how long? There was a nice-looking crew-cut college type squatting next to me waiting his turn to lie down.

"What are we waiting in here for?" I asked. "Honor farm?"

He smiled a wry smile. "You've got a good sense of humor."

I wasn't feeling very funny. "What are you in for?" I asked. "502?"

It has had a new number for some time, but people still call it a 502, or a DUI—Driving Under Influence.

"No," he said offhandedly. "Manslaughter."

It was terrible not being able to see the sky. Unlike Oscar Wilde in *Reading Gaol*, I had no window in order to look:

> With such a wistful eye
> Upon that little tent of blue

211

Which prisoners call the sky,
And at every drifting cloud that went
With sails of silver by.

Dawn finally came. I knew it was dawn because a guard came and unlocked the door and announced, "Chow, you lucky bastards," and Manslaughter said, "Five o'clock," as we got in line in the corridor. We walked single-file down a long slanted tunnel into a big brightly lit room filled with other prisoners eating at benches. I got a tray with different-shaped depressions in it and shuffled behind Manslaughter along a counter. Disembodied hands reached out from under a partition and slopped watery oatmeal, burned toast, leathery scrambled eggs, and greasy hash browns on the tray. I ate some of the oatmeal and drank the carton of milk.

During breakfast I wanted to ask my new friend what man he'd slaughtered and what a nice guy like him was doing in a place like this, but we just ate in silence.

When we were through and were marched back, a guard said to follow him and we were given a bedroll and a comb and toothbrush and led to a new cell. Club Med it was not, but it *was* much bigger and brighter. That was the good news. The bad was that there were already 35 people in it, their gray pallets almost touching each other. Through the haze of cigarette smoke, I found a narrow space between a gigantic fat Mexican and a muscular black.

The Mexican smelled of a variety of odors, like a pet shop, and the black had a scar that ran down his face from his forehead to his chin like a zipper. I had the distinct feeling that neither of them was in here for spraying graffiti on walls or spitting in the subway. I said hello and they grunted as I spread out the two-inch-thin "mattress."

The black was reading a book.

"They told me no books," I said.

"They'll give you a Bible if you ask for it. Trouble is they won't give me my glasses, so I can barely read it. They figure you can cut your wrists with lenses."

I looked around. No windows, three seatless toilets on a dais at the end of the room, five shower heads, guards walking by the bars about every twenty minutes.

"What are you in for?" I asked the Mexican.

"Liquor store," he said laconically.

I turned to the black.

"Me? B and E."

I looked quizzical.

"Breakin' and enterin'." He winked. "I was framed."

"How about you?" asked the Mexican.

I was almost embarrassed at the tameness of my crime. "502."

The black yawned and returned to his Bible. "Figured," he said contemptuously.

I went to wash my hands, clutching my beltless pants and watching my step as I made my way gingerly around bodies. There was no soap, no paper towels, no toilet paper, and one safety razor to be used by all the men in turn.

"Is it always like this?" I asked when I returned to my place.

The Mexican shrugged. "Lot of new customers this week for some reason.

I watched the man take a Hershey bar and eat it. I yearned for it.

"How do you get one?" I asked.

"They's ways," said the black.

I watched a young Mexican across the aisle trying to draw an eagle on a pad. He was copying a photo from a newspaper clipping and having a terrible time of it. After the third total erasure, the pedagogue in me could stand it no longer.

I went over to him. "Give you a hand?"

He looked up at me uncomprehendingly.

"Quiere usted que le ayude?" I ventured.

He nodded, suspiciously. I sat down, took his pencil, and began to draw. I like to draw birds, especially raptors, and it came out pretty well under the circumstances. Wide-eyed with admiration, the man said, *"Mil gracias,* Professor. My girl will think I'm great."

From under his pillow he fished out a package of cigarettes. *"Gracias,"* I said, "but I don't smoke."

Out came two Hershey bars. "Weeth or weethout nuts?"

"Weeth," I heard myself say. I was ravenous, and practically snatched it out of his hand. Nothing from the Tour d'Argent could have tasted as good. I wondered if he had a little bottle of Old Verdugo under that pillow—a drink of anything would have gone great about then.

My new amigo showed his eagle around to his neighbors. A Yul Brynnerish head from an adjacent mat said shyly, "Can you do a picture of me for my wife? I don't got no Hershey bars but I got soap, lotta soap."

I took my time on the portrait—I wanted that soap. I spent half an hour on it and had a little crowd behind me by the time I'd finished. Then I did another for a roll of toilet paper. I stashed my loot under my pillow, an inviolate place, I gathered. Suddenly I was aware of a figure making his way toward me. Although only about 5'4", he was an imposing figure, and I noticed how people deferred to him and stepped out of his way.

"They call me Buff," he said quietly, extending his hand. He was a distinguished-looking man of about 65, somehow natty even in prison garb, and his shoulder-length yellow-gray hair was neatly groomed, as were his mustache and goatee. Of another era, it was easy to see why he was called Buffalo Bill.

He looked at my three commissions thoughtfully, nodded his approval and, like a Borgia to Michelangelo, he commanded, "Do me."

Clearly here was the boss of the cell block.

I've done perhaps 600 professional portraits since starting at 15—everyone from Manolete to Steinbeck to William F. Buckley, Jr. Yet I sensed that my portrait of Buffalo Bill could well turn out to be one of my more important assignments.

I set to with a will. I would put him in a beaded, fringed buckskin shirt. He stood and I sat so that I drew him from below, and therefore he looked nine feet tall and heroic and exactly like William F. Cody with his narrowed eyes focused on charging Indians or on some stampeding buffalo or on Annie Oakley.

I took two hours to do it, and as I drew I wondered what he could have done to land in jail; it certainly couldn't be anything as mundane as drunken driving. I finally asked him during a break in the posing.

"Safe," he replied flatly. "One lousy safe, and I drew thirteen years."

"Safe? You"—I searched for the right word—"you blew a safe?"

"Didn't blow it," he said. "Just plumb took it. Out of a fourth-story office in Phoenix. Used a crane, plain daylight on a Sunday morning." He was clearly proud of the caper. "Hauled a grand piano box empty up one side of the building, took it down full on the other side. Me and my partner split forty thousand bucks—some politicos paid us to do it."

"What was in it?"

"Never did ask. Some kind of papers. Must have been important—they said something about Goldwater. I just opened it up for them, took the money, and split."

"How'd you get caught?"

"Partner got picked up in Honolulu—ratted."

"I guess you guys aren't exactly speaking to each other," I commented.

He hesitated. "Let's put it this way," he said quietly. "He's not speaking to anyone."

We finished the portrait and he studied it. Several of the inmates watched his face and awaited his reaction expectantly. Finally he nodded his approval and smiled and everyone smiled, and I smiled. And with reason—it was good; it could have enhanced the back bar of any saloon in the West, could have graced any beer ad and taken its place next to Custer's Last Stand. Buff took it on a slow triumphal tour around the cell and was greeted with respectful attention at each pallet stop and murmurs of admiration.

He took out a blue canvas sack from under his pillow, extricated a roll of Scotch tape, and attached the drawing to the wall above him about where his head would be if he were as tall as the portrait indicated he was.

He motioned me to come over to his pallet and sit next to him. He handed me an apple and a banana.

"How do you get this stuff?" I asked as I wolfed it down. "Couldn't eat the food."

"Time and knowing the guards," he said. "You'll get store privileges after a bit. What else you need?"

"I'd like to make a phone call to my lawyer."

"Ha," said another prisoner. "I been here two months and no call."

Buff rubbed his goatee. "We'll get you one in a week or two. What else?"

"I sure would like a shave," I said. "That thing up there is rusty and blunt as hell."

Buff motioned a young prisoner over to get the razor. He examined the blade. "Terrible."

"How come they take away belts and shoelaces and leave a razor?" I asked.

A prisoner next to us said, "Man, that there's solid state—can't nobody get the blade out. Not even Buff."

Buff studied the handle of the razor for a moment. "I can get it out in five minutes."

The other prisoner said, "Two packs says you can't."

Buff answered, "Five packs says you just made a bad bet."

Buff took a stick of chewing gum from his sack, chewed it a moment, then put a tiny piece on the end of a wooden match. Then he inserted it all the way into the small hole in the end of the razor's handle. He withdrew it, now with the impression of a minute Phillips screw head in the gum. He found a nail file in his sack and carefully filed the end of another match in duplication of the impression. Then, inserting the match into the handle, he gently turned it. In a moment the blade tinkled to the cement floor.

Buff handed it to the prisoner, saying, "Here, cut your wrists."

The other prisoner shook his head in admiration and handed over five packages of cigarettes.

The miraculous sack produced a new blade. Buff installed it and handed it to me. "You been in jail long as I have, you learn things."

"How long is that?" I asked.

"Did thirteen years in the Arizona pen. Was doing my final six months at the honor farm here in Santa Barbara. Then, like a fool, I couldn't wait. Wanted to see my wife, went over the fence. Free a week, then my brother-in-law turned me in and they gave me another six months in here." His eyes went into slits and he no longer looked like a distinguished older gentleman but a confirmed and dangerous criminal. "Now I got me twenty-eight days left—twenty-eight days and six hours left—before I see that sonofabitch!"

From the set of his jaw and the look in those diamondback eyes, I would not have liked to have been his brother-in-law.

"Where *is* the honor farm? I thought I was going there."

"Right near here," he said. "Must have been a foul-up, Professor. I'll talk to the guards in a few days. It's better'n here, that's for sure."

As we were talking, several prisoners came up to admire the portrait.

"Man, Professor, that sure is good."

"Looks like a goddamn *photygraph!*"

"Prettier'n you, Buff. Makes you look almost honest."

"Ought to be on a friggin' postage stamp."

It would appear that I'd created the greatest piece of prison-inspired artistic endeavor since the *Ballad of Reading Gaol.* Wow, my teachers back at Taft and Yale and my beloved parents and my grandfather, the judge who'd sent so many people to places like this, would all be so delighted to see me now, little Barny Conrad, barely sixty years old, only 13 days left to go in here, incarcerated less than 24 hours, and already the pride of the Santa Barbara County Jail!

How could I have ended up in this place? One word— alcohol. The End.

I stopped and looked around me, smiling. There was silence instead of the applause I'd sort of expected, counted on, yearned for.

Jerry sighed. "Well, group, what do you think?"

Terry, reliable old Terry, was first, of course. "Bullshit!"

"Why?" asked the counselor. "Why do you say that, Terry?"

"I don't believe all that happened. And I think he wrote it not to tell us about the evils that alcohol can lead you to but to show how good he was at drawing!"

"I agree," Essex jumped in with a will. "Showin' off!"

"And racist," said Chico. "How come only the Mexican guy smelled bad? And that 'weeth or weethout nuts' crap—some of us speak English pretty well, you know!"

"Yeah?" I said hotly in injured retaliation. "Well this guy didn't happen to! He was—"

"Shhh, Barny, be quiet and listen to your peers!" said Jerry. "Dave?"

Good old Dave—he wouldn't let me down.

"Well," Dave started reluctantly, "the article is lively enough, frivolously amusing, but what really has it got to do with addiction?"

"Exactly," said Jerry. "It is not acceptable the way it is. Barny. I didn't ask you to write a screenplay or a magazine article. I didn't ask you to amuse me. These exercises are for *you*, not for me! *You're* the sick person. Forget about impressing me! Stop being a people-pleaser for once in your life and concentrate on your recovery! I wanted you to dig down deep into yourself and scrounge up some *feelings*. For example, how did you feel when you heard the barred door slam? When you were fingerprinted? When you said good-bye to your wife? Didn't you feel humiliated, embarrassed, afraid, guilty, and so on?"

I nodded numbly. "All of those things."

"And how did she feel and how did you feel when you got out of jail?" Jerry made some notes in her binder. "I want you to do it over and this time concentrate on your emotions, those feelings of yours that are dead or buried, like every alcoholic's." She studied her assignment book. "I'm also missing your journal entries for the last two days and the rewrite on your first assignment. Where are they?"

Oh, Lord. I'd been so engrossed in the jail thing I'd totally forgotten the other work. "I don't have them. Forgot."

"You didn't forget," she said, "you hoped *I'd* forget!"

I flushed under the scolding. I had not really forgotten—

219

she was right. My intent, as it had been through much of my life, was like Paul Theroux's advice to the expatriate in Singapore: "Gain a modest reputation for being unreliable and you will never be asked to do a thing."

She shook her head. "You are in deep trouble. You know, in half an hour we're having Bradshaw's graduation ceremony—he's been here six weeks and he's graduating, sort of. But his attitude has been flip and casual and his homework has been shoddy, so we're not giving him the medallion. If he can come back in six months and prove he's earned it, we'll give it to him. The same thing can happen to you, or worse—no graduation at all. I want all your assignments, back work and all, done by day after tomorrow."

She slapped her knees. "Okay, Dave, lead us in the Serenity Prayer, and then we'll break up till this afternoon."

I was fatigued with depression, way down, as we filed out of Jerry's office. It was certainly no time to ask if I could be allowed special permission to see my daughter's TV program on Wednesday.

Dave said, apologetically, "Barny, I hope I wasn't too—"

"I know, I know," I said, angry, brushing him off, "rigorous honesty at any cost."

"It's called tough love," Dave protested.

"It's called tough shit!" I shot back over my shoulder.

When I got to the lounge and saw the telephone, I brightened. I could call Mary! At least I had that! I went eagerly to the pay phone, which was on the wall across from the little glass office of Laverne, the acerbic counselor. There was no line yet. I had a quarter and was asking the operator to reverse the call when Laverne herself materialized beside me. She jabbed the phone hook down.

"No calls for you," she ordered.

"Why not?" I sputtered. "It's the fifth day!"

"Rules say very clearly 'after five days.' Barny, you'd better start getting the rules straight in your head or you're going to be out of here on another part of your anatomy. First the room violation, fraternizing, and now this. You'll probably end up like Bradshaw—not getting a medallion."

She strode off. It isn't fair, I thought, as I slowly hung up the phone.

FIFTEEN

The next day was Tuesday and I woke up feeling full of what the Portuguese and Brazilians call *saudades,* a treasured, untranslatable word that roughly means fraught with yearnings, longings, angst, the blues, and nostalgic disquietude. I finally was allowed my coveted telephone call, and I could stop feeling sorry for myself. But what I felt, unaccountably, was apprehension. I would have my call, but not before going through the usual strenuous BFC workday.

In the morning we had a lecture by a media analyst, a female doctor from New York, who told us what we already knew—that alcohol was America's number one hard drug for all ages. She also told us that 25 teenagers die every day from alcohol, that alcohol is the number one cause of fetal abnormalities, that one in every 800 children is born defective because of a drinking pregnant mother, and that 63 percent of all patients in veterans hospitals are there because of liquor-related reasons. And yet, she said, the liquor, wine, and beer industry spends over $900 million annually on advertising to induce people to drink more!

"There were over six hundred beer spots on television on New Year's day alone for the five different bowl games," she stated. "High on the list that the media is targeting are women, minorities, the young people aged sixteen to twenty-five, and alcoholics. Yes, alcoholics. Twenty-seven percent of our nation's drinking-age population consumes ninety-three percent of all the alcohol, and the liquor industry knows damn well who their biggest consumer group is—drunks, alcohol abusers, and borderline problem drinkers.

"What alcohol ads are really selling us is happiness, wealth, prestige, sophistication, success, maturity, athletic prowess, virility or femininity, and creativity—precisely the attributes and qualities that any sane person knows are the very things that too much alcohol actually diminishes and destroys!"

She showed dozens of slides of close-ups of magazine ads, and then proceeded to go behind the scenes to where the seductive ads begin on the drawing table. She showed us how much time and attention is given to each detail, color, composition, theme, and message. She demonstrated that the use of subliminal advertising—the use of hidden images, usually sexual, works on our subconscious in the few seconds we look at the ad but are not recognized by our conscious mind or eye.

"Only when a few square inches of the ads are blown up on film—as in this slide showing the swirls in the old-fashioned glass—are we aware of the disguised images. Look at the phallic patterns and breastlike forms subtly painted into the ice in the glass in this next picture. The technique is designed, of course, to associate certain characteristics and blandishments with that particular product and make the viewer eager to purchase it. By using hidden sexual images, virility or feminine allure is implied as being inherent in the ingestion of this brand of alcohol."

As she turned off the slide machine she concluded, "What

virtually every liquor ad is in effect saying is, 'Look, sir or madam, if you want to get laid in rich and respected and fun surroundings, get plastered on our product.' They should add, 'Remember, nondrinking is hazardous to the liquor industry's health!'"

"Actually, we don't know how well it works or how effective that subliminal technique is, but it does show you that the liquor industry and the advertising companies are out to try every trick, every inducement, to create as many new candidates as possible for rehabilitation centers like this. As kind of a bone thrown to a small outraged segment of society, we occasionally see liquor ads urging moderation in drinking. I saw a cartoon recently of a lawyer defending his hung-over, contrite client, saying to the judge, 'My client was just trying to do something to stem the decline in the consumption of hard liquor.' We read regular reports that quote hard-liquor sales are down, Americans are drinking more wine and less whiskey, unquote. Just wine? Big deal! For fun, how many people here have ever gotten bombed on '*just* wine'?"

Nearly every hand in the auditorium went up.

"*Just* beer?"

Every hand went up.

"Don't you love it?" said the speaker. "They show a beer or wine ad on TV and right after it comes an ad for some new alcoholic rehabilitation facility! If alcoholism is down in the U.S., how come all these new clinics are springing up all over the country, how come this wonderful Betty Ford Center is having to expand? I blame a lot of it on the American advertising community and the liquor manufacturers of the world. Of course I wouldn't outlaw drinking—too many people enjoy and know how to use alcohol sensibly. But the fact is there are at least ten million alcoholics in America—closer to twenty million probably. If I had my druthers, I'd make it mandatory for every container of whiskey, wine, and beer to bear this simple little unmistakable warning message from the Surgeon General, exactly like any other poison." She unfolded a large piece of paper that had a black skull and crossbones painted on it. "That's *my* idea of a constructive subliminal message! I thank you." She sat down to applause.

As we filed out of the auditorium, Morrie, the real estate man, grabbed me by the arm and said in his hoarse voice; "Guy's in the hospital in total bandages, arms, legs, everything, says, 'Doc whatta you mean I'm gonna be fine; ya mean I'll be able to play the violin when I get out?' An' the Doc says, 'Of course,' an' the guy says, 'That's great, Doc. I've always wanted to play the violin!'"

He guffawed and slapped me on the shoulder.

"You look terrific, Morrie," I said. He did, too, except for the new salmon-pink sunburn on the top of his toupeeless head.

"Really good," said Dave.

"Never better," said Morrie with a wink. "You see, I can't die until the government finds some safe place to bury my liver, so I'm planning to live forever!"

He hurried off to catch up with Peter. I saw Mrs. Ford heading for her office and she smiled. "Everything all right?"

"Fine," I answered. "Thank you."

That's all she said, but I had the feeling that if I had indicated that everything wasn't all right, she would have wanted to know why and wanted to do something about it.

At group, I turned in all my work that was past due plus a rework of the jail essay with the emphasis being on my feelings—the anger, mortification, and humiliation I'd felt on going in, the loneliness and desperation once incarcerated, and the intense sense of relief coupled with guilt and remorse upon being released.

Jerry didn't comment upon my submissions. In fact, I was left alone during the whole session; the focus was on Essex. He was still wearing that ridiculous crown.

"Essex, how are you today?" Jerry asked.

The answer was barely audible. "Down, real down."

"Who are you?" she reprimanded him. "Forgot to tell us."

"I'm Essex and I'm a bad-assed drunk and addict," he mumbled.

"And dealer," said Jerry.

"And dealer," he conceded in a whisper.

"Hi, Essex!" we chorused.

There was something different about him. It wasn't just that his tough, arrogant, bullying manner was toned way down; it was his flamboyant mustache. It had been trimmed to ordinary, almost eyebrow proportions. Without it, and without the menacing grin, he no longer looked like Teddy Roosevelt. He looked like an aging, confused country boy from Texas who had come too far too fast and was equipped with too little to cope with the fast lane he'd found himself in.

Jerry riffled through the man's exercise notebook. "Essex, I read your long assignment this morning. I think it was a great effort for you to write about your mother's death when you were ten. It was very moving and too private for me to read aloud here. Your father's physical and mental brutality makes me understand many things about you now. It's amazing that you've survived as well as you have. I wasn't at all sure we could help you here, couldn't believe you could be truly honest with yourself. But the candid account in here of your two marriages and your touching relationship with your children has convinced me that you can make it. And we're going to help you."

Essex's head was bowed and a brief sob came from him.

"Are we going to help him, group?" Jerry asked.

"Yes!" came back strongly.

"Tell him then!"

"We love you, Essex!"

"We'll help you, Essex. We love you!"

The big man's shoulders shook convulsively. Chico and Bill, on either side of him, put their arms around him. Sobs like groans came from his heaving chest. We all stood up and surrounded him, including Jerry, and held him tightly for a long moment.

Then we all sat down, and Essex tried to compose himself. "Thank you," he said hoarsely. "Thank you."

"There's a lot of love in this room for you," said Jerry. "I think you can feel it."

Essex blew his nose on his bandanna. "That there's a commodity I don't know a hell of a lot about. Never dealt that."

We laughed with him.

"You'll learn," said Jerry, smiling. "And take that silly crown off your head."

After the group meeting I stayed, and Jerry handed me my new assignments for the coming week:

Goal: To gain an awareness of humility completely:

1. Name 20 ways I have tried to build up my ego—describe how it has been self-defeating.

2. Read *Ego Factors in Surrender*. Tell 2 peers daily for 5 days how I identify. Get feedbacks. Describe in journal.

3. Ask 2 peers daily for 5 days how they see me being arrogant and grandiose. Ask them to write this in my journal.

I put the paper in my notebook, saying, "I have plenty of faults, Jerry, but I don't think grandiosity is one of them."

"It has a slightly different connotation when applied to an alcoholic—grandiose in the sense more of false pride. You'll read about it. You'll recognize yourself."

As I headed out the door she said casually, "How long is that TV program tomorrow?"

I felt a jump in my chest. I started to say "Half an hour" to minimize the time spent away from my assignments. But then, the damned phrase "rigorous honesty" intruded in the back of my mind.

"One hour," I said flatly.

"One whole hour?" she said, shaking her head. "And your daughter has a big part in it?"

I almost replied "She has the lead" to make my seeing it

227

seem more urgent. But again "rigorous honesty," that damnable phrase, stepped in.

"Only a few lines, I'm afraid."

"Well. We'll see," she said. "But I'm not promising anything."

I left the office with tears in my eyes. There was a chance!

During the afternoon session with the minister, I told him about the big change in Essex.

"Looks like God at work," nodded Craig. "His Higher Power making Himself known."

"To me it looks like the BFC at work," I said.

"Well, who got him to come here?" Craig said. "And how did the BFC come into being? It just didn't happen, you know, any more than Betty Ford and her recovery just happened."

He lit his pipe and went through the files and notes in front of him. "What do you think about death? As we noted before, you seem to have had a preoccupation with it the past few years."

"I don't think about it now in here," I said, "though when drinking heavier than usual my anxieties used to turn into impending doom. Especially about three in the morning."

"Like most alcoholics," he said. "And what is death in your lexicon?"

"Well, as Groucho said, 'It's no big deal—thousands of people are doing it every day.'"

"Seriously."

"He was serious—he said it when he was dying."

"But what do *you* think death is?"

"A big sleep. I don't remember anything before I got here on earth and I don't expect to remember anything afterward. As Nabokov says, common sense tells us that our existence is but a brief crack of light between two eternities of darkness."

"Ah, simplicity itself, like the ancient Epicurus saying, 'Death is nothing to us, since when we *are*, death has not come, and when death has come, we are *not*." He puffed on his pipe. "Wouldn't it be strange, if, as Plato says—think it was Plato—'Supposing we were to find out that what we call Death is really Life and what we call Life is really Death'?"

This was getting too heavy for me so I kept quiet.

He flipped through his notes. "At one point you were going to tell me about this nightclub. How did that come about? Why on earth did you start a saloon?"

"El Matador was more of a salon than a saloon," I said. "Kind of a way of life in itself. For about ten years it was the most popular place in San Francisco nightlife. I always wanted to create a great bar, like the one in Saroyan's *Time of Your Life*, you know, a friendly casual place where great characters and gorgeous girls and literary types and actors would stroll in and explorers back from trips would spin yarns, and—"

"And where you, as the proprietor, would be the center of this little utopia?"

"I think a lot of people have dreamt of having a bar or restaurant. Does it have to be an ego trip? I've always enjoyed bars and nightclubs."

"Sure you have. Like when they asked the master thief Willie Sutton why he robbed banks he answered simply, that's where the money is! In your case, a bar's where the booze is."

"And good fellowship," I protested. "You could drink at home, but you wouldn't have the companionship."

"But just how good were those friends you made in those settings? How'd they look in the cold light of day? I'll bet your drinking chums were seldom your intellectual peers, and when you get out of here and they find out you're not drinking, they'll shun you as though you had AIDS. You're a threat to them and their life-style now."

I answered defensively. "Samuel Johnson said something to the effect that nothing yet invented by man produces so much happiness as a good tavern."

"Don't you think your tavern also produced a lot of *un*happiness? Misbegotten relationships, domestic quarrels, idleness, hangovers, to say nothing of cirrhosis?"

"I had a lot of good times there for a while. And it was a fine way to get out of the house and have fun. All kinds of fabulous people came in the Matador, and I admit to being fame-struck. I find it very stimulating to be with people who are at the top of their profession, no matter what it might be. Everyone who was anyone who came to San Francisco from 1952 to about 1962 dropped in my place."

"Who's everyone?"

"I can drop just about any name you care to hear, from the world's champion cowboy or tennis player or bullfighter or gangster or opera star or boxer. Glamorous women, like Ingrid Bergman, Hedy Lamarr, the Gabors. Over the decade our clients included such people as Tyrone Power, Sinatra, Mickey Cohen, Duke Ellington, Crosby, Judy Garland, Governor Brown, and Ronald Reagan. I especially enjoyed the literary people, like Brendan Behan, Noel Coward, Irwin Shaw, Alex Haley, Kerouac, William F. Buckley, Budd Schulberg, Alistair Cooke, Saroyan, and on and on." And as long as I was dropping names, I added: "Music has always meant a lot to me, especially the pianists, and some of the great ones would drop in and play—Ellington, Tatum, Shearing, Garner, Short, Bushkin."

"And it made you feel like a big shot to be with those big shots, to have them deign to come to your place, to sit with you?"

"I suppose so, sure."

"And you drank with them, got drunk with them?"

"I tried to pace myself, tried not to get tight on the job. Besides, I had a fifteen-mile drive across the Golden Gate Bridge every night to get home. Cops all over the place."

"But you were drinking?"

"Oh, yes, I was drinking."

"And women?"

"A plethora."

"Your general outlook on life at this time?"

"Bloodshot."

"How did Dale like your being in your saloon every night."

"Hated it. She wanted a place in the country, horses, the kids, the simple life. She was a serious, studious, private woman. Long after the divorce she went to architecture school at Stanford, when she was 45, graduated first in her class."

"You admire her?"

"Greatly."

"And Mary?"

"She's"—I stopped and thought. "She's athletic, fun-loving, impetuous, adaptable, loyal, volatile, efficient, high-strung, staunch, and—and beautiful." Then I added, "And outgoing and resourceful and ready to go anyplace with me on five minutes notice."

"Overlooked anything?"

"And impatient. And insecure."

"Run out of adjectives?"

I nodded.

"Being married to an alcoholic makes for neither patience nor security," he said. "At least, that's what my wife used to tell me." I felt quite close to him.

"So that's Mary. How long did the marriage to Dale last?"

"Thirteen years. I met Mary and that was that."

"Just like that?"

"No, not just like that. A painful divorce and a vast geographical separation from the kids and a lot of guilt. Awful. Artie Shaw, with eight marriages, says divorce is easy. 'You just pack your bag and call a cab.' Hah! For me, it was a terrible experience. Not sure I could have got through it without booze."

"You see, you're still thinking alcoholically—I'll bet booze made everything worse," he said.

"Maybe," I conceded reluctantly.

"You and Mary have the one daughter? The one who's on TV tomorrow?"

"Boy, word gets around."

"What do you think we talk about in our daily meetings?"

"Hadn't thought about it."

"And does Mary have a drinking problem?"

"Yes, but I think she's controlling it now. Easier for her—she's thirteen years younger than I. She had a bad car accident, went through the windshield, cut herself up, demolished the car. The experience shook her up badly. But she says she's quit and she can do it."

"Without help? Without AA?"

"She can do it, where I couldn't. She gave up a two-pack smoking habit twenty-three years ago and never looked back, and everyone says that's harder to kick than booze."

"Amen," he said, tapping out his pipe. "And she's coming to the family program your final week?"

"I don't know. I'm allowed to call her this afternoon. I'll ask her. I'm afraid she might not come. She's dreading the thought, I know."

"Why's she dreading it?"

"I don't know. Maybe she feels she's failed me somehow. She's a perfectionist in everything."

"It's very, very important. Liz Taylor's family came. Mitchum's wife and a son came. It makes a big difference. It's a family disease. I'm sure you know."

He stood up to indicate the session was almost over. "And how's the spiritual side of the program going for you?"

"No blinding white lights and angelic choruses yet, sorry to say."

"God works in mysterious ways," Craig said with a smile. "He doesn't always need those Hollywood props. Anyway, even if you can't quite bring yourself to believe in God, try believing in prayer, try praying. It actually works, take my word. You are at Step Two now in the program, the 'came to believe' step. It doesn't mean that we must immediately come to believe in God as He may be presented in some formal religious denomination. Because of that misinterpretation many people dismiss the AA program, thinking that it won't work for them. But it will."

We shook hands, and I went back to McCallum. I had half an hour before I'd be allowed to telephone, so I lay on my bed. I was excited about my impending call, excited, but unaccountably apprehensive; I was already a different person than when I'd last seen and talked to Mary six days before. Would it show? Would it matter? Would we be able to talk?

I could use a drink—apprehension and alcohol were made for each other. I envisioned a drink—a glorious, brown old-fashioned, a still-life canvas by Chardin, a work of art with its red cherry and its sugar, bitters and lemon peel oil mixed in just the right amounts. But this beautiful image was eclipsed by a still more lovely vision—a huge frosted glass, a shimmering julep with a sprig of green mint jutting from its crushed-ice summit. I closed my eyes, and now I was a ten-year-old boy out in the sun on our terrace, and I was helping my father prepare a half a dozen juleps for the Sunday brunch guests. He was so handsome in white golf knickers and two-toned shoes, and he and I were flapping towels at the tall glasses until they developed a lovely thick coating of ice.

"Stand closer and flap hard, Binney!" he urged. And for my efforts I was rewarded with a sip—just a sip—and, my, how it burned, but it was sugary and with one's nose buried in the mint which my father had pinched to arouse the aroma, it tasted sort of good. And then, disdaining the maid's help, I took them out on a tray to the beautiful guests in their sporty finery, playing paddle tennis and croquet out on the lawn by the pool. How beautiful my mother looked in her big hat as she sipped her julep. How glamorous it was to drink! Please, Daddy, may I have another sip, please?

I opened my eyes and shook my head. To get rid of these thoughts, I picked up the Xeroxed newspaper clipping that

Dave had slipped under my door. Where did he get these things? It was as though he'd brought a store of them and parceled them out periodically. Actually, I guess his wife sent them. They were usually very apropos, as though there was some ESP going on.

This one was from the *New York Times* and was by someone named Brian Manning. The writer, a recovering alcoholic, discussed just what Craig and I had been talking about—how he missed the good old days, the smell of the barroom, and the toasts, the songs, the jokes, the equality, and how that vague yearning might never go away completely:

I imagine my problem as an animal living inside me, demanding a drink before it dies of thirst. That's what it says, but it will never die of thirst. The fact an alcoholic faces is that this animal breathes and waits. It is incapable of death and will spring back to lustful, consuming life with even one drop of sustenance.

When I was 18 and my drinking began in earnest, I didn't play in the wine cellar at home anymore; I stole there. I sneaked bottles to my room, sat in the window and drank alone while my parents were away. I hated the taste of it, but I kept drinking it, without the kids from the neighborhood, without any thought that I was feeding the animal. And one day, I found one of those old notes we had hidden down there years before. It fell to the ground when I pulled a bottle from its cubbyhole. I read it with bleary eyes, then put the paper back into the rack. "Beware," it said, above a childish skull and crossbones, "all ye who enter here." A child, wiser than I was that day, had written that note.

I, too, was still a thirsty animal. I hadn't yet surrendered myself to sobriety. I still had a long way to go in the remaining weeks here. I'd discuss the clipping with Jerry tomorrow. I kept thinking of when I got out of here—*no drinking at all?* Not even on special occasions? What about all the fun I had drinking—the boisterous companionship that Jack London wrote about so well:

"*Glass in hand!* There is a magic in the phrase. It means more than all the words in the dictionary can be made to mean. It is a habit of mind to which I have been trained all my life. I like the bubbling play of wit, the chesty laughs, the resonant voices of men, when, glass in hand, they shut the gray world outside and prod their brains with the fun and folly of an accelerated pulse.

"No, I decided; I shall take my drink on occasion. With all the books on my shelves, with all the thoughts of the thinkers shaded by my particular temperament, I decided coolly and deliberately that I should continue to do what I was trained to do. I would drink. . . ."

I had to remind myself that Jack London had managed to find too many "occasions" after writing that and did himself in at forty. For the alcoholic, a special occasion need be nothing more than a warm handshake.

I got up and shaved and showered and put on a clean sport shirt: I wanted to look nice for my telephone call to my wife.

There was only one other person ahead of me on the phone. When I dialed Santa Barbara, I noticed my finger was trembling slightly and not from any alcoholic shakes.

Why was I so uptight?

The phone rang and rang. Please let her be there! Finally, as I was about to give up, Mary answered breathlessly. "Sorry," her warm voice said, "out in the garden!"

The conversation was stilted. She gave me all the mundane news about pets and family members and correspondence. I said there was a good chance I'd be able to see Kendall's program. She told me how thrilled my children were that I was at the BFC and that she hadn't had a drink since I'd left and never was going to have another one as long as I didn't.

"What do you do there all day?" she asked.

It was hard to tell her, to encapsulate all that had gone on

235

these past days. I couldn't find the right words. But I made an attempt and I said I'd write.

"They want you to come down for my last week," I said.

"I know," she answered. She sounded dubious. "I've got so much to do here, but they seem to think it's important."

"It is," I said.

"I'll try," she said. "But I've got so much work to do for the Writers' Conference."

And I knew she wouldn't be coming.

There was an awkward silence and I said, "People want to use the phone."

And she said, "I love you," and I said, "I love you," and I hung up, and it was time for aerobic exercise.

The much anticipated call to the outside world left me inexplicably dejected.

I was on the pity pot. I thought of Dickens's gloomy letter written toward the end of his life, and I wallowed in it: "Why is it a sense always come crushing upon me now, as of one happiness I have missed in life and one friend and companion I have never made?"

I was engulfed in *saudades*.

S I X T E E N

Mood swings were common to all of us here in BFC as we agonized and fought and clawed our way toward sobriety. For example, my *saudades* disappeared the next morning in a flash when Jerry came to my room and said, "Barny, you did a good job on your makeup work. You may watch your daughter on TV today instead of going to the lecture at one."

Ridiculously, tears of gratitude spurted from my eyes. "Thank you, thank you," I murmured. I seem to have shed more tears during this one week than I had in the past couple of decades. I don't know why seeing this TV program meant so much to me; maybe because I felt drinking had caused me to fail Kendall so many times over her twenty-one years. On her first big night, her debut, two years ago, I had gotten drunk before the elaborate ball in San Francisco and could barely execute the prescribed father-daughter dance. She has a loving nature and tossed it off the next day with "It's okay, Dad. Forget it, I forgive you!"

But it must have hurt. (My older daughter, Tani, to whom I'd done the same thing ten years before at her debut, said recently, "I didn't *forgive* you. I just gave *up* on you!")

So now I was not going to let Kendall down on her acting debut. I found out what channel *One Life to Live* was on, went into the deserted lounge at one, and turned on the set. Jack Davis, the big drawling midwestern counselor, came out of his office and joined me. And then, surprisingly, Beth and Terry drew up chairs next to me.

"*Had* to see it," whispered Beth. "Hope we don't get in trouble for watching!"

The plot of the soap opera apparently had taken the cast to Italy, and in a few minutes and after several commercials, we were at a fancy party in Venice. I kept looking beyond the close-ups of the principals to the milling extras behind them.

"Isn't that Kendall?" Beth said. I'd shown her pictures in *Vogue* of Kendall modeling dresses.

"Where?"

"There—" Beth jabbed at the screen—"behind the fat man in the tuxedo!"

But the girl strolled off camera.

"Hey, how about that one there?" said Jack. "That purty filly next to the statue?"

"No," said Beth, "that girl's blond."

"They coulda dyed her hair," said Jack.

Good old negative Terry added, "They coulda written her out of the whole thing, too!"

I was beginning to fear she might be right. We were five minutes away from the end of the program when suddenly Beth said, "Look. Wow!"

"That's her!" Terry said.

And indeed it was. A tall beautiful girl dressed in a white evening gown appeared at the party and slinked her way through the merrymakers up to the host. There was one brief close-up of Kendall's heavily made-up face. She smiled, showing the slight gap between her front teeth, and said brightly, *"Grazie!"*

And then she was gone. Gone from the ballroom, from the scene, and from the program. One word, only one word, but she'd looked great, hadn't bumped into the furniture, and my chest swelled with parental pride. I'd write her in New York today, if I could squeeze in the time. She had looked just like her mother at the same age. I'd tell her that. That would please her.

That was the highlight of my week. Word spread around "the campus" and I was repeatedly congratulated on my daughter's acting triumph, which they'd heard about but hadn't been allowed to see.

o   o   o

And the days went by at the BFC, each the same, each different.

The San Francisco columnist Herb Caen once remarked that "vacations are long in the beginning, short at the end, and round in your middle." This certainly applied to the BFC experience, though it never was a vacation. My first week at the center was surely not dull, but it seemed interminable. The second week went faster, and the final two zipped by. As for the "round in the middle"—exercise, fresh air, and an alcohol-free palate gave me a teenager's appetite and a craving for desserts.

Morrie: "Conrad's favorite dish is seconds."

Curiously, while I actually gained a little weight, everyone said how good I was beginning to look and how thin; it was merely the bloat disappearing.

There were highs and lows in my moods and attitudes during the first fortnight. Some days I was euphoric, delighted to be here, reveling in sobriety and envisioning a new life for myself. On other days I would feel surges of great anger, resentment, and impatience well up inside me, and I'd become swamped with *saudades* and self-pity. And at times I was filled with craving for a drink—not *a* drink, but a whole bowlful of liquor.

And always we complained—about the food, or lack of mail, or the tight restrictions. "Why do we put up with this shit?" I remember saying to Dave after we'd been reprimanded severely for reading a newspaper before the proper time. "They treat us like a bunch of children!"

"I guess technically we are until the day they give us their precious medallion."

But little by little the anger was dissipated as my body and mind continued to get healthier and closer to normal. There was, indeed, something magical about this place, and that was proved in so many ways.

One magical happening was in Reena's graduation. She was the courtesan-type model whom the counselor had put through the falling-over-backward experience. Before that no one had ever expected Reena to make the grade, but here she was sitting in a circle with all twenty of us in McCallum Hall, without the cheap makeup and gaudy clothes, accepting the medallion with grateful, dignified words and vowing never to forget the friends she'd made in her thirty days here.

"The most important day of my wasted life."

Terry, the nurse, stayed at the BFC, much to Dave's and my amazement, since she didn't seem to progress much in her angry attitude toward the world. It was everyone's fault but hers, always. Jerry spent a great deal of extra time outside of group with her. It was as though Terry was the ultimate challenge of Jerry's career. I found Terry thoroughly unpleasant and didn't really care what made her tick.

Essex, the dealing entrepreneur, continued to amaze with

his startling change and growth in the program. The tough-guy manner was gone, replaced by a considerate, quiet, and industrious patient.

Morrie, the pre-need cemetery-lot salesman, lost little of his ebullience when he shed his toupee; the quality of his jokes didn't improve, but we could see his demeanor change as he came closer to achieving serenity and peace within himself. When it came time for us to attend open AA meetings in the nearby town of Palm Springs, he made no bones about choosing to go to the special meeting for gays; self-assurance had come with the new self-awareness.

Fat Willy, the architect, who had beat his father in absentia with padded clubs, finally graduated with flying colors and went back to his home in Iowa and, presumably, a productive sober life.

Beth, the artistic housewife, blossomed, losing weight dramatically as she squeezed in her vigorous swimming laps between the lectures and assignments. She also always found time to make a decorative "diploma" for the graduating person using her superb calligraphy and decorative sense. She always had time for anyone in trouble, newcomer or veteran alike. There was no doubt that "the sweetheart of McCallum Hall" was going to make it out in the big wide "real" world. (We finally did finish that portrait and she sent it to her pleased husband.)

Dr. Bill, the surgeon, and my roommate, Moishe, continued with their recovery quietly and successfully. Professor Dave, being charged with verbosity both written and oral, was required to write all of his assignments with Crayolas to force him to write larger and hence theoretically to restrict his output of verbiage. Unflappable, he took it in his professorial stride on his good-natured way to sobriety.

On the other hand, Chico, our would-be veterinarian who had started out so promisingly, just wasn't there one day at breakfast. He had seemed nervous and withdrawn for days, but so were we all at times, and we paid little attention to the warnings. Peter, the granny, found a note in Chico's room and he tearfully posted in on the bulletin board:

To my beloved peers: I'll be gone when you read this. I can't hack it. The monkey on my back wins—it won't get off. It's bigger and stronger than the BFC and me combined, and it doesn't fight clean. I love you and hate myself for letting you all and Jerry and Mrs. Ford down. But you people can and will make it, I know. Stay with it! Good luck.

Chico

There was another note, folded and addressed to Beth. She read it, burst into tears, and ran from the room. She never did discuss it and no one ever asked her about the contents.

Five days later, Chico's body was found in an irrigation ditch near his hometown of Sacramento. He had OD'd. The news cast a pall over the BFC for a long time and served to reinforce the fact that in chemical substances we were up against an unseen, implacable, and powerful adversary.

This was emphasized a few days later when Dr. Spenser Mark was released from the hospital and took the place of Chico in our group sessions.

In slacks, tennis shoes, and a yellow sport shirt, he didn't look like the same person who had collapsed on Dave and me in the foyer of Firestone six days before. His gray hair was trimmed, he had his color back, and he wasn't shaking, in spite of his close brush with death. He was quiet and modest and humorous, a totally different man than when he was first admitted to the BFC. We began to see why he'd been so enormously successful as an electronics inventor and creative businessman. Yet he never played the big shot with us, and in the evening he entered into our card games and charades and pizza bull sessions with a will and easy charm.

He was totally candid, and during the group sessions he told many humorous tales of his drinking exploits. Once, when drunk, he'd bought, over the phone, a failing firm in Salinas called the Grapes of Wrath Brassiere Company simply because he liked the name.

"It went bust," he said with his charming smile.

Another time he'd rented the whole Love Boat plus Count Basie's band for a weekend cruise to Mexico for his daughter's graduation class—got drunk and missed the sailing. I remember one ingenious story of how he rigged up his Mercedes so that he could fill up the "wee-wee," the windshield-wiper reservoir, with gin and be able to drink from a rubber tube, which was pulled out from under the dash; it livened up the commute from his home to work, and also precluded the cops from finding any open bottles on his person should they stop him.

But one day he told us haltingly and in a husky voice a horrifying story of his playboy youth. He went-to Harvard to get his Ph.D., but he lived at home with his wealthy parents, and whenever he would land in jail for drunkenness, he would telephone his father to bail him out. One time he woke up in jail and told them to call his father as usual. "Can't this time," the jailer told him. "You killed him last night."

Spenser broke down and cried as he told the story of how in an alcoholic blackout he'd struck his father, who'd fallen and cracked open his head. Spenser's lawyers had got him off with a suspended sentence, but it had haunted him all these years. He said he felt relieved and cleansed for having told us, and we assured him that we loved him and supported him.

He seemed to be doing so well and adjusting so easily to the routine that it came as a shock when after ten days he announced in group that he was going to "take off a week to go to Boston on business."

"Then you're not coming back here!" said Jerry sternly.

"I'll be back in a week," Spenser protested. "I just have to wind up—"

"You leave, you don't come back," said Jerry flatly. "You're not ready, Spenser, not by a long shot. This is not just a drying out place for the rich, you know."

"Jerry, I'm not going to drink and use, if that's what you think."

"That's exactly what I think."

"Listen, I've learned my lesson. I'm never going to touch it again. I have to go on business, that's all!"

"What are you hearing, group?" asked Jerry, looking around the circle.

"Bullshit!" we chorused.

"Group, what do you think he should do?"

"Don't go, Spenser," someone pleaded.

"Stay! For God's sake, for your sake, stay!"

"You're doing so great!"

"We love you, Spenser, and we don't want to see you chuck it all!"

Spenser grew indignant as he looked around him. "Dammit, you have my word of honor. I'm not going to drink or use!"

"An alcoholic's word of honor is worth *that!*" said Jerry, snapping her fingers. "Spenser, you may think you're telling the truth, but look at your record: Three times you've been close to death in the last two years; you've gone to three different rehabilitation centers and haven't stayed the full time in any of them!"

"But this is important! A whole lot of money is riding on this shopping-mall deal for a whole lot of people, not just me! If I'm not there, it will fall through!"

"I can't stop you from going," Jerry said unhappily. "But I can sure stop you from coming back—that is, if you ever try to come back."

"I want to come back, I love this place, but if you only knew the magnitude of this deal you'd—"

"Spenser, the only commodity you have is your life! Don't you understand that simple statement? To hell with shopping malls or condos or soy-bean futures or sow bellies or whatever you're worried about at the moment. What's it all matter if you don't have your *life*? And you *are* going to kill yourself, you *are* going to be dead, dead, dead, if not in three months, then in five months or in six months!"

She stood up. "Lie down on the floor."

Startled, Spenser blinked at her.

"Lie down!" she commanded. He shrugged. He slid off the chair and stretched out on the rattan carpet, surrounded by us.

"Now close your eyes!" Jerry ordered.

He did, and she reached down and ceremonially crossed his wrists across his stomach.

"We are a few months into the future," Jerry intoned. "And you have died. Now you're in the casket, the best casket money can buy, in the best funeral parlor in Boston, and anybody who is anybody has come by to pay his last respects to you. Here's your family doctor, Dr. Carl Endicott."

She pointed at Dave and he picked up the cue. "Spenser, I'm sorry," Dave ad libbed in sad tones. "I told you to quit a long time ago. I know those other places didn't work for you, but we had high hopes for the Betty Ford Center. I'm sorry, old friend."

Jerry nodded and said, "And here's Ralph, your business partner."

She pointed at me and I improvised. "Spenser, sure it was a big deal. We all might have made a lot of money, but it could have waited, pal. Your health was more important. Rest in peace, friend, we had some good times, but we could have had a lot more."

Jerry pointed at Terry, saying, "And here's your daughter, Shirley."

"Daddy, Daddy," sobbed Terry, and she actually was crying. "I loved you so much, and when you were sober, you were so great to us and, goddammit, weren't your family and grandchildren worth more than some lousy shopping mall, and now you're gone and you won't see the new baby and we all—"

Spenser sprang up suddenly. His face was bright red and tears were streaming down his cheeks and he pushed out of the circle of our chairs, roughly, almost knocking Terry over, and he strode out of the office down the hall, back to his room, packed his suitcase, and without a word to anyone left for Boston that afternoon in his Lear jet.

Ten days later we learned that he had died. He had fallen down a flight of stairs after an office party. He left instructions that he was to be cremated with no funeral. The bulk of his vast estate went to his daughter, but his will also provided for an amount to be left to the BFC and another greater sum to go to the Boston Animal Shelter.

"Of course he didn't want a funeral," said Dave sadly. "He'd already had it at the Betty Ford Center."

SEVENTEEN

On the Sunday after Chico's death from an overdose, a dozen of us who were close to him held a little memorial service. We sat on the thick grass around the pond, and Dave spoke briefly about Chico's gentle, affectionate nature. Then I read a poem that Noel Coward had written shortly before his own death, prefacing it by saying, "With his loving heart, Chico might have written this about himself":

> When I have fears, as Keats had fears,
> Of the moment I'll cease to be
> I console myself with vanished years
> Remembered laughter, remembered tears,
> And the peace of the changing sea.
>
> When I feel sad, as Keats felt sad,
> That my life is so nearly done
> It gives me comfort to dwell upon

Remembered friends who are dead and gone
And the jokes we had and the fun.

How happy they are I cannot know
But happy am I who loved them so.

Craig said a few words, and then Beth ended it with this one sentence, so moved she was barely able to whisper the words: "Chico, dear. There is respect for a heart like yours, and if its beating stops, the spirit lives to guard the ways you wandered."

Somberly we walked back to the cafeteria and I asked Beth where she'd found that thought.

"It was in a book by Beryl Markham," she said. "The British aviatrix."

"Touching," I said.

"Actually" she hesitated—"it was an epitaph for her beloved dog, but I thought it applied to Chico, too. Do you think he'd mind that it was written to a dog?"

"I don't think he'd mind at all," I said. "He loved animals."

"Better than himself," she said, brushing away tears.

How deep did Beth's feelings for Chico go? I have often wondered if Chico ever told Beth of his love for her, but I never asked.

There were too many unfinished stories at the Center, so many potential dramas unplayed out.

For want of a better expression, I'll call it the Experience. *It* occurred that afternoon after lunch when I went to my room to catch up on homework. They said that something magical happened to people in the BFC, generally around the middle of one's stay. But it had not yet happened to me until this Sunday.

It was my third week here, and time for work on the much discussed and important Step Three, referred to by us apprehensive patients as "turning it over."

In the Big Book of Alcoholics Anonymous it reads, "Made a decision to turn our will and our lives over to the care of God *as we understood Him.*"

It is regarded by AA and the BFC as a crucial step in an alcoholic's recovery. I doubted my capability to accept it.

There was no heavy insistence on religion as such at the BFC, yet since the treatment and preparation for subsequent after-care was based on the Alcoholics Anonymous program, it perforce placed considerable emphasis on the spiritual side of the patient's treatment and development during his time there.

Interviews with the minister or priest or rabbi, after the first few times, were optional; if you felt like talking to them or attending services, they were there and always available.

It was reiterated that God, or the preferred term Higher Power, was as we perceived Him as individuals, not the way some formal church tradition or TV preacher might have pictured Him. He—or She or It—was simply a force, an energy or idea or concept that was outside of ourselves and bigger than ourselves and stronger than ourselves and more powerful than the alcohol and drugs we'd been taking, and somehow, if we prayed to this force and permitted it to, it could rid us of our consuming disease.

Many an atheist or agnostic has entered the BFC and come out still nonreligious in the traditional sense, yet imbued with a new feeling of wonder and spiritual awareness and a respect for the power of prayer.

I was one of those. I am not arrogant or wise enough to presume that there is or is not a God. But I know that I did go through some sort of spiritual awakening, and most of the other graduates of the BFC that I've talked with have told of similar happenings.

It was on my eighteenth day, and the anxieties and uncertainties of the first days were behind me. I knew what was expected of me now, and I had done my assignments as well as I could and even had drawn coveted praise for some of the

249

work from Jerry and the rest of my group. I had completed my First and Second Steps and the reading and writing connected with it. That is, I admitted to the powerlessness and unmanageability of my life in the face of alcohol, and admitted that I had been unable to do anything about it on my own. I admitted to the false pride, the grandiosity, as they termed it, which prevented me from seeing my own behavior as it actually had been, which caused me to think that unlike other mortals, I could swill down any amount of liquor I chose without being held accountable for the damage it was doing to my health, my brain, my family, and my career.

I was told that since I had made it frighteningly clear that I was incapable of curing myself of this disease, outside help must be sought, and not in the form of any medicine or hypnosis, but in some greater force, a source of energy from above and around one, a Higher Power. Step Two: "Came to believe that a Power greater than ourselves could restore us to sanity."

There was no proselytizing at BFC, and it was never made a controversial issue. Steps Two and Three simply assumed that there is a God to understand and that we each have a God of our own understanding in us. Our understanding might be that He is weak or strong, conservative or liberal, out of date or even nonexistent. We were urged not to allow our understanding of God to become an issue at this stage of our sobriety, but simply to accept the fact that if we remained abstinent and pursued the treatment, significant spiritual changes would take place in us, that as we grew to understand ourselves and other people more, we might develop a better understanding of a Higher Power. For the time being we should try merely to accept the definition suggested in the book *Alcoholics Anonymous:* a loving God as He may express Himself in our group conscience.

I grasped at the word "conscience." That I understood. I still had a conscience, at least.

It was easy enough to listen to this counsel day after day, and mouth the words, but it was a different thing to feel and truly believe.

Yet this day, this Sunday, a beautiful crisp desert day, I was in my room writing about the Third Step when something strange occurred. Suddenly I felt a tingling over my entire body. It was as though my limbs and face were glowing. And I saw as clear as the sunlight streaming in the open door that I no longer had any problems, that they had been relieved and shouldered by some unknown force. I realized with startling clarity for the first time the simplest of ideas, so simple but all important:

I didn't drink because I had problems. I had problems because I drank!

I said it out loud, and then again, jubilantly. I laughed out loud. The BFC had been hammering away at that concept for so many days, yet only now had it truly sunk in!

I had no problems in this world that couldn't be surmounted or solved if alcohol were removed from the picture.

A great warmth of serenity came over me, an absence of anger, an onrush of love, an acceptance of myself and everyone around me, and a tremendous surge of gratitude as I took inventory of my many blessings.

The magic that Craig had predicted was happening. I wanted to thank someone or something for all of it, for my realizing it finally, for my having found my way to this place, for the love I had rediscovered for people, for my wife and my children and friends.

I found myself on my knees, my hands clasped together, looking upward and mouthing fervently the words, "Thank you, thank you!"

And, as long as I was in an attitude of prayer, I felt I might as well pray for Mary to see her way clear to come here for family week.

I don't know how long I stayed there, but when Peter, the

granny, knocked and came in to say I was wanted on the phone, I wasn't embarrassed to be seen on my knees.

I went down the hall to the telephone, my legs a little shaky. I was wet with perspiration and the skin over my entire body was sensitive and achy, as though I had the flu.

It was Mary, and her voice was full of optimistic resolve and support as she said that in a few days she would be driving down for my final week. I gasped. Then I finally found my voice and answered that was great and I could hardly wait to see her.

I had prayed for that and already it had happened!

Yet I was apprehensive about her coming; beware of answered prayers. I felt I was finally doing so well; I didn't want to upset any apple carts. I started to tell her about the spiritual experience I'd just gone through, but it was still too fresh and fragile to be examined, and I couldn't risk any levity or skepticism at this point. I didn't want to let go of the vision of tranquility and serenity I'd been permitted to see.

When I hung up, I walked over to see Craig in his office. I haltingly tried to tell him what had happened to me and how marvelous I was feeling, euphoric, serene. And the answered prayer! He listened to me quietly, then he stood up, extended his hand, and said, simply "Welcome to the club."

EIGHTEEN

The jubilation of knowing that the final week was at hand was dimmed by Beth's graduation and departure. A great deal of the life and gaiety of McCallum seemed to revolve around her, and all nineteen of us cried and hugged her after she had accepted the medallion. She made a charming little talk, saying that she felt sorry for nonalcoholics since they could never know the tremendous experience she'd been lucky enough to go through during her month here. Looking much slimmer, dressed up, hair done, very pretty, she added, "I never thought when I walked in here thirty days ago that I'd be sorry to leave it, but I am, oh, I am!"

She kissed me good-bye tearfully and wrote in my *Alcoholics Anonymous* book that she would never forget the Geezer. We vowed to write often. And then she was gone, and gloom descended upon McCallum Hall, especially over Dave and me; our cheery little mascot was gone.

Except she missed her plane, by accident on purpose, and

came back that noon. Unable to cut the umbilical cord, she stayed for two days. We were all glad to see her, but it wasn't the same anymore. Someone new had already taken the bed in her room, so she stayed at a motel, but she came over in the afternoon and sat in on the bull sessions and the card games at night. But it was different. She was a "normie" and a "civilian" now; she didn't fit in, dressed in her hat and tailored city clothes and high heels. It was as though she'd come to stare at the zoo inhabitants, us unfortunates who hadn't been sprung yet. She tried to enter into our conversations as before, but we were too immersed in our day-to-day rituals and busy with assignments and treatments, and she was an outsider looking in. We saw what a wrench it was for her finally to return to reality, but after two days she made herself leave and catch the plane to the East. She telephoned us that night from her home to say how much she missed us all already, but that it was good, really great, to be home.

The next day Mary arrived in Rancho Mirage. She hadn't had a drink, not even a glass of wine, for a month and it showed; when she strode into the lobby of the Center, her leather purse slung over one shoulder, tall and tan, dark hair flowing, she was radiantly beautiful. She reminded me of our daughter on the TV program. She looked to me the way she had twenty-four years before when she'd first walked into my bar, El Matador, in San Francisco.

I was wearing a sport shirt with "Camp Betty" stenciled across the chest, and she laughed nervously at it as we came together and kissed. We kissed again, almost shyly.

What was so different? Why did we feel so awkward?

My stomach felt the way it does when you're in an elevator expecting it to go up and it goes down. We weren't the same people we had been three weeks before.

"You look great," I said.

"So do you," she said. "You look so different. You have kind of—sort of an aura about you."

"It's my new mustache," I said.

"*That* has got to go!" Then she whispered apprehensively, "What are they going to do to me in here?"

"I don't know," I said truthfully.

After registering, Mary and Dave's wife, Helen, who also had just arrived, went to a hotel in nearby Palm Springs. Though they would be staying for a week, we would not be seeing them at the BFC, except fleetingly and frustratingly, across the cafeteria dining room at breakfast. The rest of the time they spent in the family facility, Cork Hall, a few hundred yards away from the BFC's main buildings. (It was donated by the owner of McDonalds, Joan Kroc, with her late husband's name spelled backward.)

Here, for the next five days, from eight to four o'clock, the husbands or wives or parents or children would go through intensive classes, interviews, and psychiatric consultations. Plus they would engage in psychodrama sessions, where significant alcohol-related scenes in the person's life would be reenacted, dissected, discussed, and dealt with.

Mary had a rude shock, because she thought she had been summoned to discuss my problem exclusively, and instead she learned that the focus was to be on her as a co-dependent and drinker. Yet she found the days, though long and tiring, "fascinating."

I had a frantic crowded schedule set up for my final week. In addition to completing the work for the Fourth and Fifth Steps, I had long sessions with new counselors, who prepared us for the life we'd be facing soon, in the big wide "normal" drinking and using world.

One psychodrama under the direction of the psychologist Gene involved my returning for the first time to the bar of the club I belong to. The scene was staged and acted out by my peers quite accurately based on information I assume they'd gleaned from Jerry and the minister and Mary.

"Good day to you, Mr. Conrad," said Dave, washing imaginary glasses and with a creditable imitation of Patrick the bartender's brogue. "It's your usual you'll be having this foine noon?"

I shook my head. "No, not today, Pat. Give me a Perrier and lime."

"Sure'n you must be sick, sir!"

Morrie sitting on a stool next to me said, "Pour the man a real drink, for Chrissake! It's on me, old pal! Make it a double, and I'll tell you the one about the lesbian, the alligator, and the three-legged dog."

"No, really," I said. "My doctor said to lay off the sauce. Give me a Perrier."

Terry on the other stool said contemptuously, "Always thought you were some kind of fruitcake, Conrad. Now you've proved it."

"I found out I'm allergic to the stuff. Going to lay off it."

"Yeah? How long?" said Terry, taking pleasure in the role. "Your usual three days?"

"Forever, I hope," I answered.

"Bullshit," said Terry, turning her back.

"Sorry, I'm on the wagon for good."

"And a terrible thing it is," Dave said, leaning forward conspiratorially. "But please troy to keep it quiet around the club, Mr. Conrad."

Gene smiled and said, "That's what's going to happen to you over and over out there in different ways with and without the brogue. But just remember one thing, Barny, the people who'll mind your not drinking don't matter—and those who matter won't mind. You're going to be constantly fighting off well-wishers—and not so well-wishers—who won't be able to *stand* your not drinking. They'll badger you, maybe even slip some alcohol into your ginger ale to be funny. Remember, to the hard drinker you are now a threat."

Gene gave us names of sponsors in our hometowns, recovering alcoholics who would help us get our feet on the ground and steer us to AA meetings.

"Try to make ninety meetings the first ninety days, then taper off," he urged us. "And remember, you have only done five of the twelve steps here. You really haven't completed the AA program until you work the remaining seven. Your sponsor will help you through them on the outside. And remember, respect the anonymity of the meetings and what goes on there. It's vital."

And the last thing Gene said to us that day was, "Your first months out of here are the crucial ones. You'll be sorely tempted several times in many situations. The important thing is this: *Don't take that first drink!* One drink would be too many and twenty would not be enough. Remember this word: HALT. Let it stand for don't let yourself get too Hungry, Angry, Lonely, or Tired. We alcoholics tend to want a drink most at those times. And choose your companions carefully. We generally like and gravitate toward those people who have the same faults we do."

We also experienced a new thing this week—real Alcoholics Anonymous meetings in the nearby town, where we were taken by van. These sessions were a little different from the weekly ones we'd had in the BFC, rougher, less cosmetic and tailored than the in-house "beginner" meetings. One night in a Palm Springs meeting there were three motorcycle-gang members present, and their appearance in the traditional sleeveless and studded leather jackets and unkempt beards was disconcerting at first. One of the young trio gave a sincere talk when it came his turn to speak, and he concluded with this mumbled but heartfelt line: "I thank my Higher Power for my sobriety and I am truly fucking grateful to God!"

Dave whispered to me, "I'm going to have a T-shirt made of those last five touching words and make a fortune!"

"You'll sell hundreds at Billy Graham's performances alone!"

In spite of the levity, we knew that these bikers and everyone in this room, no matter what their life-styles, were brethren, genuinely bonded together in a common cause: sobriety.

Mary and I were allowed to exchange only brief salutations and a kiss as we passed each other in the cafeteria in the morning.

"How's it going?" I asked.

She rolled her eyes heavenward. "Tough! These people don't just fool around, do they?"

I was too busy myself to worry too much about Mary's regime. I had to complete the Fourth and Fifth Steps in order to be eligible for graduation and the medallion scheduled for the end of the week.

The Fourth Step seemingly was not very difficult. The Big Book states, "Made a searching and fearless moral inventory of ourselves."

Simple enough. But how to begin?

It was an intimidating assignment that I put off as long as I could. Finally, I drew a line down the center of a page and wrote "Bad" on one side and "Good" on the other and started writing. I began with the "Bad" by free-associating and scribbling down my thoughts as fast as they came to my mind.

I wrote down all the bad things I could think of that I'd done in my life; that took two days. Then I listed all the good things; that took a coffee break.

I went to Jerry's office and told her I was having trouble thinking up good things about myself.

She sighed. "Typical of us alcoholics. We're perfectionists with inferiority complexes. We swing from abject humility— we're no damn good, rotten worms, and not fit to live—and then, hey, look at me, I'm His Majesty King Baby! I'm perfect, never make a mistake, and I can do anything I damn well feel like anytime I want to and to hell with the rest of the world!"

She helped me think of some more things on the positive side of the ledger. "Own your own behavior, but don't punish yourself. Our goal is to know ourselves and to accept ourselves. Only then can we begin to change and grow."

She appeared to be very tired, with blue circles under her eyes.

"You look a little beat," I said.

She nodded and sighed. "Up all night with Terry. She says she's leaving. Why is life a privilege for some of us humans and a painful ordeal for others? Been here six weeks; only has two weeks to go, says she's leaving. Just like that." She put her fingers to her temples. "All the work we've done, all the time we've spent, and she just ups and says she's going back to Arizona. Says she's well. Ha! She'll be using again within a month if she goes out there now. She simply won't be able to bear the pain of everyday living without her anesthesia. I was supposed to go on vacation last week and Lord knows I need it, but I just won't give up on Terry. I won't let her win. I won't! Somehow I've got to persuade her to stay. Lord, how I hate failing with her. A bad month, this. First Chico, then Spenser. I don't want to lose Terry."

I said lamely, "But look at your many successes."

She didn't answer.

As I started to leave, Jerry said wearily, "You know her story?"

"No," I said. "Actually, she's not my favorite character here."

"This, of course, is no explanation of her addiction; many people have gone through worse experiences and not turned to booze or drugs. But when Terry was thirteen, her father wobbled into the house, stood in front of her and her mother, and"—she took a deep breath—"poured a can of gasoline over his head, took out his lighter, and set fire to himself."

"God," I exclaimed.

"Yes," she breathed resignedly. "God."

By the next morning, my last full day at BFC, I was ready

for the final step, the last of the steps we would "work" at the BFC: "5. Admitted to God, to ourselves, and to another human being the exact nature of our wrongs."

This meant that we read the inventory of ourselves that we'd prepared to a man of the cloth. He was not of our choosing and not necessarily one we were acquainted with. I was assigned a young, freckled, and blond priest; I soon found he was wise and extremely understanding. To my surprise, I finished reciting my litany of transgressions with a minimum of embarrassment and pain, and we actually laughed together about certain elements in it. At the end of a fast hour and a half he stood up and took my hand in both of his and said, "That was pretty tame stuff compared to what I usually hear. You know, you're really a very nice person. I wish you believed it as strongly as I do. Maybe you will with a little more time in sobriety." He hesitated. "Oh, and do you mind my asking, what do you consider the greatest act of love you've received in your recent life?"

I thought a moment. "I guess I'd have to say my son's sending me the money to come here."

He turned to his desk, scribbled something on a pad, folded the piece of paper double, and handed it to me. "Good luck," he said.

As I walked back to McCallum Hall I unfolded the paper. It said, "God sent you that check."

That night I took those pages that represented the sins of five decades and on the patio off the kitchen of McCallum Hall all nineteen of my peers helped me burn them in a flower urn to the off-key singing of "Bye Bye Blackbird."

"Burn up all my cares and woes . . ."

"Bye Bye, anger . . ."

Just a few short weeks ago I had made fun of this ceremony. Now I found it a joyous, cleansing ritual, and the traditional ice cream and pizza afterward tasted like dinner at the Tour d'Argent.

On the way to my room I saw Jerry in her office and she signaled me to come in. She was dressed differently—a hat and a raincoat—and there was a suitcase by her desk. I was pleased to see tacked on her bulletin board a drawing I'd done for her, a gin bottle with labels at different levels down the bottle: (1) Verbose, (2) Amorous, (3) Bellicose, (4) Lachrymose, (5) Comatose.

"Barny, tomorrow's your last day, but before your graduation I have arranged for a meeting between you and Mary at nine o'clock; I think it's a very important thing for both of you at this stage, especially for you and your sobriety."

Then she sighed and added, "I hate to tell you, but I won't be here for your medallion ceremony."

She saw the acute disappointment in my face.

"I'm leaving tonight for a couple of weeks. I've got to get out of this place right away before I collapse. But I'll be thinking of you at graduation time. I want you to know that I'm proud of you. You've come a long way in a short time, whether or not you can see it yet. We'll stay in touch. You're a special person."

She gave me a big hug. "Good luck out there!"

As I turned to go with tears in my eyes, she said dully, "Terry left this afternoon. For good."

"Oh, Lord," I said. "I'm sorry."

"I tried everything."

Then she said fiercely, her eyes blazing, "God, how I hate this disease! I love the alcoholic, but how I hate his alcoholism!"

The next day, Mary and I, both dreading it, met in an office; under the guidance of her counselor and Jack Davis, who was filling in for Jerry, we talked for nearly two hours.

Jack had been well briefed in our biographies by both Jerry and Craig, and he expertly and gently led Mary and me through the maze of problems that liquor had increasingly caused in our lives and our marriage.

"You two have been in tremendous competition with each other most of your married life," he started, "and this even extended to the drinking portions of your daily routine. And there's a lot of anger on both sides, which has been exacerbated by likker. But I do believe you love each other deeply. Is that a fair assumption?"

We looked at each other, smiled and nodded, and began to relax a little.

"So let's get down to work," said Cowboy Jack.

We were awkward and reticent and embarrassed at first, but soon we were talking freely and candidly and airing wounding events and grievances that had been long buried within us. Mercilessly, the two counselors steered and goaded us into private areas we wouldn't have arrived at by ourselves, and didn't really care to explore. Then they adroitly led us into what we projected for the future and what part liquor would play in it and how we would handle our drinking friends and our liquor-saturated life-style.

I cannot reproduce or transcribe all that was said or accomplished in that short-long time, but we were drained at the end of the session. We felt good, happy, optimistic, and relieved when it was over. We kissed fervently, and then embraced our counselors.

Jack looked at his watch. "I do believe it's that there time."

Mary went to get the car, and I walked into the lounge where my nineteen peers were waiting in a circle for my medallion ceremony to begin.

I suppose I'd also made fun of this ritual when I'd first come to the BFC. Now that it was happening to me, it seemed special and moving and full of genuine love.

Jack started off lightly by saying in his Oklahoma drawl, "When you first come in here, Barny, you was all jangly from drinking, and your eyes were bugged outa your head like you'd been poked with a cattle prod. But you've straightened out fine, and I'm sincerely proud to know you."

He passed the medallion to Moishe, the roommate I so rarely saw, who said simply, "I will be missing my roomie. I, too, graduate tomorrow. Come visit with me in Jerusalem—*leshonah habah Biyrooshalayim!*"

He passed the medallion to Dave, who cleared his throat and addressed himself in his best professorial manner to the group. "Boswell said that man is the only animal that laughs and weeps, for he is the only animal that is struck with the difference between what things are and what they ought to be."

He turned to me. "Barny, when you and I drank, we thought we could make the world become the way we thought it should be, and by gosh, for a couple of hours the planet used to become that fine utopia. In here we are taught that it may not be a perfect place out there, but sober we can cope with it. You've learned the lessons well, Barny, and I know you're going to make it out in the madding crowd. In Woodrow Wilson's lovely phrase, you have come *to yourself;* it's a beautiful thing to see when a person comes *to himself.*"

The medallion finally was handed to me after everyone had spoken, and I was too moved except to say more than some halting words of thanks.

Then they crowded around me, hugs and kisses, vowing to stay in touch, swearing to write, to phone, to please drop in for a weekend or just a drink of Perrier—"Remember we're not that far from New York!" (Philadelphia, Pismo Beach, Tel Aviv, San Francisco, Perth, Atlanta, etc.).

It was like the end of a cruise, as though we'd been on a month-long trip together on a ship, sharing the many ups and downs and small adventures and intimacies of a voyage.

And indeed it had been a voyage, a voyage of discovery.

I heard Mary honk the horn, reminding me that it was time to leave. I went to my room for my suitcase and stopped at Firestone to check out. There was a man in a camel's hair coat, saddle shoes, and Pennzoiled hair who was signing in.

Of an indeterminate age, he had a face more that of a damaged young man than a well preserved older man. He was swaying slightly, and growling, "Whaddya mean I can't bring magazines in with me. My father was a friend of President Ford's in college. I want to speak to Mrs. Ford right now!"

I wondered if he'd be getting my room. Poor Moishe.

I would have liked to say good-bye to Mrs. Ford, but she wasn't there that day; you could always tell because the two Secret Service men weren't on their sofa in the lobby.

I said good-bye to the people at the front desk, went out to the car, and we drove away.

As we were driving from the town of Rancho Mirage through Palm Springs, I found myself looking around— maybe on an off chance I might spot that nice cop, the one who had put me on the right road to the BFC thirty days and a lifetime ago.

I wanted to thank him.

EPILOGUE

March 16, 1986

As I write this, it is one year to the day since I drove away from the BFC and the desert and went home.

I never did find out why I drank. After all that time and effort and money, I never did find out any definite answers except that maybe I'd inherited the alcoholic's X factor from the drunken grandfather I never knew. Yes, let's just blame everything on him; it's easier and neater that way, though I'm sure there are many other factors.

They say that the act of suicide always is killing two people and runaway drinking is suicide, but I never found out who or what I was drinking *at*.

But it doesn't make any difference. I learned the important thing: that I *must* live without alcohol and that I *can* live without alcohol; I learned I can *not* drink, which is a little different from learning only that I *cannot* drink. I finally got it through my head; I now know that there's no problem so bad that drinking wouldn't make it worse.

And I learned a lot about myself and, among other things, to like myself better. So the seeking of the answer was in itself an answer for me.

Auden said that no two people ever read the same book. One could say that no two people ever went to the same rehabilitation center. I happened to respond well to the BFC, but there are many other fine treatment centers in America whose names are available to anyone who cares to call the National Council on Alcoholism or the Alcoholics Anonymous center in any city or town. At last report, there are some 39,000 beds for alcoholics in American hospitals and treatment centers!

An important fact that I did not know is that a great many health insurance policies will cover treatment of the disease. And while the $6,000 cost of the Betty Ford Center may seem high, it is far lower than most such places.

Since leaving the BFC, I've had an incredibly good year. Craig said, before I left the Center, "You'll find all sorts of good things happening to you, things that seemingly have nothing to do with your abstinence."

And that has been true—too many to enumerate. But the good things attributable directly to the absence of alcohol are obvious: health, for instance. When I went into the Center my GGTP (short for gamma glutamyl transpeptidase) count was a stratospheric 594; this is an indicative and important blood test for liver damage, and any count over 53 should be watched. Last week I repeated the test and the GGTP was an astonishing 41, to amaze even my blasé doctor. My blood pressure, even with medication, had been consistently around 170/110; now, with no medication, it is a consistent 130/70.

But above and beyond the sense of optimism and physical and mental well-being, my relationship with my family has never been better.

I don't know all that went on in Mary's week, an intense

week of lectures, interviews, acting out of situations, and the exchanging of ideas with other co-dependents, but I know that she learned that alcoholism is a family disease, no matter who is doing the heavy drinking. Since then we have been able to communicate as never before and have not felt so close and loving in two decades. We have a far better relationship with our children, who now readily come to visit and bring friends, without the embarrassment of encountering drinking parents.

I try to be available to anyone who has a drinking problem and needs advice such as I can provide, or a hand or a lift to the nearest AA meeting. And I try to remember, as I was taught, that I am dealing with sick people who want to get well, not bad people who want to be good.

I have been elected to the board of the National Council on Alcoholism in Santa Barbara, and I am proud and humbled by that; on behalf of that organization I recently had the honor of introducing the famous Dr. Pursch, probably the most visible expert on alcohol in America, at a lecture-dinner for 300 people.

Do I miss drinking?

Not really. I don't think about it much. I dream about it occasionally: Someone offers me a drink and I take the glass, I hesitate, but before I can drink it I wake up, like in the dreams where you almost fall off a cliff but wake up in time.

Awake, the idea of drinking doesn't occur to me. When I play tennis, at the end of a match I no longer think, Thirty-forty, hooray! Only three points away from a scotch and soda.

I no longer have to check my long-distance phone bills to find out why I have a $133 call to Málaga, Spain.

I no longer have to wonder what's in the funny-shaped package from Horchow's or Gump's or Johnson Smith Co. that the mailman delivered, ordered in a fit of "exuberance."

Totally strange people no longer show up at our house

with a suitcase swearing I insisted on their spending the weekend when we met in a Greenwich Village bar.

I no longer drool mentally when I see the hero of a movie pour brandy into his snifter glass.

I'm no longer delivered home after midnight through the kindness of strangers.

I no longer wake up in the morning with an archipelago of unexplained magenta bruises on my body that look like a map of the Marquesas.

At our parties, I still take pleasure, perhaps perverse, in making cocktails for the guests, but I am no more tempted to sample the results than I would be if I'd been asked to mix up a batch of Lysol and gasoline.

Both Mary and I are gregarious animals and we still get to social functions; we just don't stay very long. Every once in a while I find myself at a party or situation stuck with excruciating bores who are drinking, and for a few terrible moments I yearn to fight back in kind, to get plastered in defense, to make them disappear. As Mencken said, "I drink to make warts go away from other people's faces."

But I don't give in to the urge to drink, as before, so as to make other people interesting, and I try to avoid the bores. There's always one, at most parties, who weaves across the room and slurs, à la Foster Brooks, "Heard you went to Betty Ford. Sho proud of you. I'd go, too, if I thought I needed it. 'Course, m'wife's the one who should go, y'know."

And to those kind hostesses who zealously press drinks upon me, I simply explain I have an allergy to alcohol.

As Gene, the after-care psychologist at the BFC, warned, "If you come right out and say, "No, because I'm an alcoholic,' they tend to get that, you know, *that* look on their faces and want to know all about it. But if they keep pressing you to drink, tell 'em the truth. That's one of the great things people like Betty Ford and Liz Taylor have done—alcoholism is still a misfortune but no longer a disgrace."

I confess to missing drinking on long flights in airplanes; it was a good way to kill time (what a dumb concept anyway; we don't kill time—time kills us!) And what sort of an idiot wants time to pass quickly when that is all we truly have? That precious commodity that Ray Bradbury speaks of in this poignant prose-poem; he sent it to me with Christmas greetings and congratulations on my sobriety:

Imagine that you have been dead for a year, ten years, one hundred years, a thousand years . . .

The grave and night have taken and kept you in that silence and dark which says nothing and so reveals absolutely zero . . .

In the middle of all this darkness and being alone and bereft of sense, let us imagine that God comes to your still soul and lonely body and says:

I will give you one minute of life. I will restore you to your body and senses for sixty seconds. Out of all the minutes in your life, choose one. I will put you in that minute, and you will be alive again, after a hundred, a thousand years of darkness. Which is it?

Think.

Speak.

Which minute do you choose?

And the answer is:

Any minute. Any minute at all!

Oh God, oh Sweet Christ, oh, Mystery, give me any minute in all of my life.

And the answer further is:

When I lived I didn't know that every minute was special, precious, a gift, a miracle, an incredible thing, an impossible work, an amazing dream.

But now, like Ebenezer Scrooge on Christmas Morn, with snow in the air and the promise of rebirth given, I know what I should have known in my dumb shambles:

that it is all a lark, and it is a beauty beyond tears, and also a terror.

But I dance about, I become a child, I am the boy who runs for the great bird in the window, and I am the man who sends the boy running for that bird, and I am the life that blows in the snowing wind along that street, and the bells that sound and says live, love, for too soon will your name which is shaped in snow melt, or your soul which is inscribed like a breath of vapor on a cold glass pane fade.

Run, run, lad, run, down the middle of Christmas, at the center of Life!

What minute would I opt for, Ray?
I don't know—but I would want it to be a sober one.

o   o   o

I had no intention of writing a book about the Center when I went there, but now I'm glad I have, if only to answer the often asked question, "But what do they *do* in there?"

Perhaps this book partially tells *what* they do, but I'm afraid it hasn't fully answered the question of *how* they do it, *how* they turn desperate people's lives around. Maybe no writings could totally explain the experience and why BFC enjoys the reputation it does. Perhaps one has to *feel* in person the atmosphere of relentless honesty, the "tough love" and dedication of the Center, and see first hand the healing effect one's companions have as they react to one another's problems in the recovery process. Peer activity, peer pressure and peer caring is at the core of this unique institution's success.

And just what is the success rate of the BFC? It's hard to gauge precisely, but the authorities guess it this way: Some 70 percent of the graduates stay completely clean of alcohol and drugs; 15 percent go back to using and drinking, but they return to sobriety and AA. So ultimately, 85 percent can be said to have made it, while 15 percent go down the drain.

As for the success rate of my peers, it would seem to be excellent for those who completed the program. I hear from some of them occasionally, and from Dave and Beth and my counselor, Jerry, regularly.

I also have received many supportive letters from many people in different parts of the world, including my eldest son and younger daughter in Paris, my youngest son in Tahiti, and my older daughter in Italy. I am always surprised when people congratulate me, as though I'd done something remarkable, as though I had had a choice: It was *survival,* pure and simple.

Probably the letter that meant the most to me was one from my favorite contemporary writer, Elmore "Dutch" Leonard, and I have it framed over my desk.

Dear Barny,

The first AA meeting I ever attended I said to a guy, "Aren't parties boring if you don't drink?" The guy said, "If you think the party's gonna be boring, why go?" On the Donahue show with Dennis Wholey, Grace Slick, Shecky Greene and Gale Storm, I said that I drank a lot at parties because I was afraid talking to businessmen there might be boring. And Grace Slick said, "They are." I don't know why we have this fear of being bored, but since I stopped eight years ago I haven't been.

Don't look back. Or stew about time wasted. Doing that is a waste of time in itself. There's no need even to look ahead. Live in the present, right now, and get a handle on the Eleventh Step if you haven't already. The idea is that you make yourself available to your Higher Power and act as his instrument or as his agent. You let him use you, work *his* will through *your* work. His will is that we love one another. To do that we have to get out of ourselves, and to begin to do that we have to *listen* to others and become aware of what's going on around us. You develop a sensitivity, an affection for other people, even the bores, and you become a better writer.

I'm proud of you.

Dutch

Since completing the Betty Ford Center program, I have tried to do what Elmore Leonard suggests—I've been letting my Higher Power do as much of the work and worrying as I can get away with. It's not always an easy collaboration, but I like the feeling of knowing that my partner is always around—somewhere.